W9-BHE-760

TIME FOR KIDS

BIG BOOK OF SCIENCE EXPERIMENTS

powered by Mad SCIENCE

PRODUCED BY

DOWNTOWN BOOKWORKS INC.

PRESIDENT: Julie Merberg
EDITORIAL DIRECTOR: Sarah Parvis
SENIOR CONTRIBUTORS: Patricia Janes, Allyson Kulavis, Susan Perry, Renée Skelton, Jenny Tesar
SPECIAL THANKS: Patty Brown, Matt Shay, Barbara Gogan, Heather Lockwood Hughes, Stephen Callahan, Liz Reitman, Sana Hong

DESIGNED BY
Brian Michael Thomas/Our Hero Productions

ILLUSTRATIONS BY
Darin Anderson/Shay Design

powered by Mad Science

Experiment Development: Lindsay Milner, Evelyn Tsang, Elke Steinwender, Sharon King-Majaury

Mad Science® is on a mission to spark the imagination and curiosity of children everywhere. We provide fun, interactive, educational programs that instill a clear understanding of what science is really about and how it affects the world around us. Visit www.madscience.org to find a location near you!

TIME FOR KIDS

PUBLISHER: Bob Der
MANAGING EDITOR, TIME FOR KIDS MAGAZINE: Nellie Gonzalez Cutler
EDITOR, TIME LEARNING VENTURES: Jonathan Rosenbloom

Time HOME ENTERTAINMENT

PUBLISHER: Richard Fraiman
VICE PRESIDENT, BUSINESS DEVLOPMENT & STRATEGY: Steven Sandonato
EXECUTIVE DIRECTOR, MARKETING SERVICES: Carol Pittard
EXECUTIVE DIRECTOR, RETAIL & SPECIAL SALES: Tom Mifsud
EXECUTIVE DIRECTOR, NEW PRODUCT DEVELOPMENT: Peter Harper
EDITORIAL DIRECTOR: Stephen Koepp
DIRECTOR, BOOKAZINE DEVELOPMENT & MARKETING: Laura Adam
PUBLISHING DIRECTOR: Joy Butts
FINANCE DIRECTOR: Glenn Buonocore
ASSISTANT GENERAL COUNSEL: Helen Wan
ASSISTANT DIRECTOR, SPECIAL SALES: Ilene Schreider
DESIGN & PREPRESS MANAGER: Anne-Michelle Gallero
ASSOCIATE BRAND MANAGER: Jonathan White
ASSOCIATE PREPRESS MANAGER: Alex Voznesenskiy
ASSOCIATE PRODUCTION MANAGER: Kimberly Marshall

SPECIAL THANKS: Christine Austin, Jeremy Biloon, Alex Borinstein, Jim Childs, Susan Chodakiewicz, Rose Cirrincione, Jacqueline Fitzgerald, Christine Font, Jenna Goldberg, Lauren Hall, Carrie Hertan, Suzanne Janso, Raphael Joa, Jeffrey Kaji, Mona Li, Amy Mangus, Robert Marasco, Amy Migliaccio, Georgia Millman-Perlah, Nina Mistry, Myles Ringel, Dave Rozzelle, Sasha Shapiro, Soren Shapiro, Adriana Tierno, Emily Wheeler, Vanessa Wu

For information on TIME FOR KIDS magazine for the classroom or home, go to TIMEFORKIDS.COM or call 1-800-777-8600.

Published by TIME FOR KIDS Books, an imprint of Time Home Entertainment Inc.
135 West 50th Street
New York, New York 10020

ISBN 10: 1-60320-885-2
ISBN 13: 978-1-60320-885-7

We welcome your comments and suggestions about TIME FOR KIDS Books. Please write to us at:

TIME FOR KIDS BOOKS
ATTENTION: BOOK EDITORS
P.O. BOX 11016
DES MOINES, IA 50336-1016

If you would like to order any of our TIME FOR KIDS or SI KIDS hardcover Collector's Edition books, please call us at 1-800-327-6388 (Monday through Friday, 7:00 a.m.–8:00 p.m., or Saturday, 7:00 a.m.–6:00 p.m. Central Time).

1 QGT 11

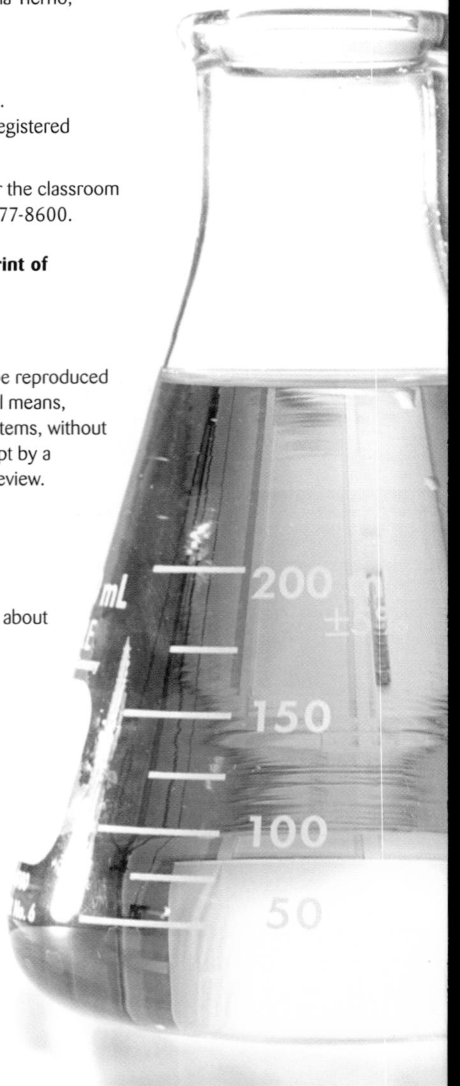

CONTENTS

Experiments marked with a green test tube can be set up and performed in less than one hour.

Experiments marked with a yellow flask can be completed in a matter of hours.

Experiments marked with a red beaker will take more than a day to complete. See individual experiments for time requirements.

Life Science (continued)

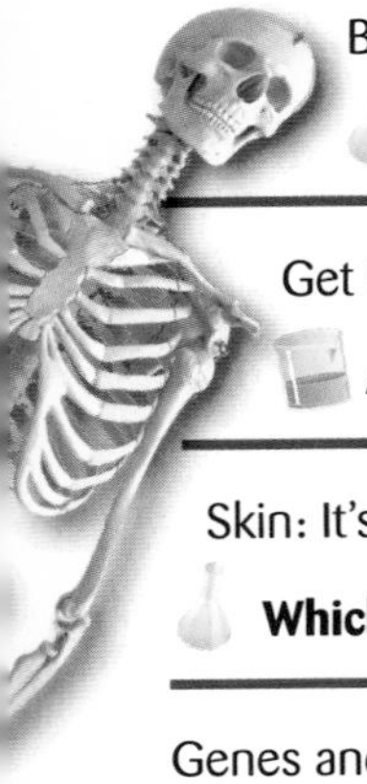

Physical Science 94

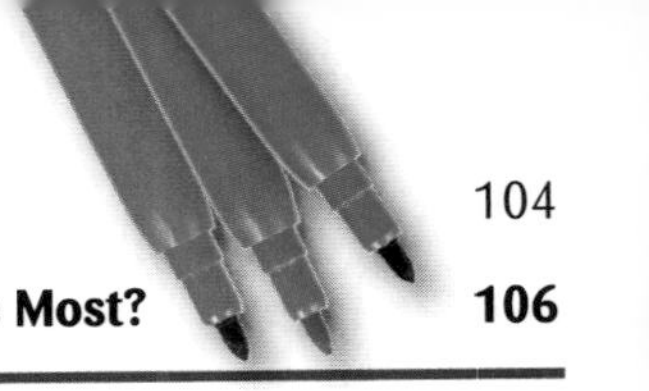

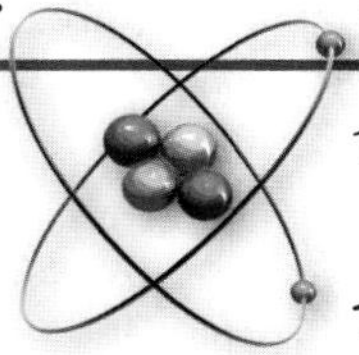

The experiments and activities in this book require adult supervision. Time Home Entertainment Inc., TIME For Kids, Downtown Bookworks Inc., and The Mad Science Group disclaim all responsibility and liability for any damage or injuries caused or sustained while performing any of these experiments or activities.

WHAT DO SCIENTISTS DO?

Scientists observe, study, look for patterns, and try to find general rules to explain how things work or why things happen. A scientific law describes something that has been observed many times. Understanding these rules often helps scientists create or improve processes that we use in our world every day. The laws of gravity, for example, explain why we stick to the Earth instead of floating away.

The Scientific Method

Scientists follow a set of steps called the scientific method. They begin by making observations that lead to generalizations about why an event happens. These "first guess" generalizations are called **hypotheses.** Scientists test a hypothesis many times to make sure a certain outcome is not an accident or a fluke. As scientists test a hypothesis and observe the results of experiments, they look for evidence to support a hypothesis. If they can support the hypothesis, it may lead to a theory or a law of science.

All scientists use six basic skills in the scientific method: observing, communicating, classifying, measuring, inferring, and predicting.

A paleontologist is a type of scientist who studies the remains of organisms that lived long ago.

OBSERVING We use our senses to get information about the world around us. We can also use tools, such as microscopes, magnifying glasses, and telescopes. Scientists do not include opinions in their observations. They only record what they observe.

COMMUNICATING Scientists share observations, discoveries, and results in many ways. They write, draw, and use visual aids such as graphs, charts, maps, diagrams, and multimedia presentations.

CLASSIFYING Classifying objects is grouping them according to how they are similar, how they are different, or how they are related to one another. Scientists classify everything from animals to planets.

MEASURING Scientists use tools to take precise measurements of what they observe. Tools measure things like temperature, mass, distance, volume, and time.

INFERRING Inferring means using observations and what you know to figure something out. Here's an example. A scientist observes that every time a large insect comes near a smaller one, the smaller insect releases a dark, sticky liquid from its body. The larger insect flies away. If the scientist saw this many times, she could eventually figure out, or infer, that the liquid helps the smaller insect defend itself.

PREDICTING A scientist can use what he or she knows and observes to predict the outcome of an action. In the case of the small insect, a scientist could predict that the small insect would release the sticky fluid the next time a larger insect came near.

An agricultural engineer takes soil measurements.

General Steps in the Scientific Method

1. QUESTION

What makes you curious? Look around and observe the world. Think about the materials you have available. What are these things made of, how do they work, and what can you do with them? What do you want to find out? Do some research online or at a library. Decide what question you want to answer.

Research a topic that interests you before you plan your experiment.

2. HYPOTHESIS

Think about how you could answer your question. Based on what you've seen and read, what do you predict will happen? What do you think the outcome of the experiment will be? Why do you think this is so? Make a prediction using an "If _________, then _________ because _________" statement format. For example, your hypothesis could be, "If I give a plant more water, then it will grow taller because plants need water to grow."

Be precise with measurements.

3. EXPERIMENT

Create a list of the materials you need. Write out each step of your experimental procedure. Carry out each step carefully. Make sure you work safely and accurately. Record what you observe with words and pictures.

4. RESULTS

What happened? Record all your results. Use graphs and charts to clearly show your findings.

Write down all of your observations.

5. CONCLUSION

What do your results tell you? Analyze your results and compare actual results with your hypothesis. Decide whether or not your results support your hypothesis. Think about further research you could do on your topic. What new experiment ideas do you have now? Write up your findings to share with other scientists.

PLAY IT SAFE!

Remember to be safe when you do the projects in this book.

- ✔ Be sure safety equipment is nearby. If you are doing an experiment with heat, know where you can find a fire extinguisher.
- ✔ If you are going to handle something hot, use pot holders, oven mitts, or thick gloves.
- ✔ Read all the instructions before you begin.
- ✔ Do not eat or drink any parts of an experiment unless you are told to.
- ✔ Pull back long hair so it's out of the way.
- ✔ Be sure to clean up all surfaces when you're done with experiments.
- ✔ Wear shoes with closed toes when you are doing experiments.
- ✔ Get adult help with anything sharp, electric, or hot.

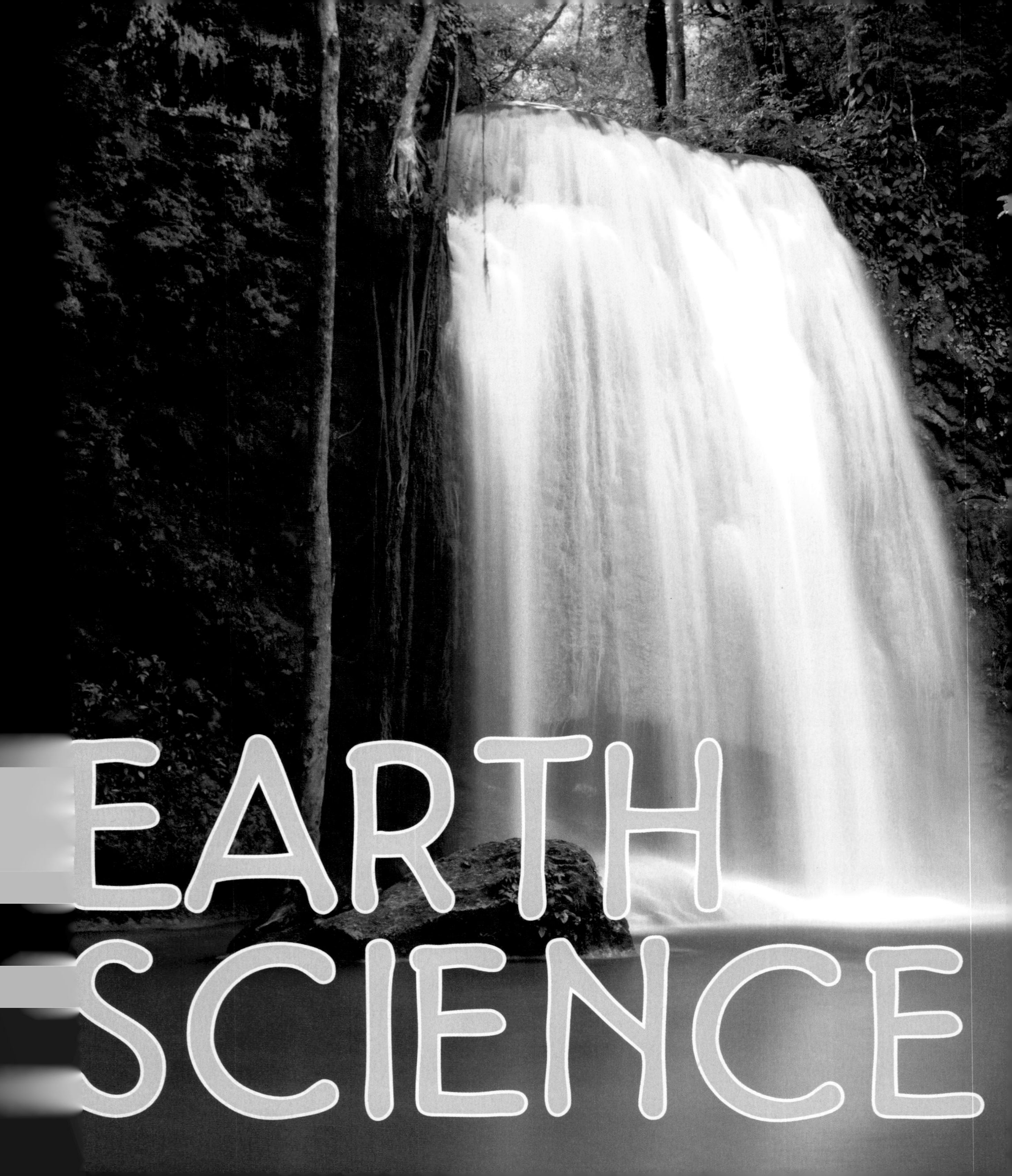
EARTH
SCIENCE

How do hurricanes start? What is the greenhouse effect? Where do fossils come from and how are diamonds formed? Earth science is the study of Earth and all of its land formations, bodies of water, weather, and the universe that surrounds it. Oceanography, the study of Earth's oceans, and meteorology, the study of weather, are both Earth sciences. Geology focuses on the rocks and minerals that make up Earth, as well as how it changes over time.

IN THE CLOUDS

Some clouds look white and fluffy. Other clouds look like soft sheets of gray. The truth is, clouds are not fluffy or soft. They're wet, because they are made of water. But how are clouds formed?

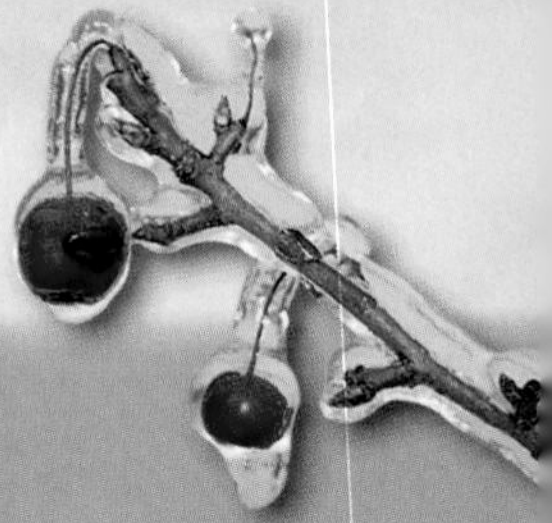

Water Changes State

The **state** of a substance refers to the form it takes. The three most common states are solid, liquid, and gas. There is only one substance that exists as a solid, liquid, and gas in Earth's atmosphere. That substance is water. We know it as ice when it is solid, water when it is liquid, and water vapor when it is a gas. Water changes from one state to another when heat is either added or taken away. Evaporation and condensation are opposite processes. Freezing and melting are also opposite processes.

CONDENSATION
When water in the gaseous state loses heat, it changes into liquid water. The process in which a gas loses heat and becomes a liquid is **condensation.**

EVAPORATION
When water in the liquid state absorbs heat, it changes into a gas called water vapor. The process in which a liquid gains heat and becomes a gas is **evaporation.**

FREEZING
When water in the liquid state loses heat, it changes into a solid called ice. The process in which a liquid loses heat and becomes a solid is **freezing.**

MELTING
When water in the solid state gains heat, it changes into liquid water. The process in which a solid gains heat and becomes a liquid is **melting.**

When the water vapor in the air comes in contact with an ice-cold drink, it cools down and turns back into water. That's why beads of water, or condensation, will appear on the outside of a glass on a hot or humid day.

Icicles form when water drips from an object and freezes. In cold weather, icicles often form on roofs, cars, fences, and tree branches.

How Clouds Form

Water from Earth's surface changes state to form clouds. Clouds are made of billions of tiny drops of water or pieces of ice. This is how clouds form:

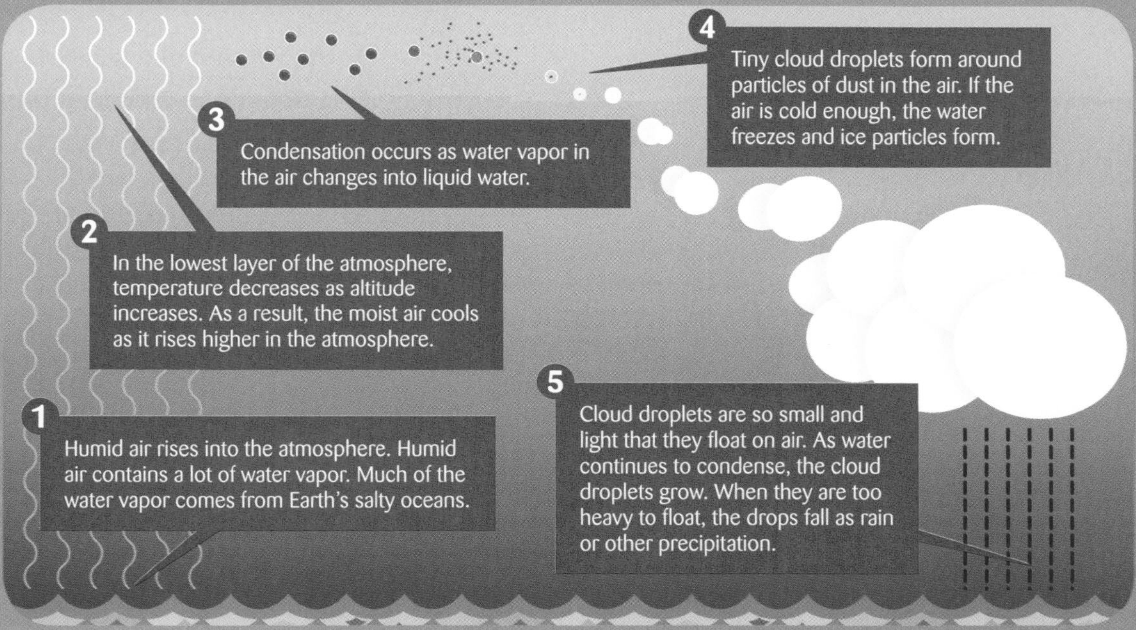
1 Humid air rises into the atmosphere. Humid air contains a lot of water vapor. Much of the water vapor comes from Earth's salty oceans.
2 In the lowest layer of the atmosphere, temperature decreases as altitude increases. As a result, the moist air cools as it rises higher in the atmosphere.
3 Condensation occurs as water vapor in the air changes into liquid water.
4 Tiny cloud droplets form around particles of dust in the air. If the air is cold enough, the water freezes and ice particles form.
5 Cloud droplets are so small and light that they float on air. As water continues to condense, the cloud droplets grow. When they are too heavy to float, the drops fall as rain or other precipitation.

Cloud forests, like this one in Costa Rica, form around high-altitude rain forests. Warm air rises out of the forest, cools, and condenses into clouds. The peaks are constantly surrounded by clouds.

DISTILLING WATER

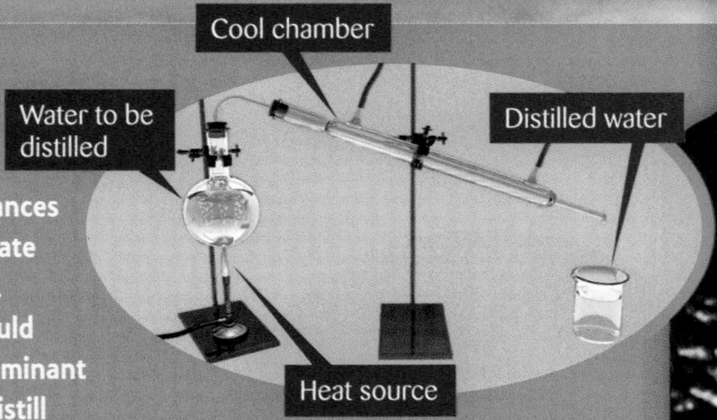
Cool chamber
Water to be distilled
Distilled water
Heat source

When water is completely mixed with another substance, it is said to be miscible. The two substances will not break into layers. To separate them, you will need to distill them.

One reason to distill water would be to remove salt or another contaminant and make it safe for drinking. To distill undrinkable water, the water is heated to its boiling point. Once it starts to boil, the water vaporizes. When water vaporizes, it evaporates and goes into the air as water vapor. The boiling point of water is lower than the boiling point of salt and most other contaminants. So the salt stays behind. The water vapor then enters a cool chamber. The water cools and condenses. So it becomes liquid again. The "pure" water is then collected in a container for use.

HIDDEN SALT

Clouds are formed with water vapor that has evaporated from the Earth's surface. Much of that water vapor comes from salty ocean water. Does that mean that the clouds are salty like the ocean water?

The volume of a cloud drop is about one-millionth the volume of a raindrop.

Are Clouds Salty?

YOU WILL NEED:

- 2 bowls
- Water
- Marker
- Tape
- Salt
- Spoon
- Plastic wrap
- Refrigerator

1. Fill both bowls with warm water.

2. Using the marker and a piece of tape, label one bowl "salt." Add 3 spoonfuls of salt to the bowl, and stir to make the water salty. This is like the water in the ocean.

3. Cover the bowls with plastic wrap and leave them in the fridge for 1 hour.

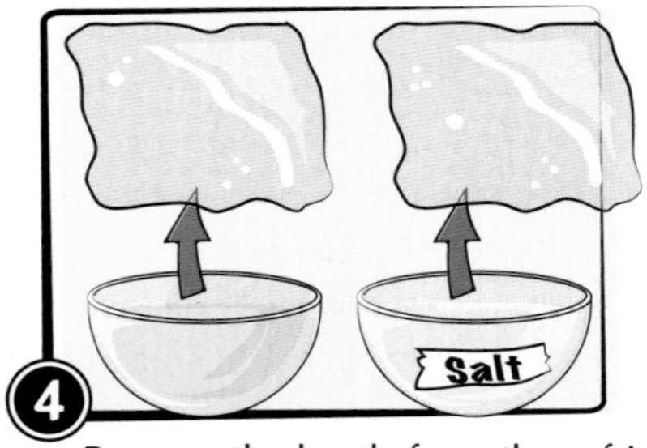

4. Remove the bowls from the refrigerator, and observe the plastic wrap to see how clouds form. Carefully remove the plastic wrap from each bowl. Taste the condensation on the plastic wrap. Did the salty water make salty condensation?

science fair tip

Research instances of salt water being purified in nature (rain, dew, seabirds, mangroves, willow trees). Include pictures and a short description of a few examples in your presentation.

DESALINATION

Everyone needs fresh water for drinking, cooking, and growing food. But there are many places in the world that don't have enough. Millions of people now use desalination to solve this problem. Desalination is a process that makes fresh water from salt water. Some desalination plants use distillation. At these plants, salty seawater is heated until the water evaporates. The water vapor is then cooled. It condenses back into fresh water—leaving the salt behind.

The largest desalination plant in the United States turns seawater into up to 25 million gallons (95 million L) of clean drinking water each day.

Change it UP!

☞ Repeat the experiment. Only this time, fill the bowl with sugar water or colored water. Determine how evaporation and condensation remain the same—or are different.

☞ Find out which form of water makes the best cloud—warm water, cool water, or ice water.

The SCIENCE Behind It

The salt water you placed in the refrigerator was a solution. The salt and water were mixed. Although the two substances looked like they had become one, they were not joined chemically. That is why you can separate them by distillation.

The air inside the bowl was full of water vapor that evaporated from the warm water. When the bowl was placed inside the refrigerator, the water vapor cooled. Some of it condensed to form droplets on the plastic wrap. During the process of distillation, only the water evaporated and condensed. Salt cannot turn into vapor at this temperature, so it stayed in the bowl. That's why the condensed water did not taste salty. Salty ocean water often evaporates from Earth's surface to form clouds. Based on the results of this experiment, do you think clouds are salty? How do you know?

Some seabirds, such as gulls and pelicans, have a special gland near their eye sockets that helps them remove the salt from seawater so they have fresh water to drink. They collect this briny solution, which then moves into the birds' nasal passages, where they "sneeze" to get rid of it.

THE SUN

Most of us enjoy being outside on a sunny day. The sun's warmth and light make us feel good. But if you stay outside too long, you might become dehydrated or get a sunburn. What's the best way to protect yourself?

Energy from the Sun

The sun's energy is electromagnetic radiation (ER), which travels through space to Earth as waves. The way we sense electromagnetic waves is different depending on the wavelength (the size) and frequency (speed of movement) of the wave.

Visible light is the only type of ER that we can see. You can feel infrared radiation (IR) as heat. You can't see ultraviolet (UV) radiation, but it has a lot of energy and can be harmful.

UV Radiation Can Damage Skin

There are three types of UV radiation. Each one has a different effect on the skin.

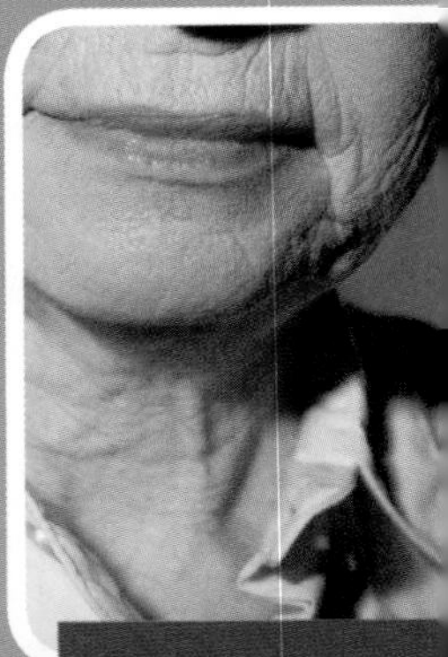

UVA radiation toughens, wrinkles and ages the skin.

UVA – Up to 95% of the UV we get from the sun is UVA. UVA penetrates deeply into the skin, beyond the top layer. UVA can also increase the risk of skin cancer.

UVB – Earth's atmosphere absorbs much of the UVB that reaches the surface of the planet. So it is less common at Earth's surface than UVA. UVB also doesn't penetrate the skin as deeply as UVA. Still, it can be harmful.

UVC – This is a very dangerous form of UV. But Earth's atmosphere blocks it. As a result, UVC is not a major concern for people on Earth's surface.

THE ELECTROMAGNETIC SPECTRUM

The electromagnetic spectrum refers to a variety of types of radiation, arranged according to their wavelength, energy, or frequency. There are many kinds of electromagnetic waves. Radio waves, which make it possible for you to tune in to music on a radio, are types of electromagnetic waves. Microwaves, like the ones that heat up food quickly, are also on the spectrum. Radio waves and microwaves are invisible and have different wavelengths. Visible light also travels in waves, but you can see it. Each of the colors you see has a different wavelength.

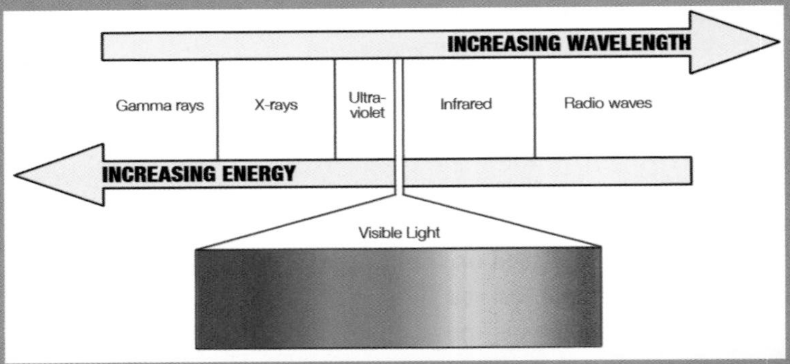

What Is a Suntan?

Many people think a deep suntan is a sign of health. But it's really a sign of skin damage. UV exposure can make the skin sag and look tough and wrinkled, even in people who are not old. UV can also cause skin cancer. A tan is just your body's attempt to block the sun's harmful UV rays.

When UV from the sun hits your skin, it triggers the release of melanin. **Melanin** is a brown pigment. It darkens the cells of the epidermis, which is the upper layer of the skin. This darkening of the skin is what we call a suntan.

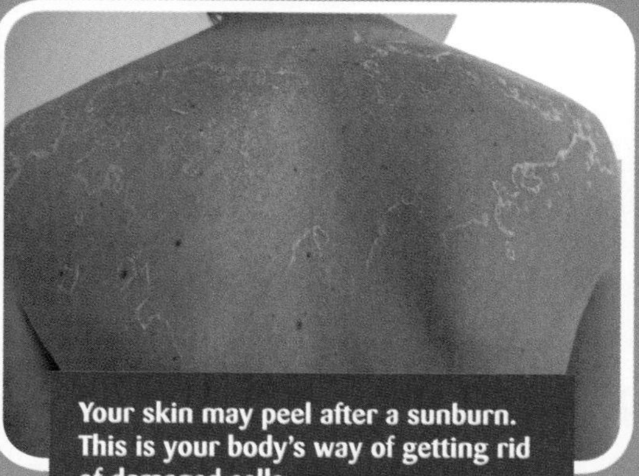

Your skin may peel after a sunburn. This is your body's way of getting rid of damaged cells.

It's important for kids to protect themselves against the sun. Most people get between 50% and 80% of their lifetime sun exposure before they reach the age of 18.

People with darker skin have more natural protection than light-skinned people. Why? Because they have more melanin in their skin. Still, not even people with dark skin are safe from UV damage. Everyone needs protection from UV when they are out in the sun.

SUN PROTECTION

Do you rub on sunscreen when you go to the beach? Do you wear a hat or sunglasses to keep the sun out of your face on a bright day? People have many ways to protect themselves from the sun. Which ones work best?

Does Paper Need Sunscreen, Too?

YOU WILL NEED:

- Colored construction paper
- Plastic wrap
- Colored notepad paper
- Newspaper
- Shiny colored paper
- Thick colored paper
- Sunscreen
- Sun hat
- 5 pairs of sunglasses
- Sunshine
- Scissors

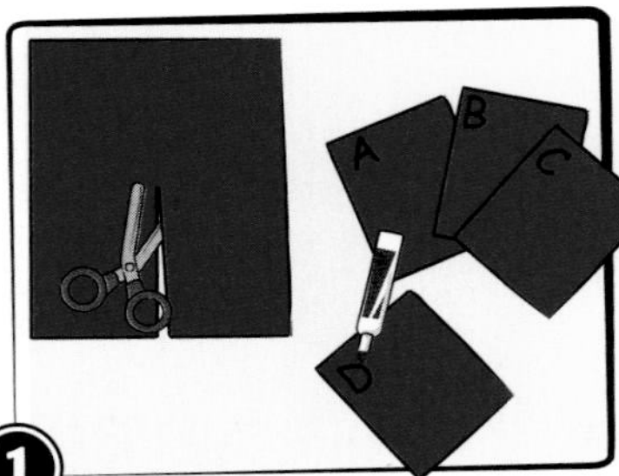

1. Cut the colored construction paper into four equal pieces. Write the letter A, B, C, or D on each piece.

2. Wrap each piece of paper in a sheet of plastic wrap.

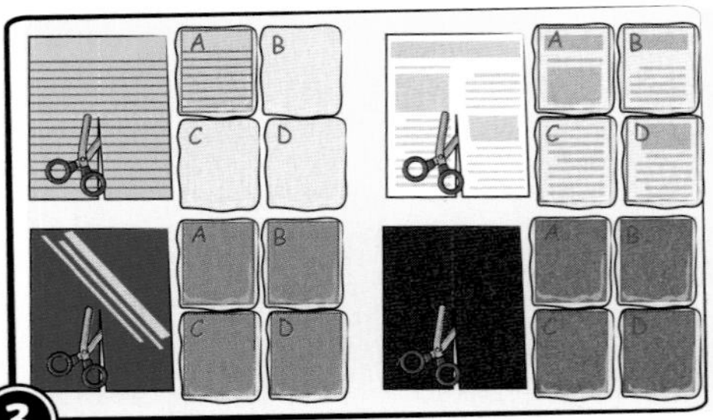

3. Repeat steps 1 and 2 for the four other types of paper.

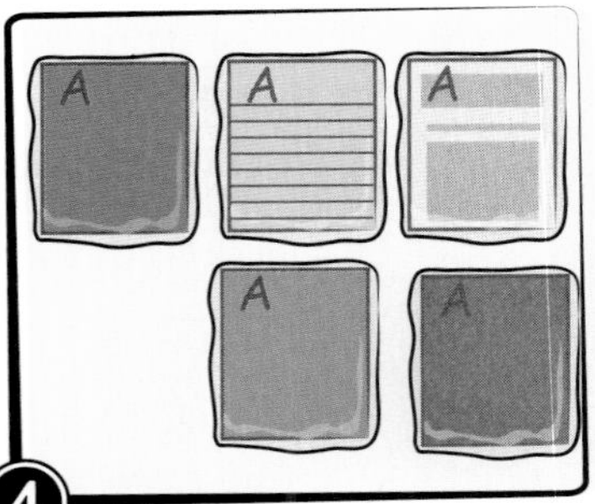

4. The papers marked with an "A" are your control papers. Place all five As out of the sun for the duration of the experiment.

5. The papers marked "B" are for your sunscreen test. Coat the plastic wrap of all five Bs with sunscreen and set them in the sunlight.

science fair tip

If you plan to use poster board to make a trifold display, buy an extra piece of the same type of poster board, cut it into four pieces, and include it as one of the types of paper in your experiment.

UV PROTECTION

It's not just our skin that needs protection against the sun's harmful UV rays. UV from the sun causes coatings on the exterior surfaces of many objects to fade or deteriorate. As a result, many exterior paints and coatings for cars, airplanes, and buildings include substances that help block or protect against the sun's UV rays.

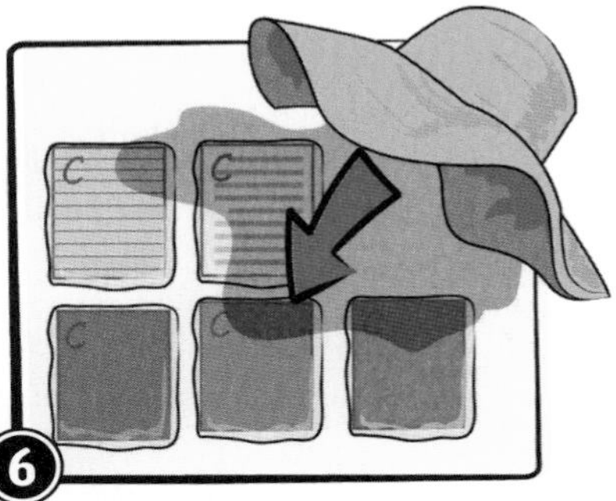

6 The papers marked "C" are for your sun hat test. Place all five Cs in the sunlight and cover them with the sun hat.

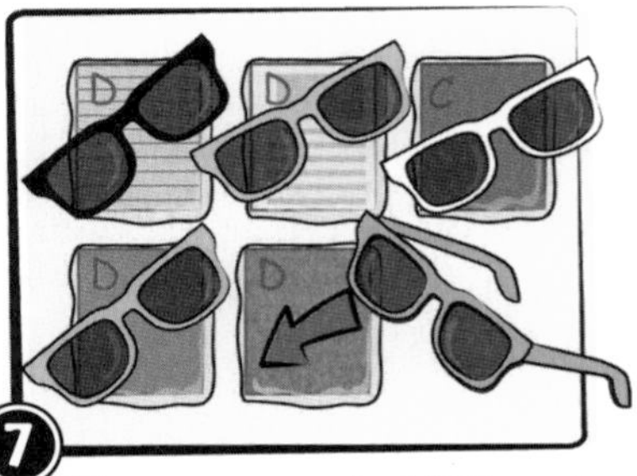

7 The papers marked "D" are for your sunglasses test. Place all five Ds in the sunlight and put sunglasses on top.

8 Check on your papers every day for one week. Compare the three tested sets of paper with the control set. Is there a difference in the colors? Did any of the papers fade?

Change it UP!

☞ Sunscreen comes in different strengths. The Sun Protection Factor (SPF) indicates how well a sunscreen protects your skin. Design a version of this experiment that allows you to test sunscreens with different SPFs.

☞ Do some paint colors or types of paint stand up better against sun damage than others? Paint several pairs of identical wood surfaces with different color paints of the same type, or different types of paint. Leave one half of each pair inside and expose the other to the sun for several weeks. Observe changes during that time. Take photos every day to contrast the way the surfaces look at the start of the experiment with the way they look at various stages of the experiment.

The SCIENCE Behind It

What determines whether a hat, sunglasses, or sunscreen gives protection from the sun? That depends on how well it protects against the sun's UV waves. If the paper under the sun hat or sunglasses faded, then the hat or glasses did not provide good UV protection. The thicker the layer of sunscreen and the higher the SPF, the better the protection should have been.

Your results also depended on the type of paper you used. Some kinds of paper do not break down easily in UV light. As a result, these papers would not fade easily, even if the protection of the hat, glasses, or sunscreen offered little protection.

EARTH ON THE MOVE

Imagine that you are on top of a mountain. You bend down and pick up a piece of rock, you crumble the rock into smaller pieces, and it blows away. You are now part of a process called erosion.

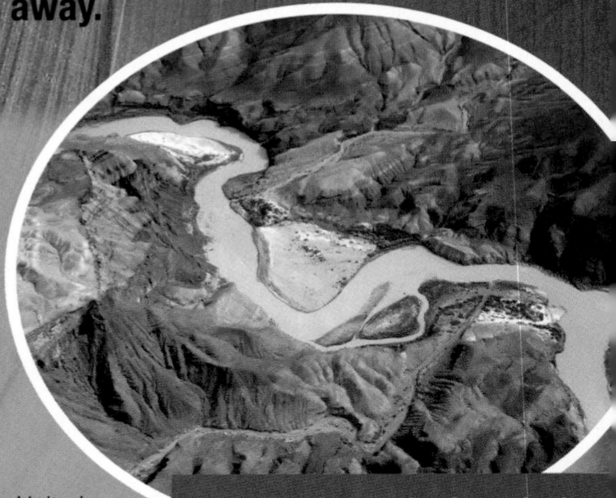

The Colorado River has been slowly carving its way through the Grand Canyon by a process called erosion.

The Breakdown

Wind, water, and temperature changes break rock into smaller particles in a process called **erosion.** Wind, water, and gravity can rearrange these particles into new landforms.

Erosion in U.S. History

In the 1930s, wind erosion caused a problem in the southern Great Plains in the United States. The Plains (a flat area between the Mississippi River and the Rocky Mountains) grew grasses that held the soil in place. But over time, people began to grow wheat as a crop. They built houses where there used to be only fields of grass. People also raised more and more cattle, which ate the grass. The strong roots of the grasses helped to hold the soil in place. Without the grass, the soil was exposed to the wind. Rain and heavy winds eroded the soil. In some places four inches (10 cm) of soil was blown away.

The Colorado River snakes through the rock that makes up the Grand Canyon. Over time, this great river has dug out a mighty canyon. When rain falls on hard, dry ground, it cannot soak into the soil. Instead, the water moves fast and breaks up the soil and rocks. The erosion forms canyon walls over millions of years.

The Great Plains were known as the Dust Bowl in the 1930s.

Flash floods are particularly dangerous, because they come on without warning.

IN A FLASH

Floods are a natural disaster caused by weather. Quick, heavy rainfall combined with hilly terrain create the recipe for flash floods. Rainwater runs off the steep hillsides into narrow streams. The water level rises rapidly as the streams rush downhill. This raging water can move cars and boulders, uproot trees, and destroy roads, houses, and bridges.

Can Grass Slow Soil Erosion?

YOU WILL NEED:

- 1 jelly roll or roasting pan
- Soil (moisten it a bit)
- 2 to 3 books
- Cup
- Grass seed (1 Tbsp or 15 mL)
- Plastic wrap
- Water

1. Cover one-half to two-thirds of the pan with moist soil. Gently slope the soil to form a "hill" at one end of the pan.

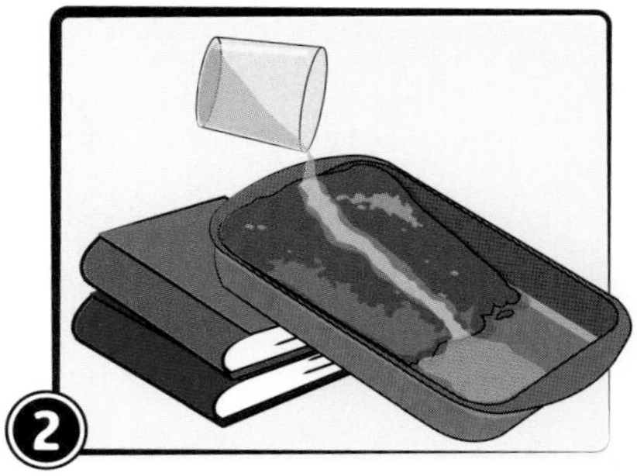

2. Use the books to lift the end of the pan with the most soil. Fill the cup halfway with water. Carefully pour the water onto the highest part of the pan, forming a river.

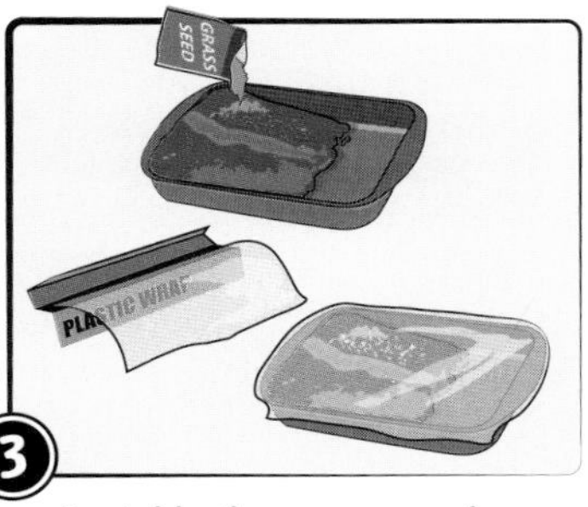

3. Sprinkle the grass seed on one side of the river. Cover the pan with plastic wrap and set it in an area that gets plenty of sunlight.

4. Be sure that the soil in the pan stays moist. Wait about a week, until the grown grass presses against the plastic wrap.

5. Remove the wrap. Use the books to elevate the end of the pan with the most soil in it.

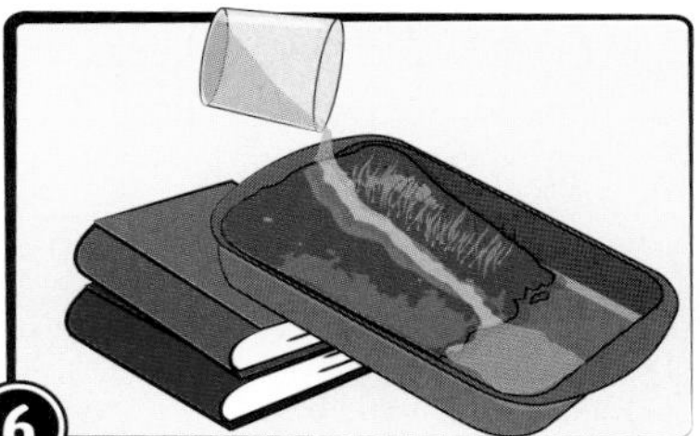

6. Fill the cup with water. Carefully pour the water into the riverbed. What happens to the soil along the river? Does one side suffer more damage than the other?

Change it UP!

☞ Redo the experiment with several different types of grass. Do you observe a difference?

The SCIENCE Behind It

Moving water carries soil from one area to another and may destroy crops and farms. The roots of some plants make the soil more resistant to flooding. Planted soil may still suffer damage, though, if there is too much water for it to soak up. When the waters recede, or go back to normal, they leave behind deposits of soil and other debris that can bury or damage plants.

WHAT MAKES CLIMATE?

Why is the desert hot and dry? Why are some places in the world forests and others grasslands? Why do certain plants and animals live only in some parts of the world? The answer is climate.

The "Recipe" for Climate

Climate is the long-term weather of an area, usually recorded over a period of 30 years or longer. Two important things that help to make up climate are the amount of precipitation (rain or snow) and the usual temperature of an area. Here are some factors that affect climate.

LATITUDE: The farther a place is from the equator, the larger the temperature difference is between winter and summer.

TERRAIN: The higher a place is, the colder it is.

WATER: Near large bodies of water, the winters are milder and the summers are cooler.

WIND: Global winds shift during the different seasons. In spring, winds move toward the poles. In the fall, they move toward the equator.

Weddell seals, which live in ice cap climates, have dense fur and a thick layer of fat to keep them warm.

Climate Spotlights

Tropical wet climates like the Amazon rain forest are perfect for trees and other vegetation.

TROPICAL WET CLIMATES

Tropical wet climates are hot and humid all year round. The average rainfall can top 100 inches (254 cm) in a year.

ICE CAP CLIMATES

Climates on the polar ice caps are the coldest climates on Earth. Temperatures don't go above freezing, even in summer.

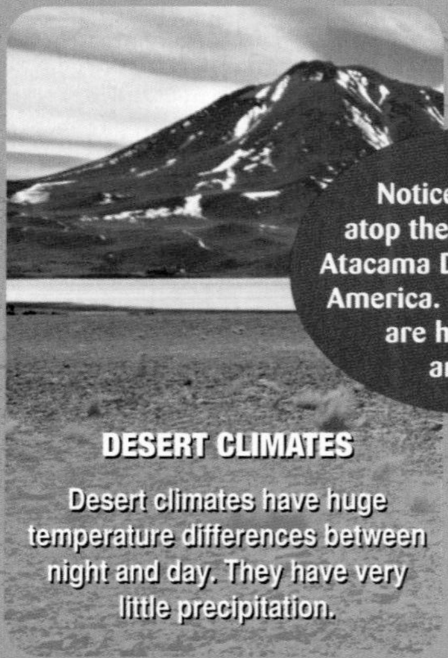

Notice the snow atop the peaks in the Atacama Desert in South America. Not all deserts are hot, but all are dry.

DESERT CLIMATES

Desert climates have huge temperature differences between night and day. They have very little precipitation.

Can You Capture Heat?

YOU WILL NEED:

- 2 pieces of black paper or black cloth
- 2 large glass jars, same size
- 2 thermometers that will fit inside the jars
- 1 jar lid
- A very sunny day
- Oven mitts

1. Put a piece of black paper or cloth inside each jar.

2. Place a thermometer in each jar, on top of the paper or cloth.

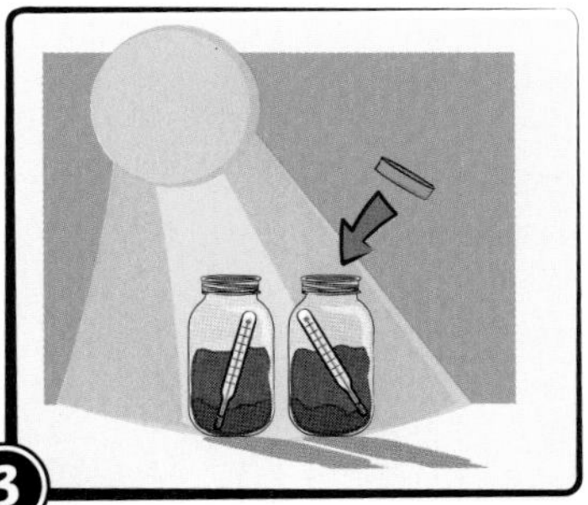

3. Put the lid on one of the jars, and place the jars outdoors in the sun.

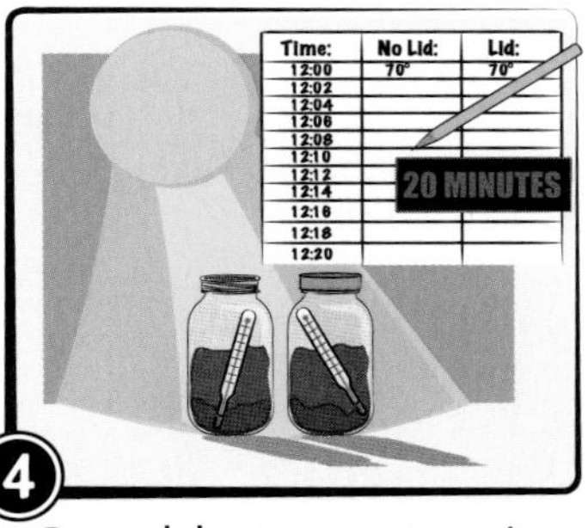
Time:
No Lid:
Lid:
12:00
70°
70°
12:02
12:04
12:06
12:08
12:10
12:12
12:14
12:16
12:18
12:20
20 MINUTES

4. Record the temperatures in both jars every 2 minutes for 20 minutes.

5. Wearing oven mitts, move the jars to the shade. Remove the lid from the covered jar. Compare the temperatures of the two jars. Can you feel the difference?

The SCIENCE Behind It

You made a model of the greenhouse effect! Sunlight shines on the objects and heats them up. An item inside a closed container heats even more quickly, because the heat cannot escape.

THE GREENHOUSE EFFECT

Greenhouses are buildings covered with glass or plastic that use the same science that we see in this experiment to keep the air warm for the plants and crops inside.

The greenhouse effect is a similar principle. There is a layer of gases building up around the planet called greenhouse gases. When sunlight strikes Earth's surface, some of it is reflected back toward space as infrared radiation (heat). The greenhouse gases absorb this infrared radiation and trap the heat in Earth's atmosphere. The greenhouse effect is warming up the Earth, which can lead to climate changes.

Change it UP!

☞ Use light-colored paper or cloth. How different are the results?

☞ Instead of closing the lid, place a tiny potted plant with moist soil or a small tray of water inside the jar and repeat the steps.

ALL ABOUT WEATHER

Weather can ruin a picnic or make a day at the beach even better. White fluffy clouds can form beautiful "pictures" in the sky. Weather forecasters use terms like *fronts* and *pressure.* What are they talking about? Let's find out more.

It's All About Air

You might hear a weather forecast about a cold front coming in. With the cold front, the temperature will plunge. But what is a cold front exactly? **Fronts** are borders between air masses. An air mass is a large body of air that has pretty much the same temperature and amount of moisture throughout.

When air masses meet, they create a front. In a **cold front,** for example, a cold air mass is moving in to replace a warm air mass. The winds usually shift, too. Before a cold front comes through, the winds blow from the south. After the cold front, the winds may blow from the north instead.

Clouds

Cirrus clouds

Clouds are an important part of the weather. A cloud is a collection of tiny droplets of water or ice crystals in the air. Scientists classify clouds according to how high they are above Earth, their shape, and what they're made of.

Cirrus clouds are highest above the ground. They are so high, they are made of ice. These clouds are thin and wispy.

Alto clouds are the middle clouds. They are made of ice crystals and water droplets and usually cover the entire sky. They can signal approaching thunderstorms.

Stratus clouds are the lowest clouds. They look like fog that's just higher than the ground. Sometimes light mist falls from these clouds.

Cumulus clouds aren't classified by their height. They are flat on the bottom and rounded on the top. If you see those round parts grow taller, watch out! The clouds signal that heavy rain, snow, hail, or even tornadoes are on the way.

Thunder and Lightning

There's definitely a recipe for a thunderstorm. It requires a mix of unstable air and moisture. You also need something that lifts unstable air, like a front, a strong breeze, or even a mountain. Thunderstorms can happen anytime, although they usually happen in warm weather and in the afternoon and evening. All thunderstorms have lightning.

Lightning causes more deaths every year than hurricanes or tornadoes.

CITY HEAT

Cities create their own weather. Scientists are studying the consequences of the fact that, as cities grow, buildings and paved surfaces replace the natural landscape and can soak up heat to raise air temperatures by as much as 10°F (12°C). This bubble of heat is called an "urban heat island."

Chicago

How Strong Is Air Pressure?

YOU WILL NEED:

- Water
- 1-liter or 2-liter plastic soda bottle
- Saucer or pie pan
- 3 quarters
- Scissors
- 3-inch x 5-inch (7.6-cm x 12.7-cm) index card
- Tape
- Pencil

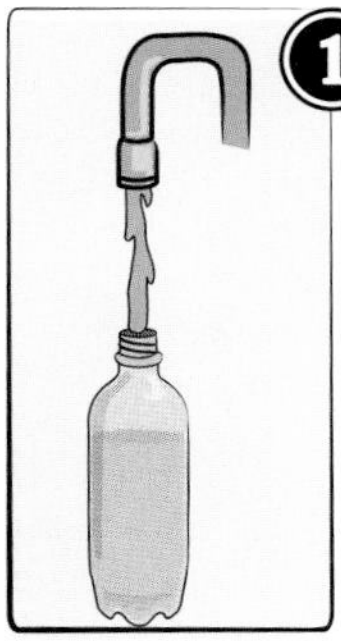

1 Pour water into the bottle until it is about three-quarters full.

2 Fill the saucer halfway with water. With your thumb over the mouth of the bottle, turn the bottle upside down and hold it in the water in the saucer.

3 With the mouth of the bottle under the surface of the water, remove your thumb and rest the bottle upside down in the saucer. Slide three quarters under the mouth of the bottle so the bottle is balanced on them.

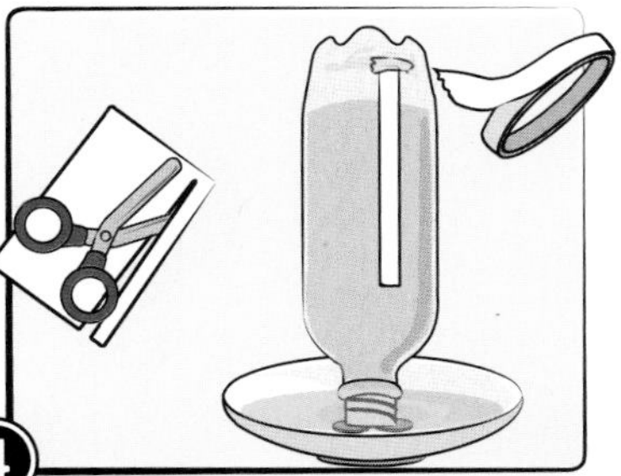

4 Cut the index card into thin strips. Place a strip of index card vertically along the outside of the bottle, toward the top. Tape it in place.

5 Using your pencil, gently mark the level of water on your index card, and write the date next to your mark. Continue to mark the level and record the date on the card every day for a week. What do you notice?

Change it UP!

☞ Repeat the experiment, but note the temperature as well. Do you begin to see a pattern?

The SCIENCE Behind It

The weight of the air in our atmosphere presses down on the water in the saucer, keeping water inside the bottle. The weight of the air in the atmosphere and the force it exerts is called air pressure. Air pressure changes slightly from day to day. When there is a decrease in air pressure, the water level drops. An increase sends the water up. What did you notice about the temperature on days when the water level rose or fell?

Air pressure, also known as barometric pressure, is measured by an instrument called a barometer.

MAGNETIC EARTH

What does a refrigerator magnet have in common with planet Earth? Believe it or not, they're both magnets.

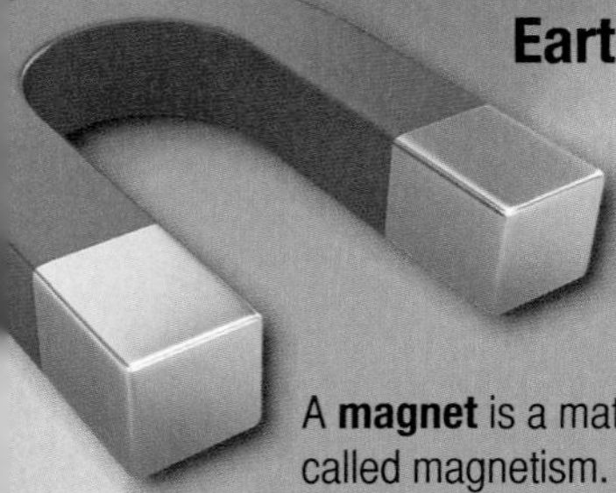

Magnets

A **magnet** is a material that attracts iron and iron compounds with a force called magnetism. Steel can become a magnet itself when stroked against naturally magnetic iron ores called **lodestones.** Magnetic force can pull metal objects toward the magnet and sometimes even push them away. It's strong enough that a small refrigerator magnet can hold papers on your refrigerator. But there are also large magnets that can hold much heavier loads. Magnets create areas of space around them called **magnetic fields.** The magnetic field becomes weaker at a distance.

Earth's Magnetic Field

Just like all magnets, Earth has a magnetic field around it. You cannot see Earth's magnetic field, but it is all around you.

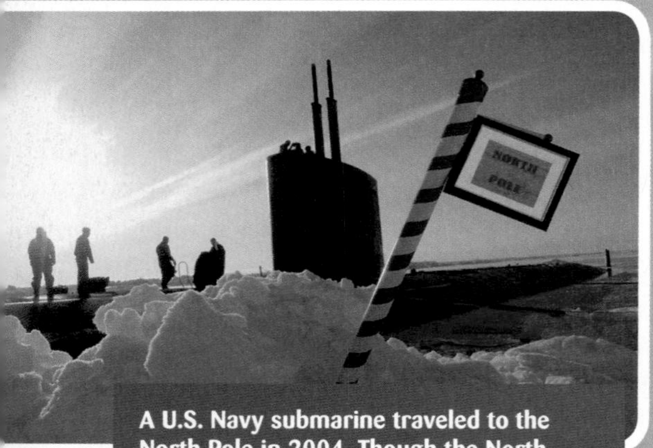

A U.S. Navy submarine traveled to the North Pole in 2004. Though the North Pole is located in the Arctic Sea, the water is usually covered with sheets of sea ice that constantly move and shift.

A Pair of Poles

The magnetic North Pole moves slightly over time because of changes in the Earth's core.

Magnets have two poles. A **pole** is another name for the end of a magnet. One pole is called the north pole. The other is the south pole. The magnetic force is strongest at a magnet's poles. Where else do you use the terms *north pole* and *south pole*? Exactly—when talking about two very cold areas on our planet. Earth has a North Pole and a South Pole, although Earth's magnetic poles and geographic poles do not match exactly. In magnets, like poles repel and opposites attract. You can try this with small magnets. If you put the south poles of two magnets near each other, they won't stick together. In fact, the magnetic force will push them apart.

How Do Paper Clips Respond to Magnets?

YOU WILL NEED:

- Box of uncoated paper clips
- Bar magnet with the north (N) and south (S) poles

1. Make a pile of paper clips on a table.

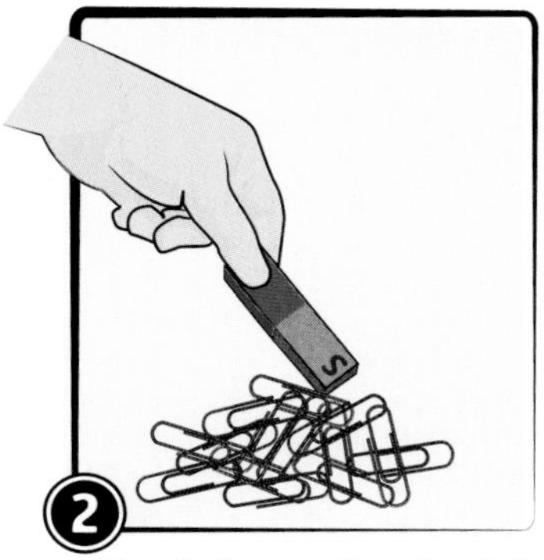

2. Touch the south pole of the magnet to the paper clips. Lift up the magnet. What happens?

3. Touch the north pole of the magnet to the paper clips. Lift up the magnet. What happens?

4. Touch the side of the magnet to the paper clips. Lift up the magnet. What happens?

ANIMAL MAGNETISM

Scientists believe many animals are influenced by Earth's magnetic field. Some study migrating birds to find out if Earth's magnetic field guides the birds in the direction they travel. Other scientists aim to determine if Earth's magnetic field influences sea turtles as they swim across the oceans.

Change it UP!

☞ See how the magnet interacts with metal objects such as a coin, an earring, an aluminum can, a fork, a bolt, scissors, and some foil.

The SCIENCE Behind It

A magnet is a special metal. Magnets attract things made of steel or iron, like paper clips. Magnets have north and south poles with space between them. A magnetic field is like a big bubble around the magnet that starts at the magnet's north pole and loops around to the south pole. The magnet attracted the paper clips when you touched its poles, or the ends of the magnet, to the pile because a magnet's pull is strongest at its poles. The attracted paper clips form a loop when you dip the side of the magnet into the pile. This loop shows what the magnetic field looks like.

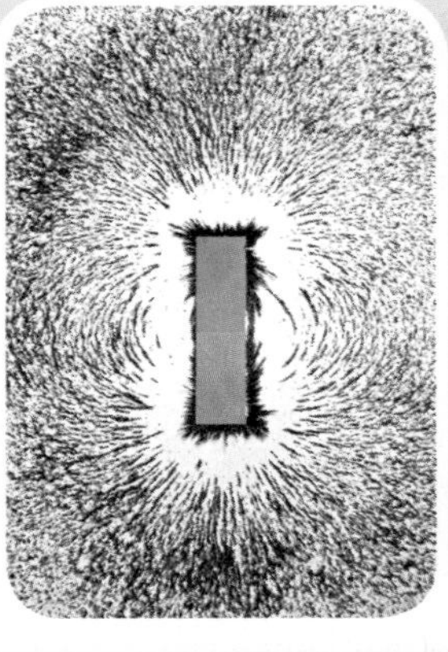

LIFE SCIENCE

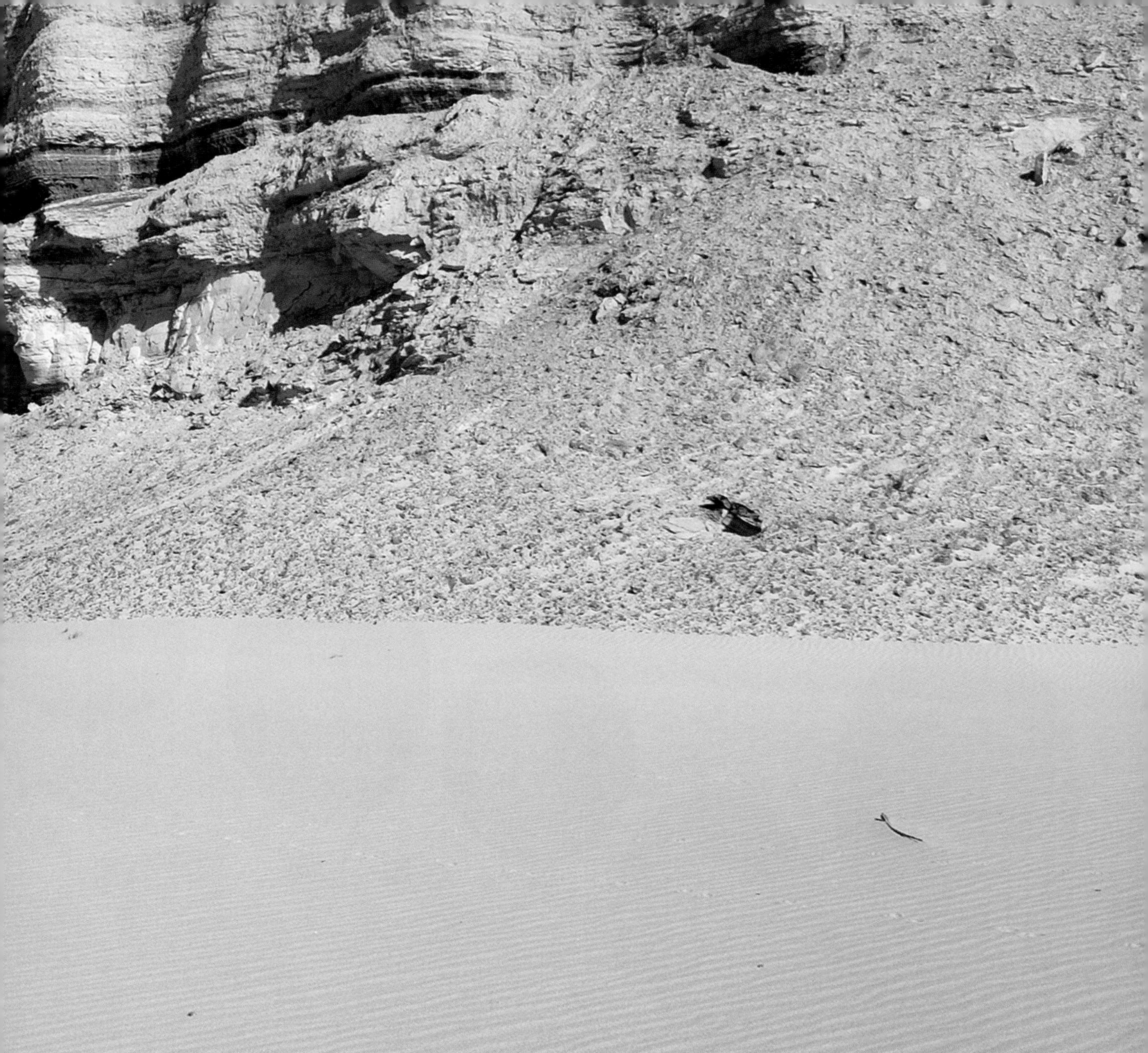

How do plants survive in the desert? Why are some animals endangered while others are just fine? What's up with camouflage? And how does the human body work? Life science explores living things, like plants and animals (including humans). Biology is a life science that includes the study of life, from cells and genes to every kind of animal and how it evolves. Microbiology is the scientific study of microscopic organisms. Botany focuses on plants, and zoology is the study of animals.

SEED GERMINATION

Seeds are how plants reproduce themselves. For a seed to grow into a plant, it must first sprout, or germinate.

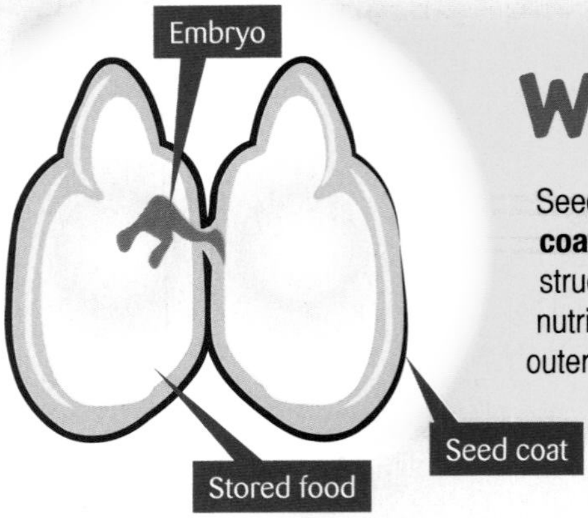

What's in a Seed?

Seeds have three basic parts: an **embryo,** a **food storage area,** and a **seed coat.** The embryo is the undeveloped plant. It contains either one or two leaflike structures, called **cotyledons** (kot-i-*leed*-un). The food storage area contains the nutrients that the embryo will feed on as it starts to grow. The seed coat is the outer layer of the seed. It protects the embryo from getting damaged.

Once a seed is exposed to the right growing conditions, it begins to take in water and oxygen through its seed coat. This sends a signal to the embryo to start using the nutrients in the seed's food storage area. As the embryo feeds on the nutrients, it begins to swell. Eventually, the embryo gets so big it causes the seed coat to break open.

A root then begins to grow downward, searching for more water and nutrients. This first root is called a **radicle** (*rad*-i-kul).

Soon after, a shoot emerges. It grows upward, seeking light and air. This shoot is called a **hypocotyl** (hy-puh-*kot*-l), and it produces the plant's first leaves.

During the germination of some plants (such as sunflowers), the hypocotyl pulls the embryo's cotyledons out of the ground with it. When other plants (such as peas and corn) germinate, the cotyledons remain in the soil.

The cotyledons will wither away once the plant has grown its first true leaves.

In 2005, scientists were able to get a 2,000-year-old seed to germinate. The seed was from a date palm tree. It was found in the ancient palace of Herod the Great in Israel. The seed is now a little tree. Scientists named it Methuselah, after the oldest man in the Bible.

A Seed's "Quiet" Time

To **germinate,** a seed needs the conditions in the environment—things like air temperature, moisture, and light—to be just right. Some seeds are always ready to sprout if the conditions are good. Other seeds are programmed to stay inactive, or dormant, for a period of time before they start to grow. Many seeds stay dormant through the winter. They contain a natural chemical that keeps them from germinating until spring, when the conditions for survival after germination are at their best.

HOW FRUITS ARE FORMED

Flowering plants enclose their seeds in an ovary. As the seeds mature, the ovary becomes a fruit. Apples, grapes, strawberries, and oranges are examples of seed ovaries that have developed into fruits. Many other foods that we eat are also fruits, although we don't usually call them that. These foods include tomatoes, cucumbers, pumpkins, eggplants, and pea pods.

Not all plant fruits are edible. The dandelion's fluffy parachutes are fruits, for example, as are the hooked burrs of the unicorn plant and the winged samaras of the elm tree.

In addition to protecting seeds until they are ready to germinate, fruits help make sure the seeds inside them are spread as widely as possible. Dandelion parachutes are carried long distances on the wind, and burrs travel on the hairs and feathers of animals. Animals also help spread the seeds of berries and other juicy fruits. They eat the fruits. The seeds then pass through the animals' digestive systems, and get deposited in the animals' droppings, often far from the original plant.

GERMINATION OR TERMINATION?

Not all seeds are able to grow into plants. Several factors can destroy a seed's viability, including the wrong amount of water or heat. A simple experiment can be used to demonstrate how one of those factors—heat—affects a seed's ability to germinate.

Are Seeds Alive?

YOU WILL NEED:

- 2 clear containers
- Water
- Raw, unsalted sunflower seeds
- Roasted sunflower seeds
- Tape
- Marker

Fill each container with water.

Place 10 raw sunflower seeds in one container and label it with a piece of tape.

Place 10 roasted sunflower seeds in the other container and label it with a piece of tape.

Let the seeds soak in the water for 10 hours overnight.

Drain the water and remove any seed skins that have come free from the seeds.

science fair tip

In your display, include a labeled diagram of the germination of a seed.

DOOMSDAY SEEDS

Not all seeds germinate, even under ideal conditions. The seed may be improperly formed. A predator or plant disease may have damaged or killed the seed. An environmental condition, such as too much water or too much heat, could also cause a seed to lose its viability. The age of the seed is another factor. Some seeds remain viable for only a short time.

Because healthy plants can be lost to diseases, environmental disasters, and wars, scientists keep seeds from all kinds of plants in seed banks. In the event that a particular plant is wiped out in nature, it will not be lost forever. The Svalbard Global Seed Vault is an enormous high-security, underground storage facility on a remote arctic island in Norway that houses backup versions of seeds from all around the world. It is also known as the "doomsday vault."

6 Add fresh water to each bowl.

7 Place the containers in indirect light and change the water daily.

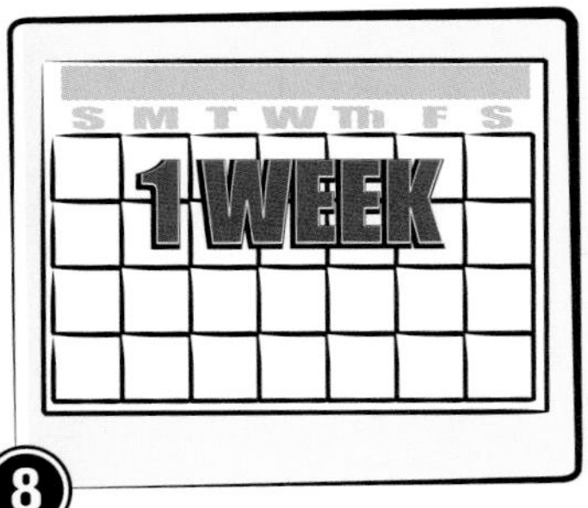

8 Observe the results twice a day for a week. What do you see?

Change it UP!

☞ Using only the raw sunflower seeds, try different temperatures of water and observe the results.

☞ Soak raw seeds in plain water, in water with salt added, and water with sugar added, and compare the results.

☞ Try germinating the seeds in complete darkness and direct sunlight, in addition to indirect light.

☞ Are other liquids better or worse than water for sprouting raw sunflower seeds? Soak sunflower seeds in water, orange juice, milk, iced tea, vinegar, soda, and seltzer, and observe the results.

☞ See what germinates most quickly: lentils, garbanzo beans, sesame seeds, brown rice, or almonds.

The SCIENCE Behind It

Raw seeds are alive! Germination is what happens when a seedling grows from a seed. This is possible because a seed contains a plant embryo, just like a pregnant human mother contains a human embryo. During germination, the seed embryo soaks up the water, causing it to swell and split the seed coat. Water can penetrate some seeds more easily than others. Those seeds germinate faster. For a seed to germinate, however, it must be viable (alive). When seeds are roasted, they are no longer viable. The heat from the roasting has killed the embryo—and destroyed many of the nutrients in the seed's storage tissue area.

GROWING PLANTS

Plants are all around us. They give us food, shelter, and medicines—even the oxygen we breathe. But what do plants need to grow? What helps them grow best?

Plants Make Food

Plants cannot live and grow without **photosynthesis.** Photosynthesis is the process plants use to make food. Plants need three ingredients for photosynthesis: carbon dioxide, water, and light.

- Plants take in carbon dioxide from the air through holes in their leaves called **stomata.**
- Plants take in water (and minerals) from the soil through their roots.
- Outdoor plants get light from the sun. Indoor plants get light from lamps and indirect sunlight.

During photosynthesis, plants make sugars such as glucose. Plants change the sun's light energy into chemical energy and store it in glucose. Many animals eat plants. For example, horses munch on grass, rabbits love to raid the vegetable garden, and you've had plenty of apples and ears of corn in your lifetime. When an animal eats a plant, the animal's digestive system breaks down the glucose to release the stored energy. The animal's body then uses that energy to move, grow, and stay alive.

An animal that only eats plants is called an herbivore. Giraffes, elephants, guinea pigs, and grasshoppers are herbivores.

Food Chain

A simple food chain shows how the energy that plants get from sunlight is passed along from that plant to one animal, then another, then another. For example, a plant takes energy from the sun to grow, then the plant is eaten by a grasshopper, which is eaten by a rabbit, which is then gobbled up by a fox. When the fox dies, decomposers such as mushrooms, earthworms, and bacteria help to break down the animal's body into nutrients. These nutrients return to the soil, where they help to feed plants.

Humans are at the top of many food chains. Here's one.

Photosynthesis

This equation explains photosynthesis:

$$6CO_2 + 6H_2O \xrightarrow[\text{produces}]{\text{with light energy}} C_6H_{12}O_6 + 6O_2$$

Plants take in carbon dioxide (CO_2) and water (H_2O). Using light energy from the sun, the plants produce sugar ($C_6H_{12}O_6$) and oxygen (O_2) from these ingredients.

About half of Earth's oxygen comes from single-cell, plantlike organisms called algae.

The Steps of Photosynthesis

Carbon dioxide from the air enters plants through stomata. Water from the soil enters plants through roots.

Light shines on leaves, which contain structures called chloroplasts (*klor*-o-plasts). Chloroplasts contain a green pigment, chlorophyll (*klor*-o-fill), that absorbs light energy.

The plant uses the light energy to split molecules of water into hydrogen and oxygen.

The plant gives off oxygen through its leaves as a waste gas. Most of the oxygen we breathe is released as waste by plants and algae during photosynthesis.

The hydrogen bonds with substances in the chloroplasts. This creates energy the plant can use to continue the process when there is no light.

The plant combines carbon from the carbon dioxide and hydrogen from the water to produce glucose. Plants use some glucose. They store extra glucose as starch.

Chlorophyll gives plants and leaves their green color. During the spring and summer, the leaves on many deciduous trees have lots of chlorophyll and are green. In the fall, the leaves are exposed to less sunlight and the chlorophyll absorbs less light energy. The chlorophyll begins to break down, and the leaves lose their green color.

LIGHTEN UP

Plants need light. Yet how much do they need to grow? In this experiment, you will grow plants in different amounts of light to find out.

Where Do Plants Grow Best?

YOU WILL NEED:

- 6 healthy carrots
- Knife
- 3 shallow dishes
- Water
- Pencil
- Paper

SAFETY NOTE
Do not handle sharp knives. Have an adult helper cut the carrot tops for you.

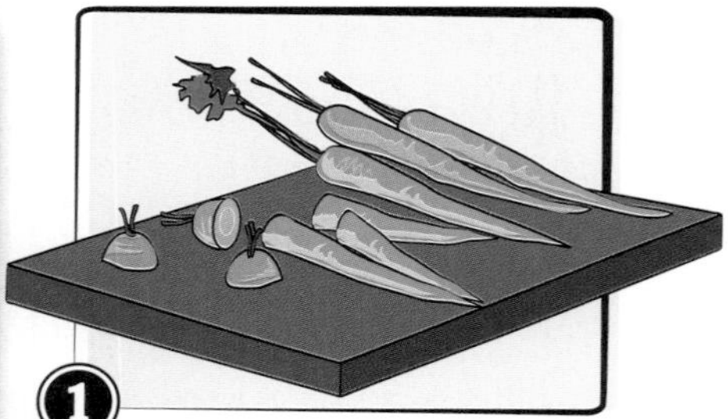

1. Have an adult helper cut the tops off six carrots about 1 inch (2.5 cm) from the top. Have your helper also trim the stems short and cut off any leaves.

[Note: You will not need the rest of each carrot. Set them aside for a snack!]

2. Add a shallow layer of water to each dish. Place two carrot tops stem-side-up in each dish. Make sure the tops stick up out of the water.

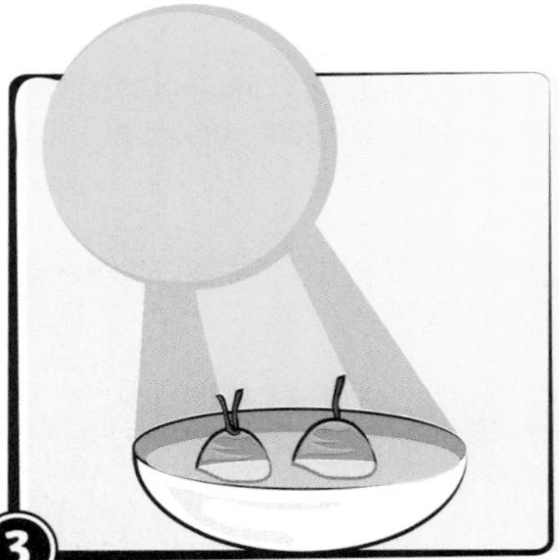

3. Place one dish in a sunny spot by a window.

4. Place the second dish away from direct sunlight.

science fair tip

Create a graph that shows the growth of the plants under different conditions. The x-axis can be the time, and the y-axis can be the length of the plant. Represent each plant as a different-colored line on the graph.

An astronaut inspects a plant-growth experiment aboard the International Space Station.

FARMING IN SPACE

Plants need light. So how do you grow plants where there is very little or no light? Scientists at NASA are trying to solve that problem because growing plants on space stations or on other planets will be difficult. There is either no sunlight or not enough. NASA is developing LED (light-emitting diode) lights for growing gardens in space. A LED is a light source made from a material that an electric current can pass through—but only under certain conditions. LED lights are smaller, cooler, and weigh less than traditional lights. That's great for space transport. LED lights can provide the light plants need for photosynthesis—even when there is no sunlight.

5

Place the third dish in a dark closet.

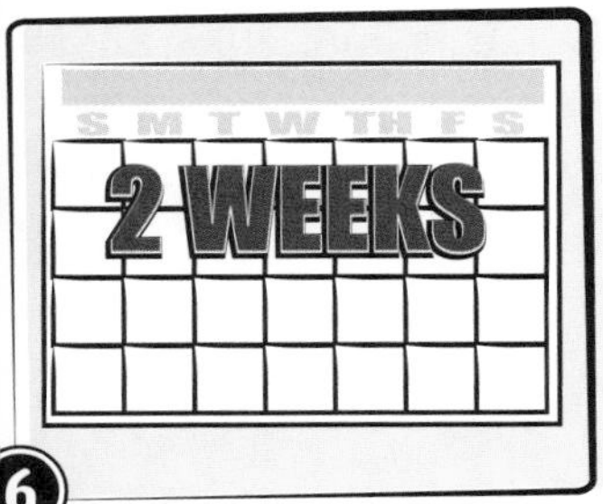

6

Check your carrots each day for two weeks. Measure the length of the stems, and write down what happens to each carrot top. Add water as needed, and change the water if it becomes cloudy or smelly. What do you observe?

Change it UP!

In this experiment, you varied the amount of light that reached your carrot tops. To learn more about how plants grow best, perform the experiment again, changing a different variable.

☞ Try growing carrot tops with both natural and artificial light. Compare the effects of sunlight with those of incandescent light, fluorescent light, and LED light. Be sure to keep the other growth conditions the same.

☞ Mix different substances with the water to find the one that grows the best leaves. Add sugar to one dish, plant food to another, and leave plain water in a third.

☞ Redo the experiment with grass or chia seeds in cups of soil or damp paper towels. What happens if you plant some seeds deeper than others?

☞ Which grow faster: seeds or carrot tops?

The SCIENCE Behind It

Like all living things, plants need food to live and grow. To make their food, plants must have water, carbon dioxide, and light. In this investigation, the plants got plenty of carbon dioxide from the air. You supplied the water. The only uncertain condition was light. After about one week, you probably started to see leaves sprouting from some of your carrot tops. Which carrot tops grew the most? How does the presence or absence of light change the way plants grow?

THIRSTY PLANTS

Like you, plants cannot live without water. But when you water a plant, you pour the water onto the soil around it. How does the water get into the plant? Are there conditions that make it easier for plants to "drink"?

You can see a part of a plant's vascular system simply by looking at a leaf.

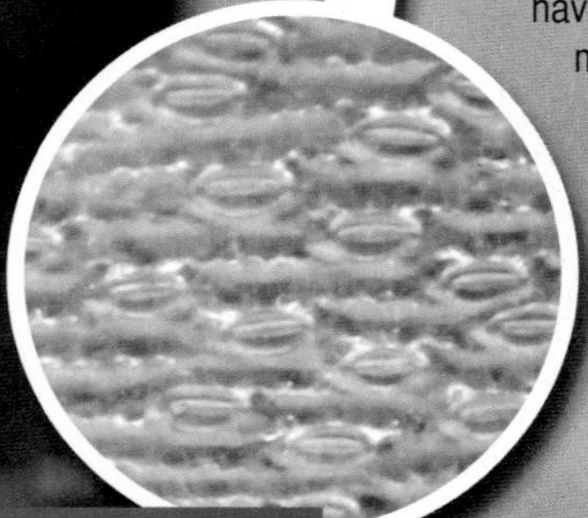

This leaf has been magnified to appear 40 times larger than its actual size. Now the stomata are easy to see.

The Vascular System

Plants don't drink the way we do. But like us, they do need to ingest water. If you look closely at any leaf, you can see veins running through it. The veins are the plant's **vascular system**—a system of tubes that carry water and nutrients throughout the plant. In plants, there are two types of vascular tubes: phloem and xylem. **Phloem** (*flow*-em) tubes carry sugars and other nutrients the plant makes during photosynthesis to all parts of the plant. **Xylem** (*zye*-lem) tubes carry water and minerals from the roots up to the stems and leaves. Water evaporates and exits the leaf through stomata. **Stomata** are small holes in the top surface of leaves.

Similar to the vascular system in plants, humans have a cardiovascular, or circulatory, system. Its main organ is the heart. Instead of carrying water and minerals, our veins and arteries carry blood all over our body.

This microscopic image shows a cross section of the root of a buttercup plant.

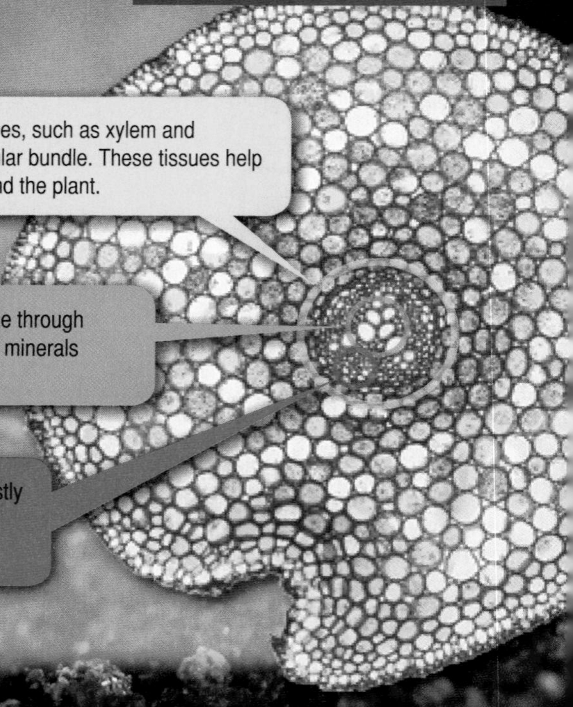

This is the **vascular bundle.** Tissues, such as xylem and phloem, are found inside the vascular bundle. These tissues help to support and conduct liquid around the plant.

Xylem tubes begin at the plant's roots and continue through the stems, leaves, and flowers, carrying water and minerals throughout the plant.

Plants make food during photosynthesis. This takes place mostly in the plant's leaves. **Phloem** carries food produced during photosynthesis from the leaves to all parts of the plant.

Fluid Movement in Plants

Water doesn't just flow upward through xylem on its own. It has to fight the downward force of gravity. Water is sucked upward because of transpiration. **Transpiration** is the loss of water from plants through the stomata on the surface of the leaves, mostly by evaporation. As water evaporates through the leaves, a vacuum is created at the top of the xylem tube. This vacuum pulls water up through the xylem.

Transpiration happens faster at higher air temperatures than at lower ones. Why? Because water evaporates faster as temperature increases.

Warm water also flows through xylem faster than cold water. That's because warm water is less viscous, or thick and sticky, inside the xylem tube than cold water. Think of what it's like to drink a milk shake through a straw. When the shake is cold, it is thick and harder to suck through the straw. But as the shake warms up, it gets thinner. You can pull it up through the straw more easily.

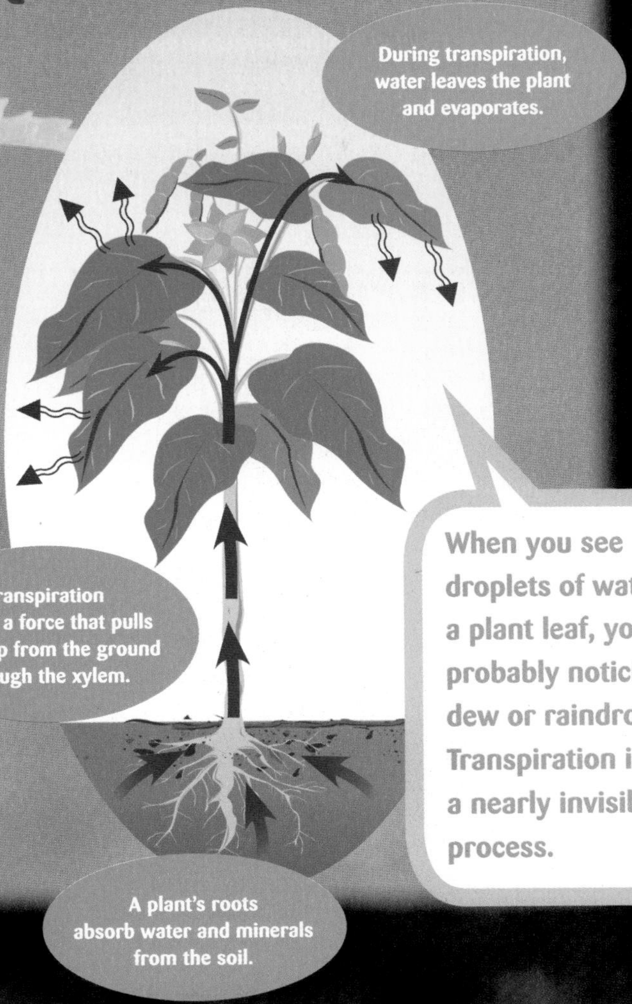
During transpiration, water leaves the plant and evaporates.
Transpiration causes a force that pulls liquid up from the ground through the xylem.
A plant's roots absorb water and minerals from the soil.

When you see droplets of water on a plant leaf, you are probably noticing dew or raindrops. Transpiration is a nearly invisible process.

A large oak tree can transpire 40,000 gallons (151,000 L) of water in a year. That's a lot of moisture being released into the atmosphere!

WATER ON THE MOVE

How does temperature affect the movement of water through plants? In this experiment, you will observe the movement of cold and warm water through two plants to see if there is a difference.

How Do Plants Drink?

YOU WILL NEED:

- Marker
- Tape
- 2 drinking glasses
- Very warm water
- Ice-cold water
- Food coloring
- Room-temperature water
- Bowl
- 2 white carnations
- Scissors
- Watch or clock timer

1. Write "cold water" on one piece of tape and "warm water" on the other piece. Put one of the tape labels on each glass.

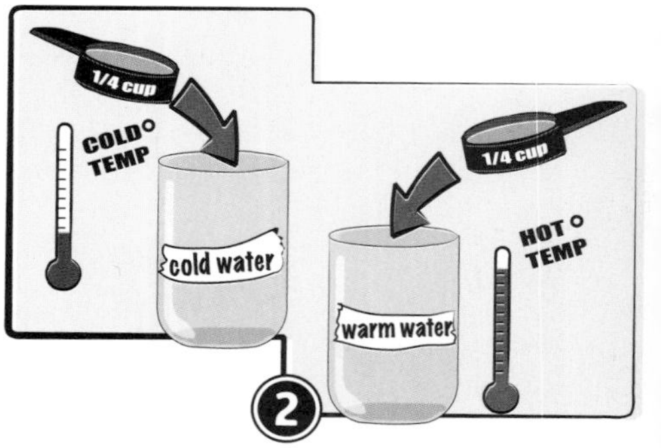

2. Add ¼ cup (60 mL) of very warm water to the "warm water" glass. Add ¼ cup (60 mL) of ice-cold water to the "cold water" glass.

3. Add 20 drops of food coloring to each glass to give the water a deep color. Set the glasses aside while you complete step 4.

4. Fill the bowl with room-temperature water. Place the ends of the flowers in the bowl of water. Cut the ends at an angle while keeping them underwater. The stems should be the same length, about 1 to 2 inches (3 to 5 cm) longer than the height of the drinking glass.

science fair tip

The morning of the science fair, set out two glasses filled with water and a different color food coloring. Place a white carnation in each glass. Encourage visitors to your booth to return later in the day to see if they can detect a difference in the flowers' appearance.

COOLING OFF, NATURALLY

Having tall trees around a house is a good thing—especially in summer. In hot weather, a house with large trees around it will be cooler than one that stands in direct sunlight. Part of the reason is the shade provided by the leafy branches. But transpiration also helps cool the house. When it's warm outside, a lot of transpiration occurs in the trees. The water vapor the trees give off helps keep the air under the treetops—and around the house—cooler than the air in direct sun.

5 Put one flower into each drinking glass. Record the time.

6 Draw or photograph the flowers at regular intervals for two days. Compare the colors in the flowers. What do you observe?

The SCIENCE Behind It

You just traced how plants drink. The colored water was pulled up the xylem all the way into the flowers' petals. Water evaporates out of the petals, leaving the color behind. The evaporation from the flower petals also helps pull water up the xylem in the stem. Notice how the color moves along the petal. By studying how the petals change color, you can see the xylem's structure. Think about your observations in this experiment. Based on what you saw, what statement can you make about the difference in the movement of cold water and warm water in a plant?

Water is made up of tiny particles called molecules. Water molecules move around more quickly when they are warm. This makes warm water move up the xylem faster and color the plant faster than cold water.

Change it UP!

☞ Using several stems of the same type of plant and keeping all other conditions equal, redo the experiment at several temperatures, ranging from very cold to very hot. Observe the plants carefully, and measure the advance of the colored water in the plants' stems and leaves over time. Graph the results. Determine the best temperature for water movement in the plant.

☞ Do all plants drink water the same way? Try your experiment again with a different type of flower, or another type of plant such as celery stalks.

☞ See what happens when the water solution contains either salt or sugar.

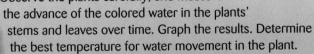

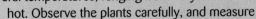

PLANTS AND WATER

Water is good for plants. They need it for photosynthesis, which provides the energy they need to grow and reproduce. Water also helps plants to maintain their structure.

Plant Cells

Most of a plant cell is water. A lot of that water is in the cell's central **vacuole. Cytosol,** the liquid around the structures in the cell, is also mostly water. Water moves in and out of cells through tiny openings in the **cell membrane.** The **cell wall** surrounds the cell membrane. It forms a protective barrier.

Plant cells collect water in their central vacuoles. Full vacuoles press out against the cell wall. This makes the cell rigid, which helps the plant stand upright and keep its structure.

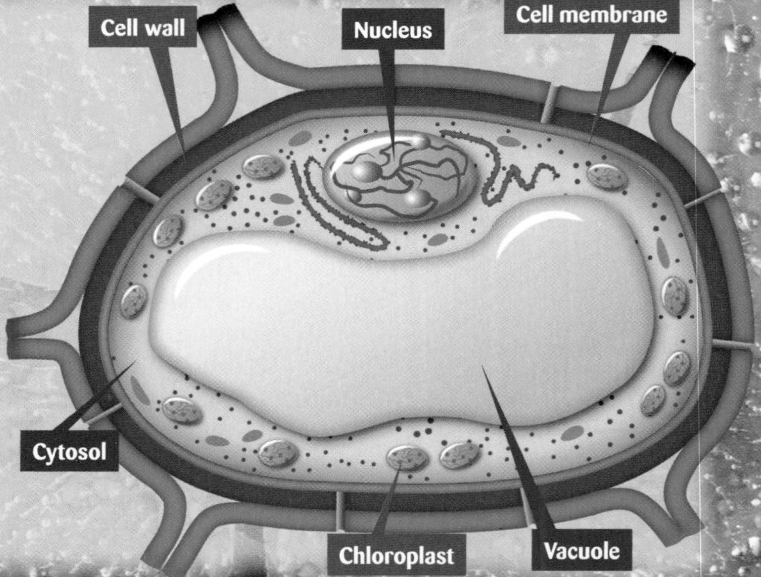

A Plant Drinks In Its Environment

Plants are largely water for a reason. They can't survive without it. But not just any type of water will do. Each plant is adapted to the water in its environment. Most land plants, such as apple trees or roses, must have fresh water. Salty ocean water would kill them. Yet there are plants that thrive in wetlands at the edge of the sea and take in salty ocean water.

Mangrove trees are among the small group of plants that are able to live in and around salt water.

Water Pollution

Human activities can pollute water, leaving it unsuitable for some plants. Pollution that pours into rivers or bays from ships or factories can poison water—and the plants that live on or in that water. Pollution from the burning of fossil fuels can cause acid rain, which changes the chemical composition of soil and contaminates water. Acid rain removes nutrients from soil that plants usually absorb along with water. It can also lead to the release of substances in the soil and groundwater that are toxic to plants.

Help prevent water pollution. Do not pour oil, paint, or nail polish remover down the drain.

Oil Spills

Oil from the Deepwater Horizon oil spill in 2010 seeped into this cove, killing the marsh grasses by the water.

Water pollution can be harmful when plants take it in through their roots. But pollutants such as oil can also be harmful when they coat the surface of plants. Oil comes from wells on land and on the ocean floor. Deep ocean wells produce a lot of oil, but accidents sometimes happen. On April 20, 2010, there was an explosion and a fire at an oil well in the Gulf of Mexico. Oil gushed from the damaged well for months. Almost 5 million barrels of oil poured into the Gulf and the wetlands around the Gulf.

After the leak, there were many pictures of beaches and animals covered with oil. But oil spills also affect plants. Oil coated plants in the marshes and swamps around the Gulf, too. What happens if plant leaves are coated with oil? Oil can clog the leaf's stomata (see page 36) so that carbon dioxide cannot enter the plant. Without carbon dioxide, photosynthesis cannot take place. Water also cannot leave the plant through the clogged stomata. Oil can prevent water from moving through the plant to the cells. With the plant unable to get water to its cells, the cells shrivel and the leaves wilt. If the plant cannot carry out photosynthesis, the plant will stop growing and eventually will die.

OIL AND WATER DON'T MIX!

Plants need water to live and thrive. Unfortunately, some environmental disasters have resulted in huge amounts of oil polluting waterways. In this experiment, you will explore one way oil can impact plant leaves.

What Effect Does Oil Have on Plants?

YOU WILL NEED:

- Vegetable oil
- 4 plates
- Water
- Lettuce

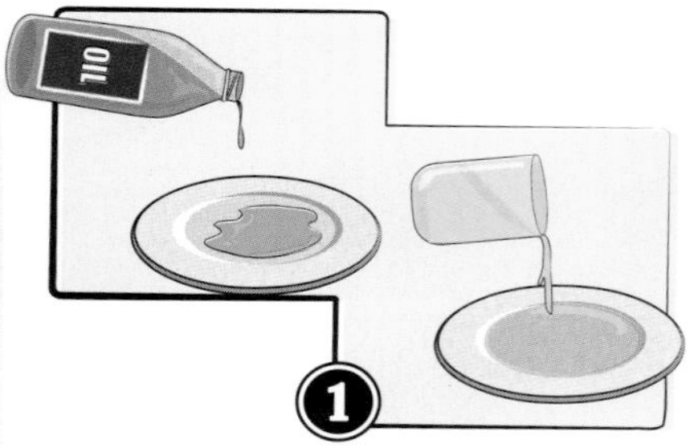

1. Pour a layer of oil onto one plate. Pour a layer of water onto a second plate.

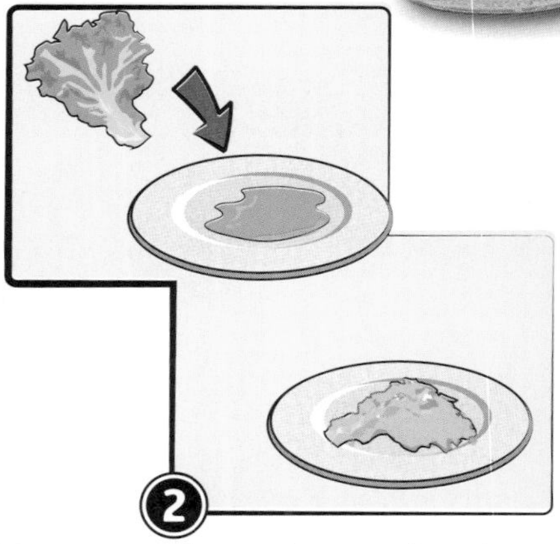

2. Dip one crisp lettuce leaf into the oil to coat it. Place it on a clean plate.

3. Dip a second crisp lettuce leaf into the water to coat it. Place it on the other clean plate.

4. Observe the two leaves every 10 minutes for an hour. What do you observe?

science fair tip

Set three plates in front of your display: One with a piece of lettuce, one with a waterlogged lettuce leaf, and one with an oil-coated lettuce leaf. Let visitors to your booth see and touch the lettuce for themselves. But make sure to have napkins on hand!

The water supply inside a lettuce leaf is important, because lettuce is 95% water.

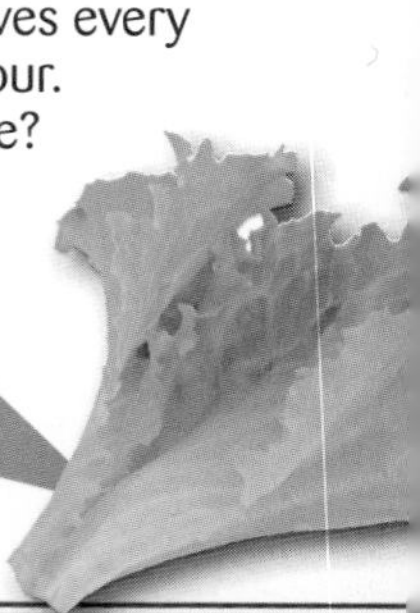

The SCIENCE Behind It

The outer surface of a lettuce leaf has a waxy coating that protects it. So when you put a lettuce leaf in water, the water beads up on the leaf and rolls off the outside. But the vascular tubes in the leaf can still take in water. So the leaf cells will remain plump and full. Oil is a different matter. The oil blocks the leaf's stomata and vascular tubes. It can even seep into the leaf cells. The oil blocks the inflow of water, causing the cell vacuoles to shrivel.

Change it UP!

☞ Experiment with different liquids to see how the lettuce reacts. Some options:

- sugar water
- salt water
- vinegar
- dish soap
- a sports drink, like Gatorade

Compare and contrast how the lettuce leaves react to these different liquids.

☞ Try the experiment again with different kinds of plants. You might see how grass, flowers, or spinach react to oil.

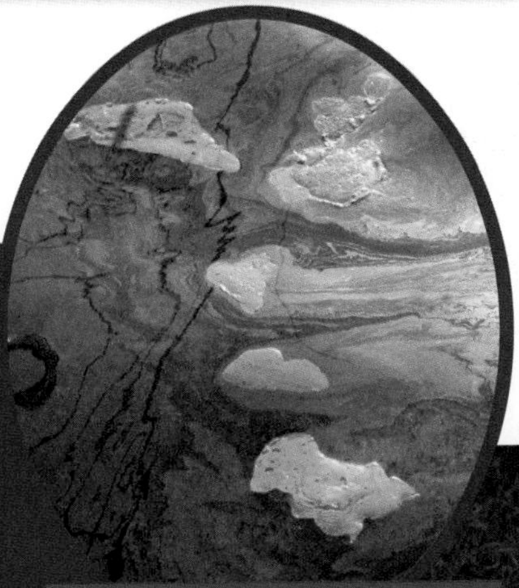

BREAKING UP

Oil spills are difficult because big globs of oil coat everything they touch. Scientists have developed chemicals called dispersants that break the big globs of oil into smaller bits. Tiny bits of oil cannot form a slick surface on plants and wildlife. The tiny bits also have more surface area, so bacteria can break the oil down more easily. Still, some dispersants contain chemicals that harm the environment in other ways. Scientists are trying to create new chemicals that can break up oil slicks without harming ecosystems.

Oil leaves a shiny sheen on the surface of the water. The orange splotches above are from a chemical dispersant used after a 2010 oil spill in the Gulf of Mexico.

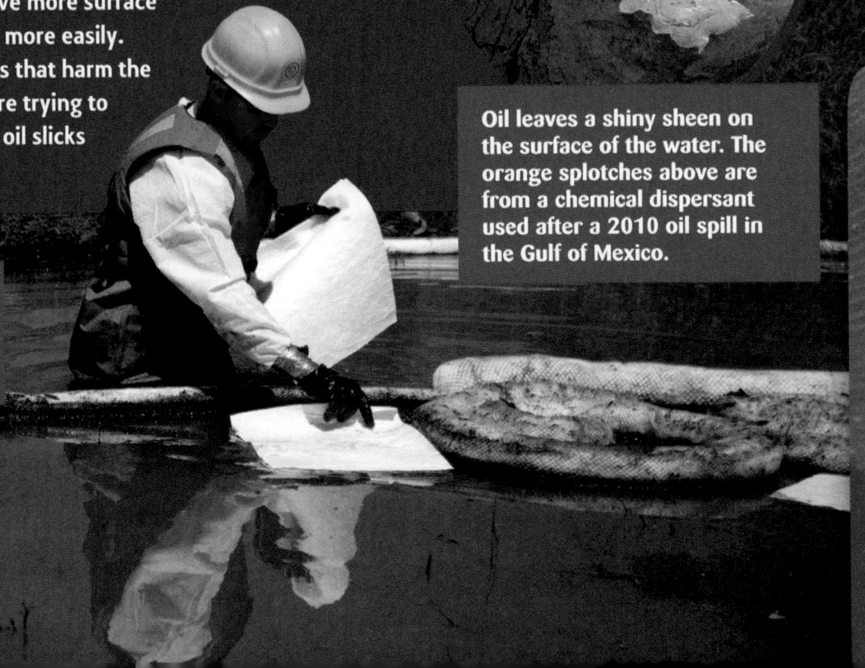

A worker uses oil-absorbent materials to try to soak up some of the oil that seeped into the Yellowstone River in June 2011.

GROWING CROPS FOR FOOD

Farmers rely on many different techniques to create foods that can grow faster or bigger or with more nutrients.

Organic vs. Conventional Foods

For thousands of years, vegetables, fruits, grains, and other foods were grown organically, or without any synthetic (human-made) chemicals. That changed about 100 years ago, when scientists learned how to create chemicals that kill weeds and crop-eating insects. Scientists also invented chemical **fertilizers,** which are added to the soil to make plants grow bigger and faster. Most agricultural (food) crops are now grown with one or more of these chemicals. In grocery stores, fruits and vegetables grown this way are called **conventional foods.**

Herbicides and **pesticides** are useful to society because they help farmers grow more crops. But they can also be harmful to humans, animals, and the environment. Many of these chemicals have been banned. One banned pesticide, DDT, killed almost all the bald eagles in the United States before it was taken off the market in 1972.

Chemicals that kill weeds are called herbicides, and ones that kill insects are called pesticides.

Making Hybrid Plants

A scientist examines a hybrid variety of grape.

Before the invention of agricultural chemicals, farmers used other methods in an effort to grow the biggest, healthiest crops. They would select their healthiest plants during the harvest season—the biggest ears of corn, for example, or the juiciest cantaloupe—and collect seeds from those plants. They would then plant those seeds the next spring. Using this method, farmers developed varieties of corn and other food crops that were not only more likely to survive but also more delicious.

Then, in the early 1900s, scientists discovered that they could grow more corn on the same amount of land by controlling the cross-pollination of different varieties of each plant. For example, they could cross-pollinate a variety of corn that grew fast with one that was resistant to disease. The seeds, or kernels, from this new hybrid corn would then produce plants the next year that contained both these desirable features. Hybrid seeds usually produce bigger crop yields than non-hybrid seeds. But growing hybrid plants has a disadvantage: Farmers can't save the seeds from hybrid plants and use them the following spring. They must buy new hybrid seeds each year. That's because hybrid plants don't usually produce seeds that grow into plants just like them.

Genetically Modifying Foods

This golden rice is growing in a greenhouse.

More recently, scientists have been using a technique called genetic modification to produce food crops with certain desirable traits. Faster-growing salmon, calcium-enhanced carrots, and insect-resistant apples are some genetically modified (GM) foods available today. The technique involves altering a seed's genes. Genes are the "instruction codes" that all living things have inside their cells.

To genetically modify a plant, scientists insert into its genetic code some useful snippets of genetic material taken from another organism. That organism can be anything that's alive, including another plant, a bacterium, a virus, or even an animal! Here are two examples of genetically modified organisms, or GMOs:

- **Bt corn** is a genetically modified corn that contains an insect-killing gene that comes from a bacterium. Farmers who grow Bt corn can use fewer insecticides.
- **Golden rice** is a type of rice that has been genetically modified with three genes. One gene is from a bacterium and the other two are from daffodils. The new genes help the rice make large amounts of beta-carotene, a nutrient that prevents some forms of blindness.

Some people think genetic modification is a useful new technology, and some people are worried about how these new foods could affect our health. What do you think?

This rice has a normal level of phytic acid. Ingesting too much phytic acid can be bad for people.

This rice has been bred to have a low level of phytic acid.

This rice has a low phytic acid level and has been given a gene to make it more golden. This way, farmers can tell the varieties apart just by looking at them.

A "FISH-TOMATO"?

One food company tried to use an Arctic flounder fish gene to create a tomato that could survive frosts. This "fish-tomato" did not succeed, but you can find many other GM foods at most grocery stores in North America.

A seed's genetic code determines what characteristics it will have when it grows into a plant, such as how big it will become and the types of nutrients it will contain.

GROCERY CHOICES

Organic fruits and vegetables are grown from seeds without synthetic chemical pesticides or herbicides. Genetically modified, or GM, foods have had their genes changed, often in a laboratory. The goal is usually to create foods that can survive harsh conditions, or grow faster or larger. Can you tell the difference between organic and GM foods just by looking? Do they taste different?

What's the Difference Between Organic and Genetically Modified Food?

SAFETY NOTE

Ask an adult to help you cut the tomatoes.

YOU WILL NEED:

- Adult helper
- 3 GM tomatoes
- 3 organic tomatoes
- 3 bowls
- 3 plates
- Knife
- Paper
- Pencil
- Camera

1. Have an adult help you buy three GM tomatoes and three organic tomatoes.

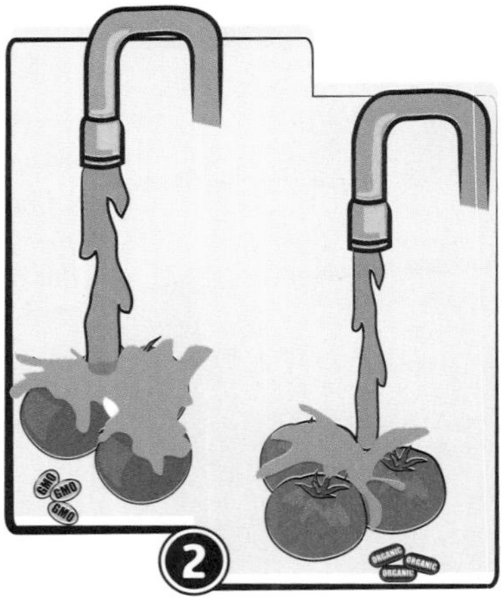

2. Remove the stickers and wash the tomatoes.

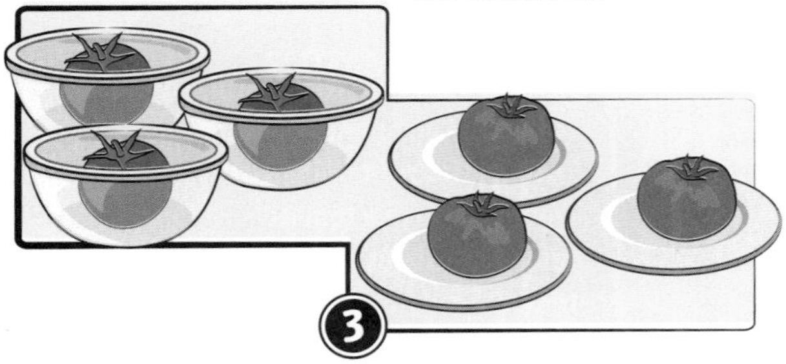

3. Place one organic tomato in each bowl. Place one GM tomato on each plate. This will help you keep track of which is which.

SHOPPING NOTE: In North America, most produce is labeled with PLU code stickers. These codes tell you if the produce is conventionally grown (four-digit code), organic (five-digit code beginning with a 9), or GM (five-digit code beginning with an 8).

Not all companies choose to use the PLU label. If you cannot find GM produce for this experiment, you can compare organic and conventional produce instead.

4 Have an adult help you cut open one organic and one GM tomato. Scoop out the seeds. Then observe and count them. Does one tomato have more seeds than the other? Which has bigger seeds?

5 Have an adult help you slice up one organic tomato and one GM tomato. Keep the GM tomato slices on the plate and the organic slices in the bowl. Gather some friends or family members. Do not tell them which tomato is which. Ask them to taste the slices and say which they prefer.

6 Leave out the last two tomatoes for several days. Write down your observations every day. Take photos to record their decay. Does one spoil faster than the other?

A SEED-FREE FUTURE?

Some fruits and vegetables are naturally seedless. For example, there are seedless varieties of watermelons, oranges, and cucumbers. People like seedless foods because they're easier to eat. The first varieties of seedless fruits and vegetables popped up spontaneously in farmers' fields due to naturally occurring gene mutations. Farmers then took cuttings from those plants to grow the following year.

Most seedless fruits and vegetables grown today are hybrid varieties. They are created through careful cross-pollination. Some seedless fruits and vegetables are also created through genetic modifications. In 2011, scientists discovered a gene mutation that causes many different kinds of plants to not have seeds. That discovery may make it easier to produce more seedless fruits and vegetables in the future.

In 2010, some Chinese farmers sprayed their watermelon crops with a chemical that would make the watermelons grow faster. But it worked too well. The watermelons grew big so fast that they exploded.

The SCIENCE Behind It

Organic farmers do not grow genetically modified foods. They grow their crops without synthetic pesticides or herbicides. Organic farmers want to keep these toxins out of the environment. Conventional farmers use chemicals on their crops, and sometimes grow GM foods as well. Organic, conventional, and GM foods usually look, taste, and feel alike. The choices you make in the grocery store can have effects on the environment and on your health.

Change it UP!

- Try this experiment with different GM and organic fruits and vegetables.
- Compare and contrast conventional and organic eggs or cookies. Do the egg yolks look different? Do the cookies taste different? Create a chart to compare the prices of conventional, organic, and GM foods.

YEAST FERMENTATION

How do bakers turn a bowl of tasteless flour and water into a delicious, aromatic loaf of bread? With the aid of a tiny organism called yeast and an amazing biochemical string of events known as fermentation.

Sugar-Eating Fungi

Yeasts are living, single-celled, plantlike organisms. They are part of the fungus family, which means they're related to molds, mushrooms, and toadstools. Unlike plants, fungi do not have green leaves that contain chlorophyll, so they can't use sunlight to create their own food (for more on chlorophyll, see page 33). Instead, yeast feeds on sugars in plants and other organisms.

It's All About Waste

There are hundreds of different kinds of yeast. Breads are made with a species called *Saccharomyces cerevisiae,* which is also known as baker's yeast. When this yeast eats sugar, it produces two waste products: alcohol and a gas called carbon dioxide. This is the yeast fermentation process—and it's why a loaf of bread is soft and plump rather than hard and flat.

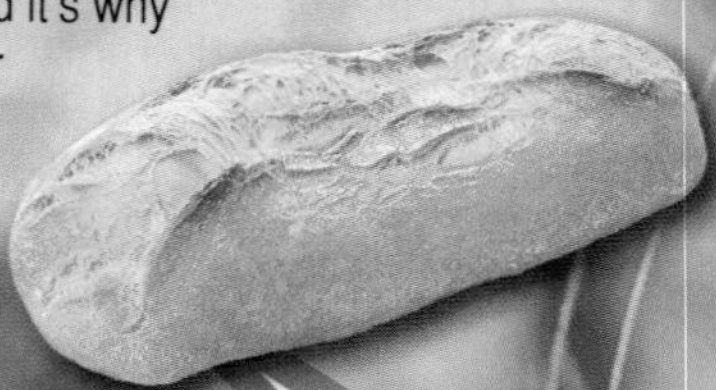

Yeast fermentation is also used to make alcoholic beverages: wine from grape juice, beer from barley grain, and hard cider from apples. In Japan, rice is fermented with yeast to make a drink called sake (*sah*-kee).

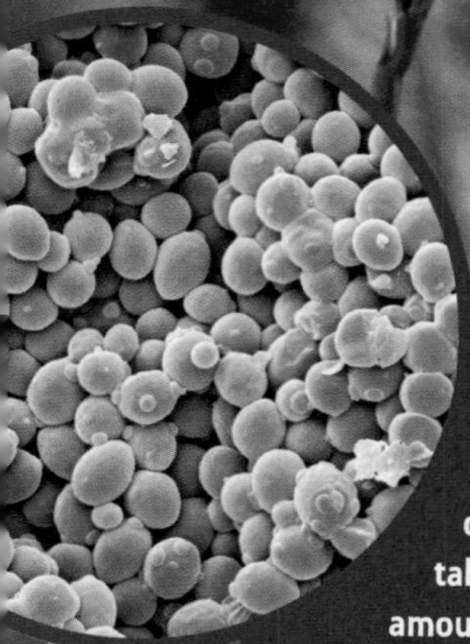

BILLIONS OF LIVING CELLS

Yeasts are so small they can be seen only under a microscope. A single tablespoon of dry baker's yeast—the amount typically used to bake a loaf of bread—contains billions of individual yeast cells.

Fermentation in Action

1. The process begins when the three basic ingredients for making bread—flour, water, and baker's yeast—are mixed together to make a dough. The water causes carbohydrates to be released from the flour. Those carbohydrates contain a natural sugar called maltose.

2. As soon as the yeast "tastes" the maltose, it begins to feed on it. That kicks off the fermentation process—and the release of carbon dioxide. Because carbon dioxide is a gas, it would, if it could, rise up and escape from the bread dough. Instead, it gets captured in little spaces, or chambers, within the dough. Those chambers are created by gluten, a stretchy, sticky, threadlike substance that is formed when flour is mixed with water.

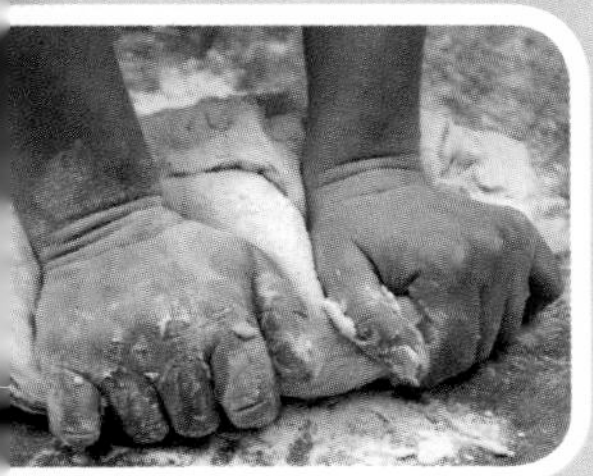

3. The stronger the gluten, the greater the number of chambers—and the more the dough rises. To strengthen the gluten, bakers repeatedly fold, press, and stretch the dough. That process is called kneading, and it can be done by hand or with a special machine.

4. Once the bread has been kneaded and the carbon dioxide is trapped in the dough, the bread is put into an oven to bake. The oven's heat causes the yeast to work even harder at producing carbon dioxide. As the carbon dioxide increases, so does the size of the air chambers. Eventually the heat kills the yeast, and the bread stops rising. The air chambers that have already formed stay in place, however. Those networks of tiny chambers give the finished bread its soft and spongy texture.

5. The other by-product of yeast fermentation—alcohol—gets burned off in the oven. But the alcohol still contributes to the final loaf of bread. Without the alcohol (and the maltose), bread would not have its special flavor and aroma.

FROM HIEROGLYPHICS TO PASTEURIZATION

Ancient Egyptian hieroglyphics contain drawings of bread ovens and beer distilleries. So we know that people have been using yeast fermentation to bake bread and brew beer for at least 5,000 years. But scientists didn't know that yeasts were living organisms until 1836. By 1860, the French chemist Louis Pasteur had figured out exactly how and why yeast ferments. He also learned that if the fermentation process went on too long, it ruined both beer and wine. Pasteur invented pasteurization (the heating of a food to a specific temperature) in order to kill yeast and stop beer and wine from turning sour. That discovery saved these industries a great deal of money. Pasteurization was later used to keep other foods—most notably, milk—from going bad and making people sick.

CAPTURING CARBON DIOXIDE

One of the by-products of yeast fermentation is carbon dioxide. Although carbon dioxide is an invisible gas, you can use a simple experiment to watch and measure its release during the fermentation process.

Why Does Bread Rise?

The little holes and air pockets you see when you look at a slice of bread are formed by gas bubbles from yeast.

YOU WILL NEED:

- 2 clear, clean plastic cups or other containers
- Warm (not hot) water
- 2 packages of dry yeast
- Dry-erase marker
- 1 teaspoon of sugar
- 2 clear plastic food bags
- 2 rubber bands

1 Fill two clear cups halfway with warm water.

2 Stir a package of dry yeast into each cup.

3 Mark the liquid level on each cup with a dry-erase marker.

PAWS-itive Report

Clara Peterson Daily Progress Report: First Grade

Name: Wyatt　　Points Received: 40

Date: 10/26/15　　Teacher: Snow

Daily Goal 34　　Daily goal reached? Yes　No

☹	0 Points
😐	1 Point
☺	2 Points

GOALS	Period 1: 8:20-9:20	Period 2: 9:20-10:20	Period 3: 10:20-Recess P.E.	Period 4: Recess & Lunch	Period 5: End of Lunch-1:10 Lab tears & complaints	Period 6: 1:10- 1:35	Period 7: 1:35-3:00
Respect Yourself	☹ 😐 ☺	☹ 😐 ☺	☹ 😐 ☺	☹ 😐 ☺	☹ 😐 ☺	☹ 😐 ☺	☹ 😐 ☺
Respect Others	☹ 😐 ☺	☹ 😐 ☺	☹ 😐 ☺	☹ 😐 ☺	☹ 😐 ☺	☹ 😐 ☺	☹ 😐 ☺
Respect Property	☹ 😐 ☺	☹ 😐 ☺	☹ 😐 ☺	☹ 😐 ☺	☹ 😐 ☺	☹ 😐 ☺	☹ 😐 ☺
TOTAL	6	6	6	6	6	4	6
Comments				Rested			

Signatures	Student	Teacher	Parent (s)	

____ Copy made and sent home for parent signature　　Entered into SWISS by ______

A SALTY SLOWDOWN

Salt slows down the growth of yeast. Too much salt can keep yeast from fermenting and creating carbon dioxide. That's why bakers are careful about how much salt they use when making bread. They add just enough salt to the dough to make it taste good, but not too much to keep the bread from rising.

4 Add a teaspoon of sugar to one cup and stir.

5 Cover each cup with a clear plastic bag, and secure it with a rubber band. Leave the cups for 20–30 minutes, and observe the results.

Change it UP!

☞ Repeat the experiment by substituting other possible yeast foods. Instead of sugar, here are some foods to try:

maple syrup	molasses	flour
honey	apple juice	salt

Do they all produce gas? Which ones create the greatest amounts of gas? Those are the ones that the yeast prefers.

The SCIENCE Behind It

During the process of fermentation, the yeast feeds on the sugar in the cup, creating two by-products: alcohol and foamy bubbles of carbon dioxide. The gas then escapes from the bubbles and is captured in the plastic bag. When bread is being made, the carbon dioxide released by yeast fermentation gets trapped within the dough, causing the bread to rise.

BREAK IT DOWN

Why isn't Earth piled high with waste and dead organisms? Because decomposers break them down, causing them to rot or decay.

Understanding Decomposers

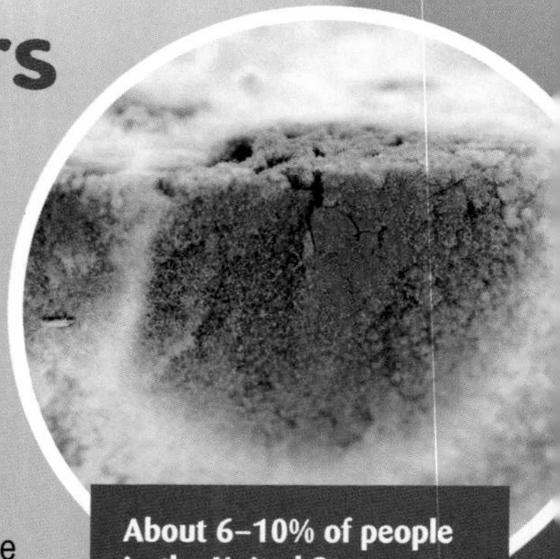

About 6–10% of people in the United States are allergic to mold.

Decomposers are organisms that consume the waste and remains of other organisms to obtain energy. Bacteria and fungi are two types of decomposers. They break down large chemicals in organic matter into smaller chemicals. The small chemicals then return to the environment in a form that other living things can reuse to grow. Not only does this help to recycle vital nutrients, it also keeps dead matter from piling up everywhere! Decomposers help maintain a balanced, healthy ecosystem.

Not all decomposers are desirable, however. For instance, mold is a fungus. You've probably spotted mold growing on foods that you've kept in your refrigerator for too long, or on the bathroom tiles in your home. When this decomposer grows out of control, it can cause health problems. People who are allergic to mold can experience sneezing, develop rashes, or even have an asthma attack.

Some decomposers grow on living organisms and kill them from the outside in. This type of killer fungus sends tiny feeding threads through an organism's body and slowly dissolves its living tissues. Then, the fungus's threads grow upward and out of the organism, ready to reproduce and attack another unlucky victim. Yuck!

Mushrooms are a type of fungus. These are called false turkey tail mushrooms, and they help to decompose dead hardwood trees.

There's a group of decomposers that mostly dine on dung. They're called coprophages (*kop*-ruh-fayj-ez), and are typically insects like flies and dung beetles. Dung beetles break up piles of waste and bury it in the soil. This provides vital fertilizer for growing plants.

Food for Fungi

Fungi are organisms that vary in size from one-celled yeasts to multicelled organisms like mushrooms and molds. Most fungi spread spores to reproduce. They may release thousands of spores, but only a few of them will fall where conditions are right for them to grow into new organisms.

Most kinds of fungi also feed in similar ways. Multicelled fungi feed using threadlike tubes called hyphae (*hi*-fee). The hyphae grow into a food source, ooze digestive chemicals that break it down, and then absorb the food.

Want to be really grossed out? Athlete's foot is a condition caused by a fungus that feeds on chemicals in a person's skin!

MOLDS THAT MOVE

Slime molds were once thought to be a type of fungus. Now, however, scientists know that they are able to move around on their own—something a true fungus cannot do. As a slime mold feeds on bacteria found on decaying organisms, it spreads out and builds tubular connections between food sources.

This type of slime mold is called dog vomit slime mold because . . . well, because it looks like barf.

Some mushrooms are edible, and some are poisonous. Never eat a mushroom that you found outside unless it has been identified by an expert.

Humongous Fungus

There are many ways to calculate the size of a living thing. For instance, you could measure its height, its length, or its mass. Some fungi are tough to measure because much of the organism is underground. A giant fungus in Malheur National Forest, in Oregon, might just be the world's largest organism by area. A honey mushroom, or *Armillaria solidipes,* it spans 5.5 square miles (8.9 sq km). Scientists can't seem to agree, though, on whether this organism is a single individual or whether it is actually a colony of smaller individuals. If it is a colony, then it would lose its world-record title. Either way, it is one enormous organism.

The umbrella-shaped portion of a mushroom is only a tiny portion of the organism. The rest spreads out under the soil. A bunch of mushrooms that seem far apart may all be part of the same fungus.

KITCHEN MOLD

To learn more about everyday decomposers, grow mold in a carefully controlled setting. Observe what happens when food begins to break down.

Which Foods Get the Moldiest?

YOU WILL NEED:

- Slice of bread
- Slice of tomato
- Slice of cheese
- Pencil
- Paper
- 3 clear, disposable containers with lids
- 3 large clear, resealable bags

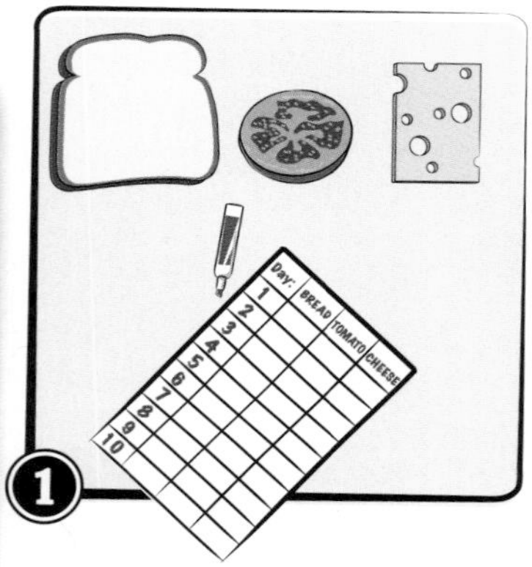

1. Write down your observations about each food slice. You may want to include the size, shape, color, or texture.

2. Place each food slice in a resealable container. If the lids are not transparent, flip the containers upside down for better viewing.

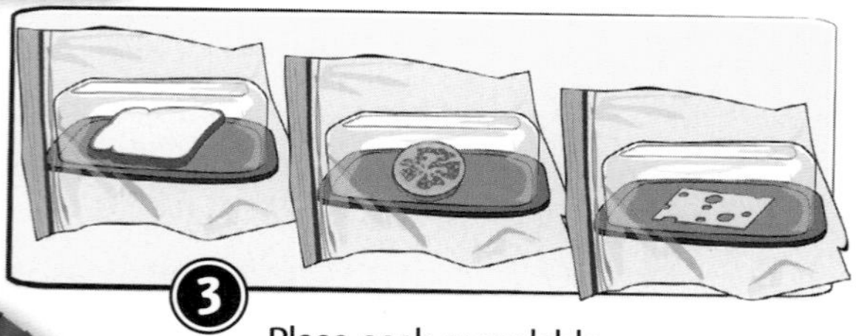

3. Place each resealable container in a resealable bag.

4. Place the three bags on a shelf or cabinet. Make sure they are out of the reach of pets or little brothers or sisters.

science fair tip

Photograph your food samples every day, and include the photos in your presentation. Don't bring any moldy food with you—you don't want to make anyone sick!

SAFETY NOTE

Check with an adult before doing this experiment. Throw out the moldy containers without opening them when you are done with the experiment. These mold spores are not good to smell or breathe.

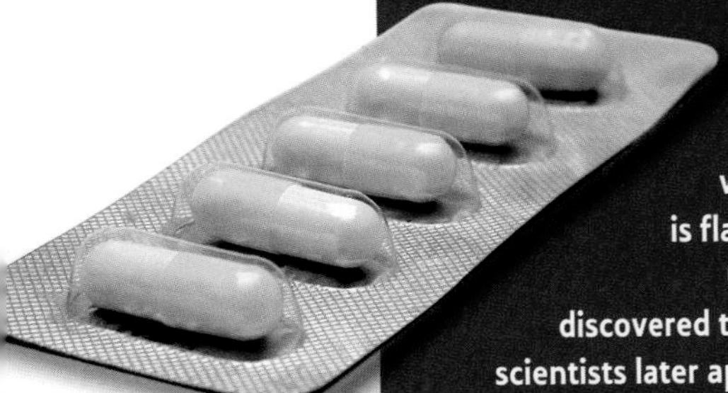

MOLD: GOOD, BAD, AND DELICIOUS

It's important for food scientists to understand molds so they can determine the shelf life of foods and keep foods safe to eat. Some molds can make you very sick, and some are very tasty. For example, blue cheese contains a mold that is flavorful and safe to eat.

Other molds are extremely beneficial. In 1928, scientist Alexander Fleming discovered that the mold *Penicillium* is an antibiotic, meaning it kills bacteria. Other scientists later applied Fleming's findings to develop penicillin for use as a medicine. You may have taken penicillin for an ear infection or strep throat.

- Try the experiment again with new types of food.
- Use two slices of bread, cheese, and tomato. Seal the slices in plastic bags or containers. Then, place one slice of each food in a dark place and one of each in a bright place. Which mold grows more quickly?
- Create a similar experiment, placing one type of food in three plastic containers. Place the containers in locations with three different temperatures.
- Compare how mold grows on wet food versus dry food.
- See if there is a difference between mold growth on a salted food and an unsalted one.

5

Observe your food slices in their containers every day for 10 days. Write down what you see. Which food starts growing mold first? Do the molds have different colors or textures?

6

After 10 days, throw away the sealed moldy containers.

The SCIENCE Behind It

Like mushrooms, molds are a type of fungus. In fact, if you look at them under a microscope, molds look a lot like mushrooms. They grow from tiny spores that float in the air, which is why they can be dangerous to people with mold allergies.

There are lots of different kinds of molds. They can be green, blue, black, or white, and they may be fuzzy, smooth, or bumpy. Different molds tend to grow on different foods. They get energy and grow by breaking down plant or animal tissues. We use refrigerators and preservatives to keep moist foods from getting rotten and moldy too quickly.

There are more than 100,000 species of mold.

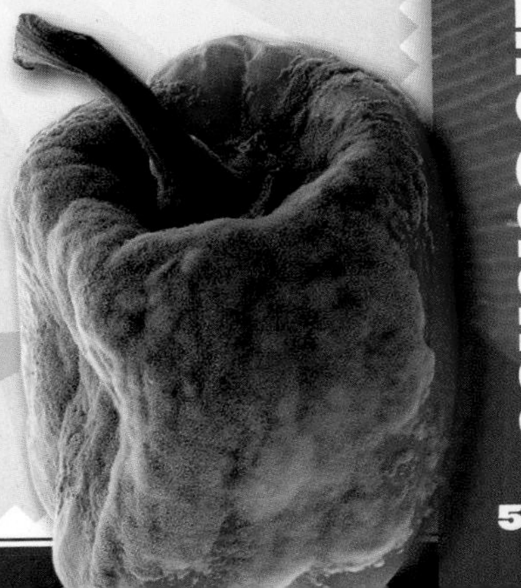

WATER, WATER EVERYWHERE

What substance covers approximately 75% of Earth and is found in every cell, tissue, and organ of your body? That's right. It is water.

Water Is Vital for Life

Water is a combination of hydrogen and oxygen (H_2O). It is essential to life on Earth. The average person could go for several weeks without food, but could survive for only a few days without water to drink. Your body relies on water to carry nutrients to your organs via your blood. Water also helps regulate your temperature, cushion your joints, and transport wastes from your body. You lose water when you go to the bathroom, sweat, and even when you exhale. It is important to replace this water to prevent dehydration and stay healthy.

People need to drink water every day. Foods with high water content like soup broths, celery, tomatoes, oranges, and melons are also good sources. And you shouldn't wait until you get thirsty to drink water. Thirst is your body's way of signaling that you are getting dehydrated. We typically don't feel thirsty until we are about a pint of water low!

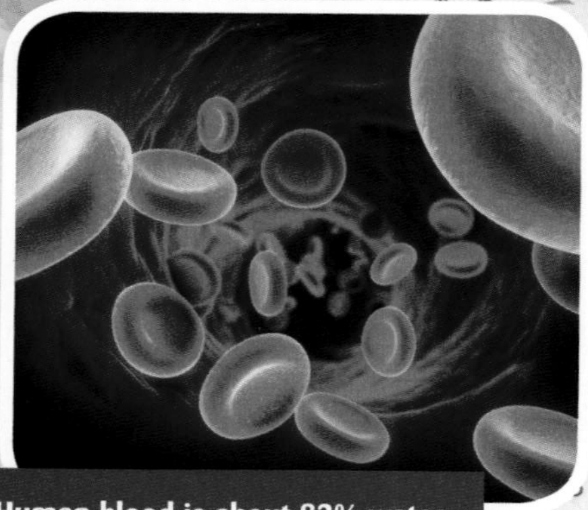

Human blood is about 83% water.

WATER WORLD

Water covers 75% of Earth, but just 1% of that water is suitable for drinking. The rest is salty seawater or is locked up in ice and snow. One way to access water is to tap into an aquifer, which is a special geological formation that provides access to underground stores of fresh water.

The Ogallala Aquifer, one of the world's largest aquifers, sits beneath the Great Plains in the U.S. When families first tapped into it in the late 19th century, water shot 100 feet (30 m) into the air. The Ogallala Aquifer made farming possible in states like Nebraska, Oklahoma, and Kansas. It is now at risk of running dry from overuse.

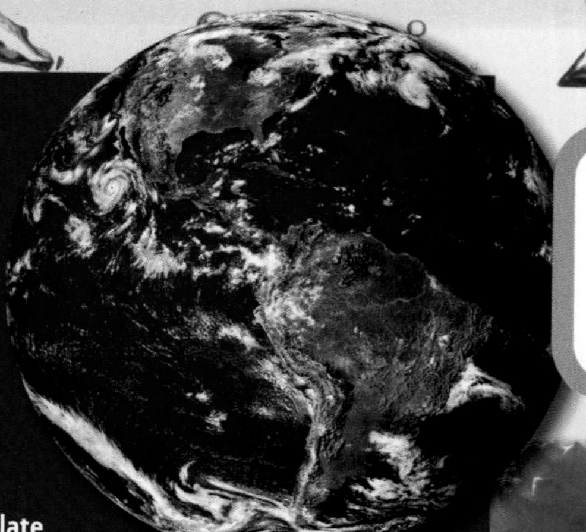

Nearly 69% of the fresh water on Earth is stored in glaciers and ice sheets.

Water Usage

Since drinkable fresh water is so scarce, it is important not to waste it or pollute it. Drinking polluted water can cause sickness and disease. Water treatment plants can filter out many chemicals and bacteria, but cleanup of industrial runoff and household chemicals like lawn-care products, motor oil, or paint removers is time consuming, costly, and often inadequate.

From turning off a faucet while you brush your teeth to running the washing machine only when a load is full, there are many ways to conserve water at home. The average person in the United States uses more water while showering than a poor person living in a developing country uses in an entire day. Inadequate infrastructure and sanitation prevent 1.6 billion people worldwide from getting the water they need.

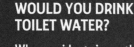

WOULD YOU DRINK TOILET WATER?

When residents in northern and central Orange County, California, fill their glasses with water from the faucet, some of it comes from an unlikely source: sewage! Water shortages have forced the county to get creative about where it gets its water. A new filtration plant purifies wastewater captured by the sewage department. Before you say "Yuck," consider this: The county's filtration process is so thorough that the water is actually too clean to drink! At the end of the process, workers have to add back in a few salts and minerals to make it more like natural water.

Bottled vs. Tap

The United States is the world's largest consumer of bottled water. Although it's good that Americans are drinking their fill of water, plastic bottles are bad news for the environment. They require massive amounts of fuel to produce and transport, and then the majority of plastic bottles end up in landfills, where they can remain intact for as many as 1,000 years. Bottled water is not necessarily healthier than tap water. In 2008, scientists tested 10 popular brands of bottled water and found an average of eight chemical pollutants per brand. Four brands were contaminated with bacteria. The majority of experts agree that buying water in bottles is unnecessary because the tap water in most American cities is perfectly safe.

Using refillable bottles is one easy way to get the water you need, without adding trash to a landfill.

In 2009, U.S. consumers recycled 2,456,000 pounds (1,114,023 kg) of plastic bottles.

THE FLAVOR OF H_2O

Some people say they drink bottled water instead of water from the faucet because it tastes better. But in taste tests, most people actually can't tell the difference between tap and bottled. Can you?

Does Bottled Water Taste Different than Tap Water?

YOU WILL NEED:

- Graph paper
- Pencil
- Ruler
- Two different brands of bottled water
- Tap water
- Filtered tap water
- White paper
- Friends/classmates
- 4 drinking glasses per taste tester
- Scissors
- Tape
- Marker

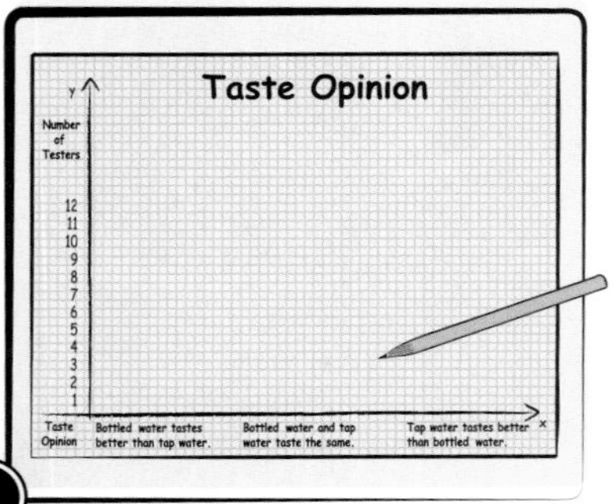

1 On the graph paper, create a bar graph with the title "Taste Opinion." Make "Number of Testers" the y-axis title and "Taste Opinion" the x-axis title. Place three choices along the x-axis:

- Bottled water tastes better than tap water.
- Bottled water and tap water taste the same.
- Tap water tastes better than bottled water.

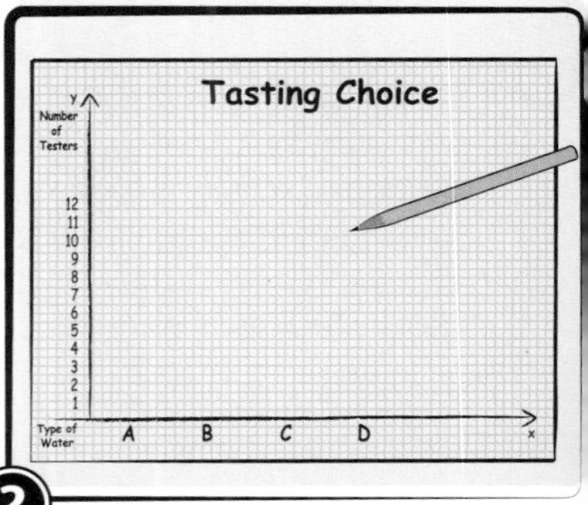

2 Create a second bar graph with the title "Tasting Choice." Make "Number of Testers" the y-axis title and "Type of Water" the x-axis title. Mark the letters for the four types of water along the x-axis.

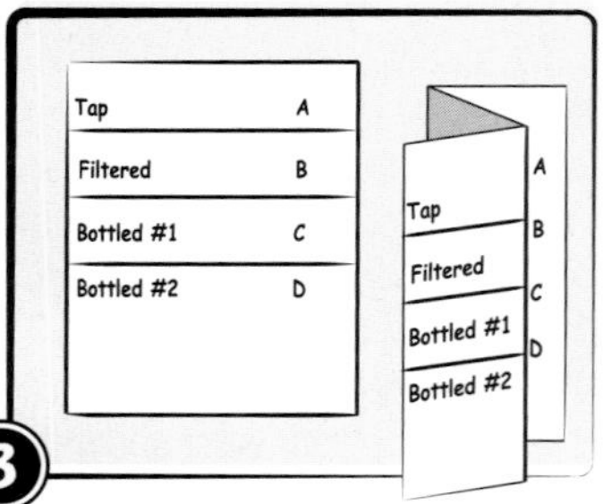

3 Write down the names of each type of water (tap, filtered, brand name 1, brand name 2). Then, assign a letter (A, B, C, D) to each one. Fold the paper and keep this information hidden from your taste testers.

4 Put a piece of tape on each drinking glass and label them A, B, C, and D. Fill each glass about one-quarter full with the type of water that corresponds to each letter.

science fair tip

Some computer programs, such as Microsoft Excel, help you make professional-looking charts and graphs. You can also visit the the NCES (National Center for Education Statistics) Kids' Zone website (nces.ed.gov/nceskids) and use the free Create A Graph program.

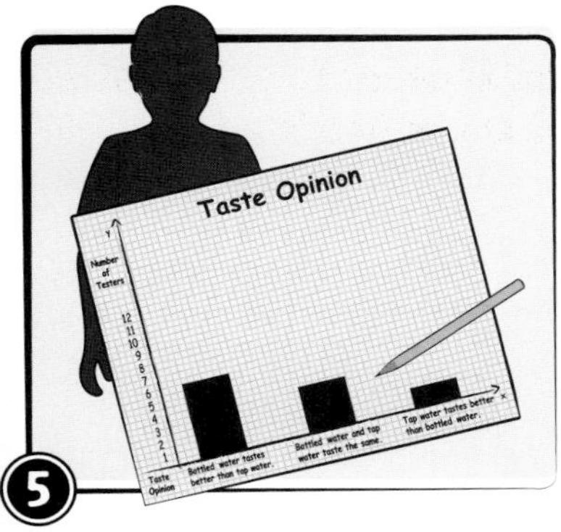

5

Before letting your tester drink from any of the glasses, ask the following question: "Which tastes better: bottled water or tap water? Or do you think they taste about the same?" Record his or her opinion in the Taste Opinion bar graph from step 1.

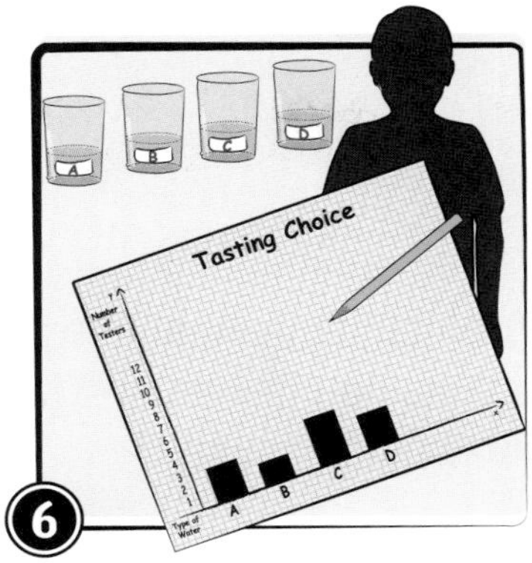

6

Have your tester taste each type of water and choose his or her favorite. Record this result on your Tasting Choice bar graph. Repeat the experiment with all of your taste testers. Make sure to change or clean the drinking glasses after each tester. What do you notice?

Change it UP!

☞ Does knowing about water treatment change your taste testers' opinions? Visit your local water treatment plant to find out how water gets treated before it comes out of your tap. Find out how water gets treated before it is poured into a bottle. Repeat your experiment, but explain how the different types of water get treated before letting the testers give their opinion.

☞ Try graphing your results using another type of graph, like a pie chart. Is it easier or harder to understand your results?

The SCIENCE Behind It

Tap water is treated by your local city to make it safe to drink. Bottled water companies market their products as a tasty or healthy choice of drinking water. The type of water you drink may be influenced by the advertisements you see or by the choices of your friends and family. A person may pick a certain brand of water because of the price or the health claims on the label. Your Taste Opinion graph shows what your testers think they prefer. Your Tasting Choice graph shows what they actually like. Your bar graphs show the difference between our influenced opinion and what we really taste.

Bar graphs are a visual way to compare your taste testers' choices and opinions. The tallest bar in the graph shows the most popular taste-tester choice or opinion. Do your taste testers' opinions of how water should taste agree with their actual water-tasting choice?

SAFETY VS. TASTY

The actual flavor of water, bottled and tap, can be affected by the way it is treated. Have you ever taken a gulp of water and thought it tasted like swimming pool water? That's because water treatment plants add the chemical chlorine to water to kill harmful bacteria and other organisms. Chlorine is used in greater concentrations to keep pools clean. Water safety officials balance the need for safety with the need for tasty tap water. The chlorine will disappear from the water after a few hours, so if you have water that smells or tastes of chlorine, let it sit out on the counter or in the refrigerator for a while before drinking it. Then it will taste just fine!

COLOR AND TEMPERATURE

Why do you choose certain colors for clothing? It's usually because you like the color. But are there other reasons to choose one color over another for clothing—or even the walls of a house?

When Light Strikes

When light strikes an object, one of three things happens:

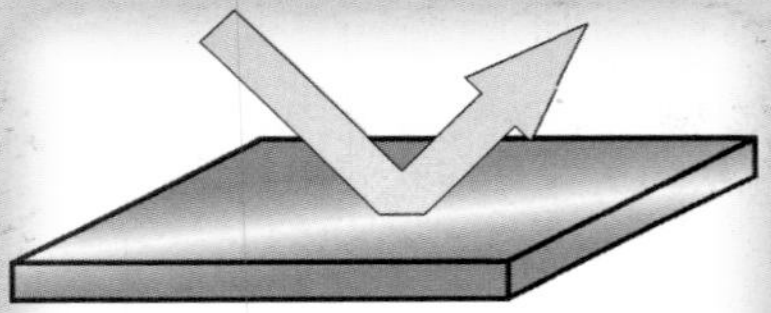

The object reflects the light. **Reflection** means the light bounces off the object. For example, a shiny surface such as a mirror reflects light.

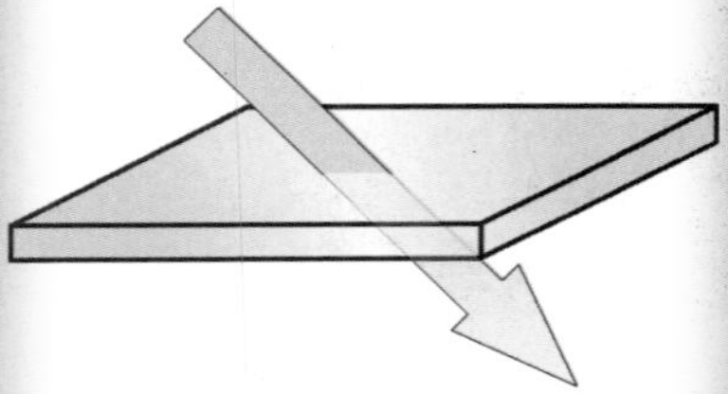

The object transmits the light. **Transmission** means the light passes through the object. A clear object, such as a glass window, transmits light.

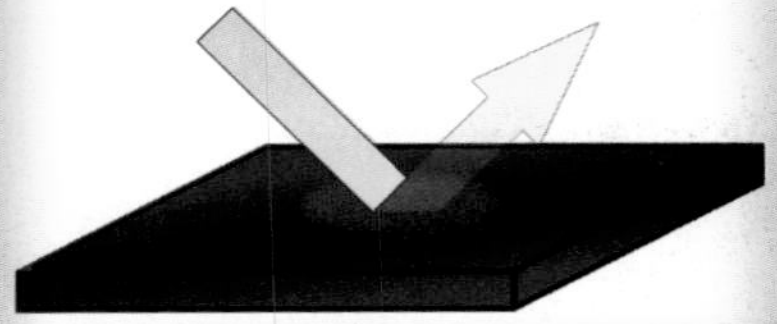

The object absorbs the light. **Absorption** means the object soaks up the light so that little or no light bounces off it. A dark object, such as a black asphalt road, absorbs much of the light that strikes it.

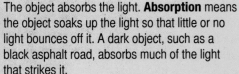

An object that is truly black would absorb all light and reflect none at all. So far, no one has been able to make an object that is totally black.

Energy Transformations

When light strikes an object that is not see-through, the object reflects some energy and absorbs some. What happens to the energy an object absorbs? That light energy is changed into heat energy. The more energy an object absorbs, the more energy it converts to heat.

Why does this happen? Light is energy in the form of electromagnetic waves. When the waves strike an object, their energy causes particles in the object to vibrate faster. This particle motion can be sensed as heat. No energy is created or destroyed when an object absorbs light energy. The energy just changes from one form to another—light to heat. The darker the color, the more light it absorbs. So, more energy becomes heat.

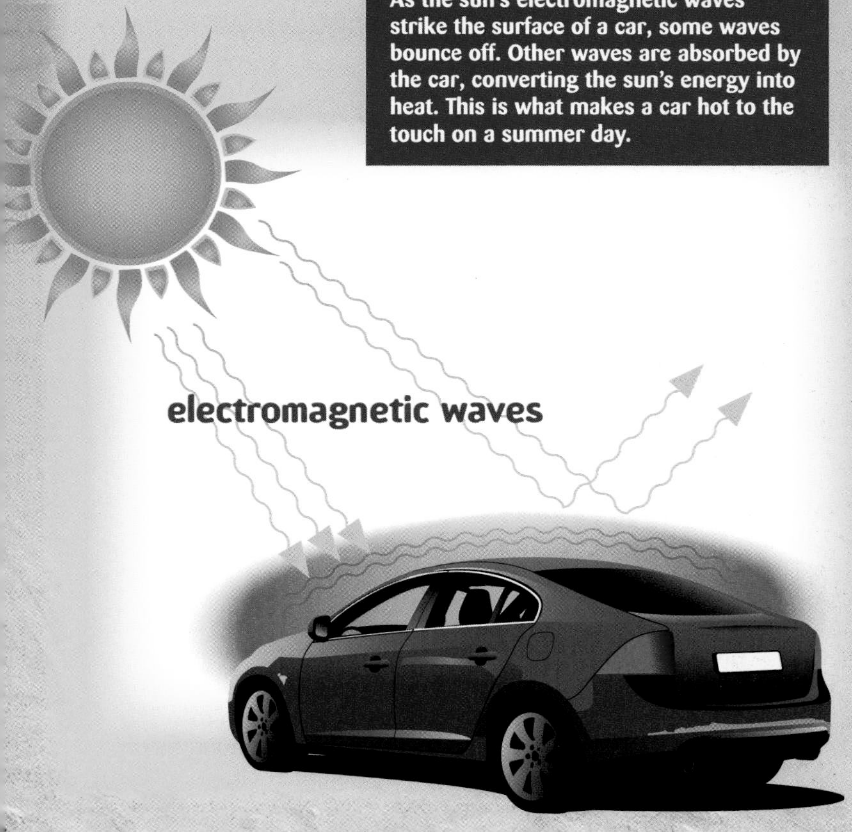

As the sun's electromagnetic waves strike the surface of a car, some waves bounce off. Other waves are absorbed by the car, converting the sun's energy into heat. This is what makes a car hot to the touch on a summer day.

ENERGY CAN'T JUST DISAPPEAR

The transformation of light energy to heat energy obeys the law of conservation of energy (see page 145). The law states that energy cannot be created or destroyed. But it can change from one form to another.

This principle is demonstrated on beach sand on a bright summer day. The sun's light energy strikes the sand. Some of the light energy bounces off the sand. But the sand also absorbs some of the light energy. The light energy changes into the heat that makes sand hot on a sunny day.

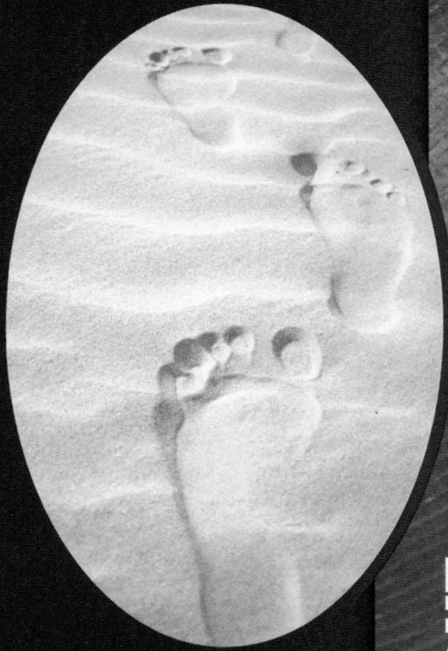

Sand will be cooler—and more pleasant to walk on—early in the morning. By the afternoon, it will have absorbed a lot of heat from the sun and can be painful for bare feet.

YOU'RE GETTING WARMER

Some colors are cool and dark. Other colors are bright and warm. But does color really have an effect on temperature? You'll find out as you complete this experiment.

Which Warms Up Faster: A Light-Colored Liquid or a Dark One?

YOU WILL NEED:

- Cold milk
- 2 clear glasses
- Dark-colored food coloring
- 2 thermometers
- Pencil
- Ruler
- Graph paper

SAFETY NOTE
Check with an adult to get permission to do this experiment. Pour the warm milk down the drain when you finish the experiment.

1. Pour cold milk into two clear glasses.

2. Add several drops of dark-colored food coloring to one of the glasses.

3. Put a thermometer into each glass. Then record the temperature of the milk in each glass.

Time:
MILK
DARK MILK
0 Mins
40°
40°
5 Mins
10 Mins
15 Mins
20 Mins
25 Mins
30 Mins

4. Place the glasses in the sun. Every 5 minutes for an hour, record the temperature of each glass. What do you observe? Does one glass of milk heat up faster than the other?

COOL HOUSES

In the past, roofs were often built with dark tiles or shingles. Some roofs were covered with thick, black tar. But as scientists, environmentalists, and people looking to save money on their energy bills have found out: roof color affects heat absorption. A white roof reflects up to 90% of the sunlight that shines on it. A black roof reflects only about 20%. As a result, white roofs keep homes cooler inside. People who live in houses with white roofs run their air conditioning less and have lower energy costs. Now, many people are painting their dark roofs white, or swapping their old, dark shingles for white tiles or shingles.

A man adds another coat of white paint to a roof in Philadelphia.

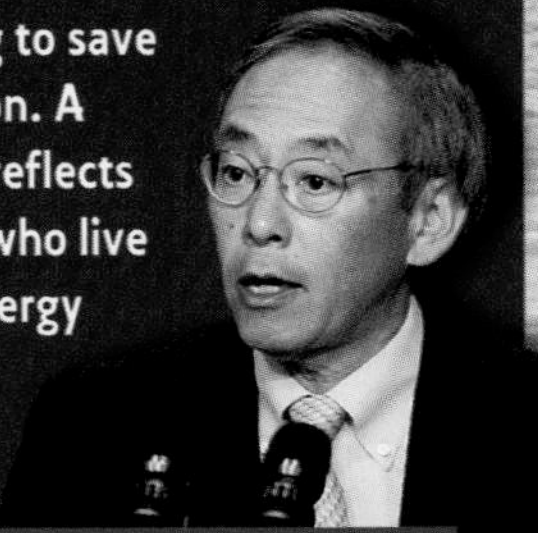

Steven Chu, the U.S. Secretary of Energy, has said, "Cool roofs are one of the quickest and lowest-cost ways we can reduce our global carbon emissions and begin the hard work of slowing climate change."

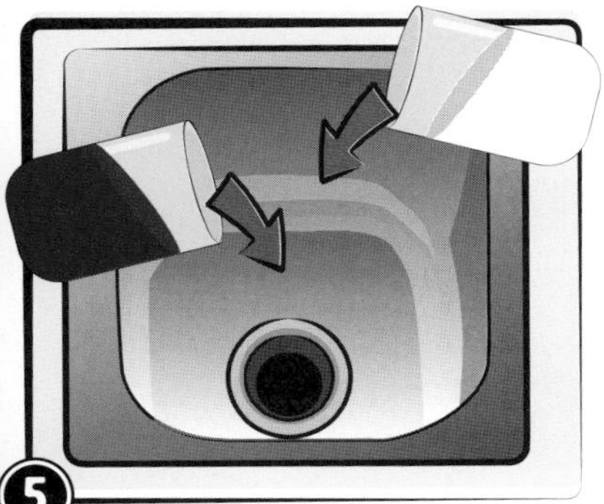

5 Pour the warm milk down the drain.

Change it UP!

☞ Take what you've learned with liquids and test out T-shirts of different colors. Find three to five T-shirts, fold them, and set them in the sun. Place a thermometer inside each folded shirt to check the temperature. Based on your results, determine which color T-shirt would keep you coolest on a sunny day.

☞ Test the effects of different house colors on the temperatures inside them. Use identical wooden or cardboard boxes for model houses. Choose several different colors—some dark and some light—to paint the outsides. Record the change in temperature when the "houses" are left out in the sun for a couple of hours.

The SCIENCE Behind It

Light-colored objects look bright because they reflect most of the light that hits them. Dark-colored objects look dark because they absorb most of the light that hits them.

In this experiment, the darker liquid absorbed more light energy from the sun than the lighter liquid. The absorbed light energy didn't disappear. It was converted to heat energy—causing the darker liquid to heat up faster than the lighter liquid. Remember that when you are having lunch outside!

KNOW YOUR NUTRIENTS

What's on that plate of food you're going to eat? Your eyes may see carrots, chicken, and rice. But what your body gets is nutrients. A nutrient is a substance that provides energy or building material for your body. The three major nutrients are carbohydrates, proteins, and fats. Vitamins and minerals are also nutrients. Your body needs all of these to stay alive, but it needs some in larger amounts than others.

Carbohydrates

Carbohydrates include sugars and starches. Starches are actually composed of chains of small sugars. When the chains are broken, energy is released. Carbohydrates are the main source of your body's energy. Potatoes, rice, wheat, corn, and cereal are rich in carbohydrates. So are fruits and vegetables. All these foods contain important vitamins and minerals, too.

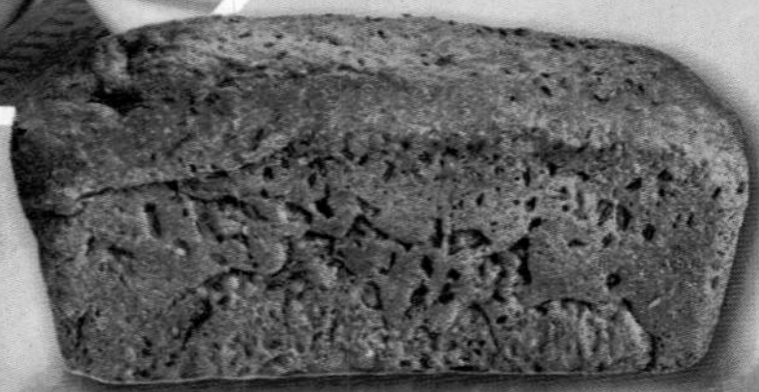

Candy, jelly, and baked goods are high in sugar, but these kinds of foods are often said to contain "empty calories." They seldom contain other nutrients, and eating too much of them can lead to weight gain.

Starchy foods, like potatoes, are high in fiber, which makes you feel full.

WHAT IS FIBER?

Foods such as avocados, kidney beans, and bran flakes contain a lot of fiber. Fiber is a carbohydrate but it isn't a nutrient. It is plant matter that your body cannot digest. Fiber passes through your digestive system and out of your body. It's an important part of a healthy diet, because it helps food move through the digestive system and makes it easier for wastes to move out of the system. Getting enough fiber reduces the risk of certain diseases.

How many calories should a person consume? It depends on several factors, including the person's age and level of activity. People who are very active burn a lot of calories.

Proteins

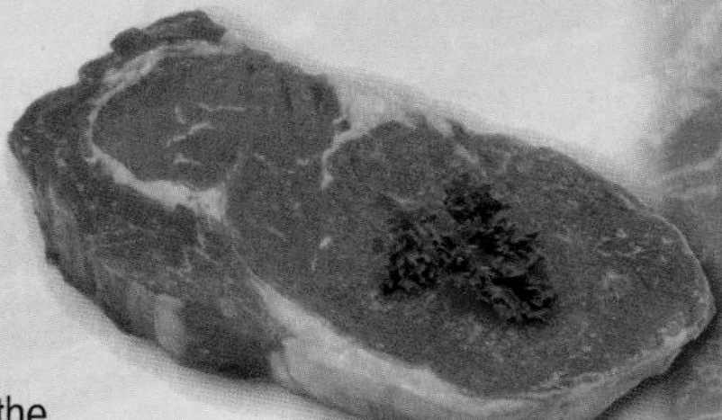

Next to water, protein is the most plentiful substance in your body. Protein is essential for growth and repair. It is the main building material of the body. Muscles, skin, blood, and most other parts of the body are made from protein.

Most food that comes from animals is rich in proteins. This includes meat, fish, eggs, milk, cheese, and yogurt. Many plant foods also are sources of protein. These foods include rice, beans, nuts, seeds, wheat, and corn.

Fats

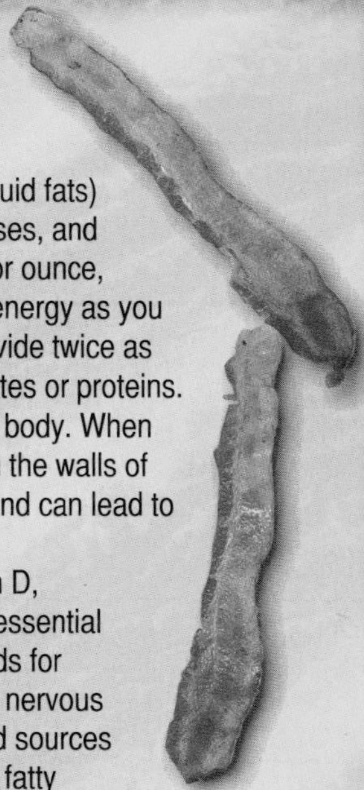

Foods that are rich in fats and oils (which are liquid fats) include butter, bacon, nuts, salmon, many cheeses, and sausages. Fats are sources of energy. Ounce for ounce, burning fats produce more than twice as much energy as you get from carbohydrates or proteins. But fats provide twice as many calories as an equal weight of carbohydrates or proteins. Fats also increase the level of cholesterol in the body. When there's too much cholesterol, the body puts it on the walls of blood vessels. This narrows the blood vessels and can lead to heart disease.

Fats make certain vitamins, such as vitamin D, available for use in the body. Fats also provide essential fatty acids. These are chemicals your body needs for certain processes, such as proper growth of the nervous system. Good sources of essential fatty acids are fish, leafy vegetables, walnuts, and sunflower seeds.

READ BEFORE YOU FEED

Packaged foods have nutrition labels on the packaging. You can look at these labels to make smarter food choices. The label provides a lot of information. For example, it indicates how many calories are in a serving. It also shows the amount of fats, carbohydrates, proteins, vitamins, and minerals in a serving.

At the bottom of the label are recommended daily values. For example, a person on a 2,000-calorie diet should eat less than 65 grams of fat each day. If the label says that one serving of the food has 17 grams of fat, then that serving provides 26% of your fat allotment for the day.

Nutrition Facts
Serving Size 1/4 Cup (30g)
Servings Per Container About 38

Amount Per Serving	
Calories 200	Calories from Fat 150
	% Daily Value*
Total Fat 17g	**26%**
Saturated Fat 2.5g	**13%**
Trans Fat 0g	
Cholesterol 0mg	**0%**
Sodium 120mg	**5%**
Total Carbohydrate 7g	**2%**
Dietary Fiber 2g	**8%**
Sugars 1g	
Protein 5g	
Vitamin A 0% • Vitamin C 0%	
Calcium 4% • Iron 8%	

*Percent Daily Values are based on a 2,000 calorie diet.

$$17 \div 65 = 0.26 \text{ or } 26\%$$

Nutrition labels also indicate serving size. Is that dish of ice cream a single serving or a double serving? If you're eating a double serving, you'll need to double the numbers shown on the label.

BEWARE HIDDEN FAT

What do you like to eat for a snack? What nutrients does it contain? Some popular snack foods contain a lot of fat, a nutrient that should make up only a small part of your diet. Test some of the snacks you often eat.

Which Snack Food Is Greasiest?

Eating fatty foods or sweets in moderation is okay, but it is important to eat lots of fruits and vegetables, too.

YOU WILL NEED:

- Paper towels
- 1 cup measuring cup
- 3 types of snack food (e.g., pretzels, potato chips, popcorn)

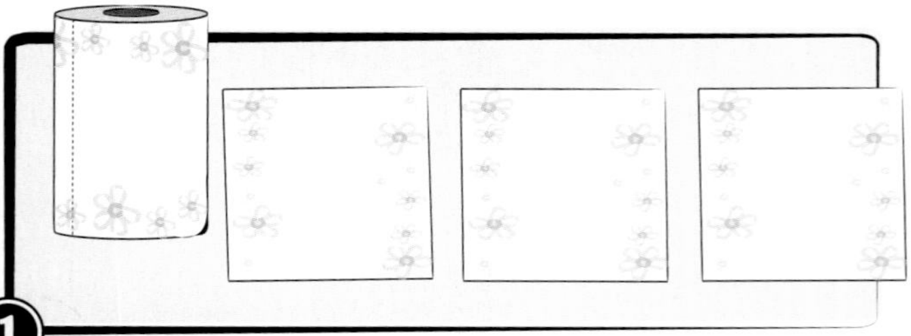

1. Rip off three paper towel squares, and place them on the table.

2. Scoop up 1 cup of each snack food, and pour it onto the center of a different paper towel. Arrange the snacks so they are lying on the paper towel and not piled too high.

3. Let the snacks sit for 10 minutes.

4. Remove the snack foods. Compare the amount of oil residue on the paper towels. Which snack makes the biggest grease mark?

MAKING BETTER FOOD CHOICES

Nutritionists and dieticians study food science, and help people make healthful decisions. Fats in greasy food are easy to see. But some foods contain "hidden fats." Doughnuts and salad dressings are examples. And some takeout foods that sound light, like baked potatoes and tuna sandwiches, may have lots of calories. So, make sure to read labels. The Food and Drug Administration (FDA) is in charge of making sure packaged foods come with nutrition labels. Right now, companies may choose whether or not to include nutrition information with fruits, vegetables, and fish. Many Americans are overweight or obese. As people confront this trend, the FDA and other agencies and school boards are constantly reviewing their food policies. In 2010, President Obama signed a law that would require many restaurants to list calorie counts and other nutritional information on menus. It has become easier for consumers to find out what is in the food they are eating, both at home and in restaurants.

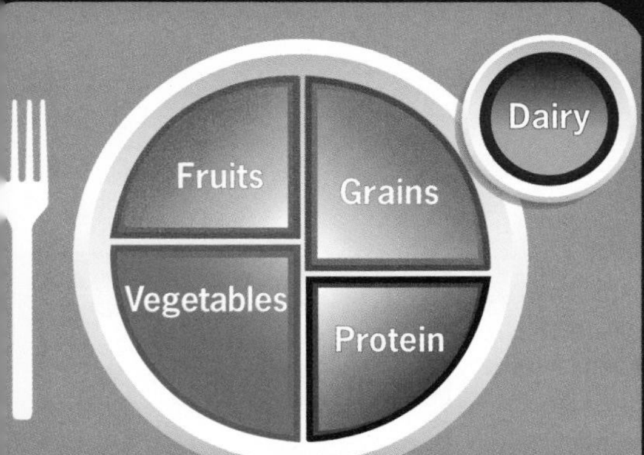

The U.S. Department of Agriculture introduced MyPlate as a symbol of healthy eating. Based on MyPlate, what should make up most of your diet? Should you eat more vegetables or more dairy products?

Change it UP!

☞ Here are some other snacks and foods that you could give "the grease test":

cookies	rice cakes	peanuts
corn chips	raisins	crackers
bread	french fries	granola bars

☞ You could compare the results of one snack food, like potato chips, from three different brands. Or french fries from three different restaurants.

☞ Another way to test snacks for grease is to dip them in water. Compare the size of the floating oil slick they create. Afterward, you can also taste the water to see how much salt the different foods release into the water. Too much salt is bad for you, too!

5 Look at the nutrition labels on the packages for each snack. Which has the most grams of fat per serving? Compare your oil residue results with the fat content listed per serving. Graph your results.

The SCIENCE Behind It

A lot of oil residue means a snack is high in fat. Some foods contain a lot of fat. Along with protein and carbohydrates, fat is one of the three fuels our bodies need to function. But, if you eat more fuel than your body needs, you will store it as fat, and you may gain weight. It's important not to eat too much of any one type of fuel. Choose a diet with a balance of fat, protein, and carbohydrates.

It's also important to get regular exercise to burn the food fuel you eat, and build strong bones and muscles.

DIGESTION

A salad. Meat and potatoes. A piece of pie. What happens to these foods after you eat them? How do their nutrients get into your body?

As you chew bread, it begins to taste sweet. This occurs because an enzyme in your mouth breaks down the starch in bread into sugar.

Breaking Down Food

The food you eat may be tasty and nutritious, but your body cannot use this food until it has been broken down, in a process called digestion. **Digestion** turns the large particles of proteins, fats, and carbohydrates into tiny, simple particles that can pass into the bloodstream.

Digestion takes place in the digestive tract. This is a long, continuous tube. It begins with the mouth. From there, muscles push the food downward through the esophagus into the stomach. From the stomach, the food passes into the small intestine and the large intestine.

In his or her lifetime, a person eats about 50 tons of food.

The Digestive System

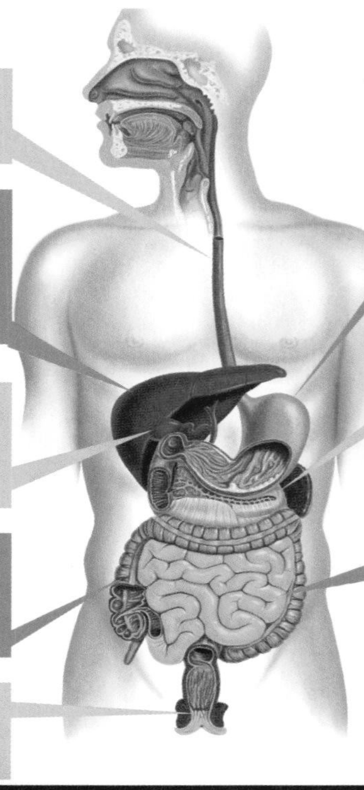

Food travels down the **esophagus** to the stomach.

Before fat can be digested in the small intestine, it must be dissolved, or broken into tiny droplets. The **liver** creates bile, a liquid that helps to break down fat.

Bile is stored in the **gallbladder,** then flows into the small intestine from the gallbladder. After the fat is dissolved, enzymes digest it.

A lot of water is used during the digestion process. Water is then reabsorbed in the **large intestine.**

Waste is passed out of the body through the **rectum.**

Food, liquids, and digestive juices mix together in the **stomach.** Protein digestion begins in the stomach.

The **pancreas** produces digestive juices containing enzymes that help to break down carbohydrates, fats, and proteins.

Protein digestion is completed in the **small intestine.** Digestion of carbohydrates and most fats takes place in the small intestine as well.

For more on protein, carbohydrates, and fats, see pages 64–65.

Nutrient Travel and Storage

Digestion breaks down food into tiny nutrient molecules. These molecules pass through the thin wall of the small intestine into the blood and lymph. **Lymph** is a lot like blood, but without the red blood cells that carry oxygen and give blood its color. It empties into the bloodstream in the upper part of the chest.

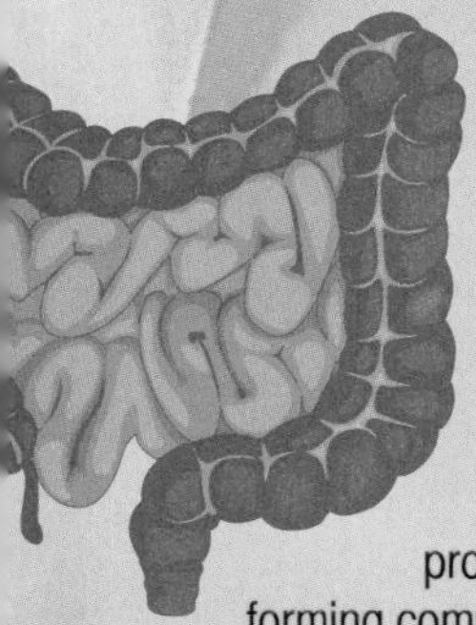

Vitamins, minerals, water, and salt are also absorbed into the blood through the wall of the small intestine. The nutrients are then carried to the liver. Some are sent to other parts of the body. Some are broken down still further. Sugar is turned into an energy-rich substance called **glycogen,** which is stored in the liver until it is needed by the rest of the body for energy. Fats can also be stored in the liver. They, too, can be broken down to provide energy. Proteins are changed in the liver, forming compounds needed to build and repair cells.

What Is an Emulsifier?

The digestive juices that help throughout the digestive process don't immediately break items down. First, they must bring together substances that do not normally interact. For example, fats are not normally soluble in water. That means they don't mix together. Bile emulsifies the fats so they will mix with water in the digestive tract. That makes it easier for enzymes to break down the fats.

TRAVELING DOWN THE TRACT

Various factors determine how long food stays in any one part of the digestive tract. Large meals take longer to digest than snacks. Meals containing a lot of fat take longer to digest than a meal that is mainly carbohydrates. For example, a plain salad may be digested in two to three hours. Add oil and bacon bits to the salad and digestion may take five to six hours. Also, if you swallow a big chunk of food without chewing it properly, the stomach needs to spend more time churning the food and mixing it with chemicals.

Part of the Digestive Tract	Time Food Spends There
Mouth	5 seconds to 2 minutes
Esophagus	3 to 5 seconds
Stomach	1 to 6 hours
Small Intestine	2 to 9 hours
Large Intestine	2 to 3 days

BRING FATS TOGETHER TO BREAK THEM APART

It's easy to rinse bits of carrot or lettuce off a plate. But when dishes are covered with gravy or bacon grease, you need detergent. Detergent is an excellent cleaner because it is an emulsifier, which means it brings together substances that naturally stay apart—like fats and water. See an emulsifier in action in this experiment.

How Does Detergent Clean Dirty Dishes?

YOU WILL NEED:

- 2 pie plates
- 2 cups (500 mL) of milk
- 3 or 4 colors of food coloring
- Water
- Dishwashing liquid/ detergent

1. Fill each pie plate with milk.

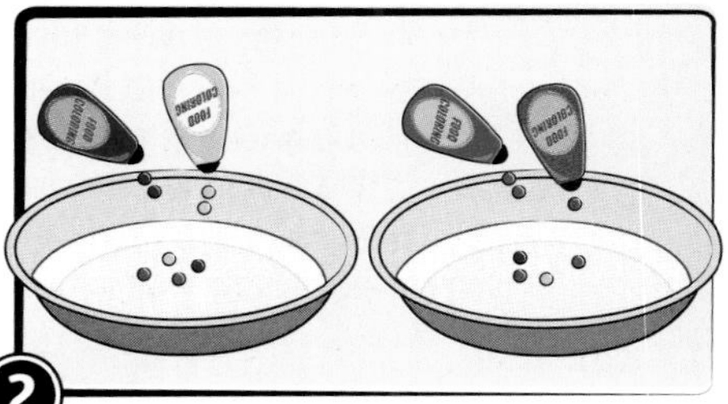

2. Add a few drops of food coloring to each plate. Use different colors!

3. Add a single drop of water to the center of the first plate. What happens?

4. Add a single drop of dishwashing liquid to the center of the second plate. What happens?

science fair tip

Take before and after photos of the milk used in this experiment. Use the photos to decorate your display.

DIGESTING FAT FROM DAY ONE

Humans need bile to digest fat. Bile is produced in the liver and stored in the gall bladder until it is needed in the small intestine. In order to properly break down and digest fat, people need each of these organs to be working just right. Many newborn babies—especially premature babies—don't have fully developed digestive systems and do not produce much bile. This is one of the reasons they are supposed to consume only breast milk for the first months of their lives. Breast milk has lots of fat in it. But it also comes with an enzyme—lipase—that breaks the fat down into smaller globules. Even before babies can produce bile, they are able to absorb the fat from human milk into the bloodstream.

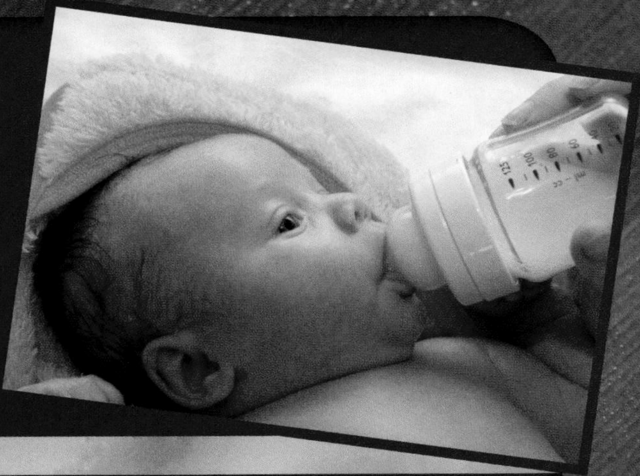

The SCIENCE Behind It

In this experiment, we see emulsification in action. Milk contains proteins and fats in solution. Any change in the solution (for example, adding detergent) affects these fats and proteins. By adding food coloring, we can observe the effect the detergent has on the molecules. The molecules begin twisting, bending, and swirling into all kinds of different shapes. The detergent also weakens the surface tension (see page 120), which is the watery skin that holds the liquid's molecules together. This helps to create the explosion of colors!

The dishwashing liquid in this experiment acts much like the bile in your small intestine. When you are cleaning a greasy plate, the detergent acts as an emulsifier. It brings together the oil or grease and the water. Once the two substances, which are not normally soluble, come together, it is much easier to wash away the slick, slimy grease. In your body, bile emulsifies fats, bringing them together with water, which makes it easier for the enzymes to get at the fats and break them down.

Change it UP!

☞ Try using warm milk. Does the temperature of the milk have any effect?

☞ What happens when you use different kinds of milk, like skim or cream?

☞ Set out five dishes of milk, and add food coloring to each dish. Add one drop of detergent to the first dish. To the rest of the dishes, add two, four, six, and 10 drops of detergent. Does the amount of detergent affect the behavior of the milk?

☞ Compare and contrast different brands of dishwashing liquid.

☞ Compare and contrast the effects of liquid hand soap to dish detergent.

Collect cooking grease, and when it is cool, toss it in the trash, not down the drain. There are about 200,000 sewer blockages every year, and more than 80% of them are caused by fat and grease.

BENEFITS OF EXERCISE

It's fun to be active. It's healthy, too. Most kids need at least 45 minutes to an hour of physical activity every day. This can be broken up into two or three periods. And it can involve different activities. You might take a brisk 15-minute walk, then play baseball. Swim in the morning and go bowling later on. Take a Zumba class or join a friend on a hike.

You still burn some calories when you are sleeping, just not as many as when you are active.

Exercise Burns Calories

To stay alive, the cells of your body constantly burn energy. They burn energy, in the form of food calories, when you're walking, eating, studying, dancing, watching television, and even when you're sleeping. The amount of calories your body burns to maintain itself is called your **metabolism.**

The speed at which calories are burned is called the **metabolism rate.** It constantly changes. You burn fewer calories when you are sleeping than when you are studying. And you'll burn a lot more when you are playing basketball or running a race.

Burning food requires oxygen. You take in oxygen through your lungs. The oxygen passes from the air in your lungs into your blood. The blood then carries the oxygen to all the cells in your body. When your body needs to burn food rapidly, it needs more oxygen. This explains why you take deeper, more frequent breaths when you are running than when you are sitting. Your heart also beats faster when you are active. It has to work harder so the blood can quickly get oxygen to the cells.

WHY DO IT?

Regular exercise has many benefits:

- ★ It builds strong bones and muscles.
- ★ It keeps your joints flexible.
- ★ It strengthens your heart and lungs.
- ★ It improves blood circulation.
- ★ It improves coordination.
- ★ It helps you keep a healthy weight.
- ★ It fights stress and helps you relax.
- ★ It helps you sleep better at night.
- ★ It helps you feel better about yourself.

I'M SWEATING!

As you exercise, your muscles change chemical energy to mechanical energy. The chemical energy stored in food is changed to movement of arms and legs. But not all of the chemical energy is changed to mechanical energy. Some of it is changed to heat energy, and your body needs to get rid of that heat. Two things happen. One, the blood vessels in the skin dilate, or get bigger. This lets more blood flow into the skin. Heat from the blood is lost to the air around you.

The second thing that happens involves your body's thermostat. This is located in a part of the brain called the hypothalamus. Nerves carry messages to the hypothalamus telling it that the body is too hot. The hypothalamus then sends messages to the sweat glands telling them to "make more sweat!" As the sweat evaporates from the skin, it removes heat and cools the body.

One pound of muscle burns 7 to 10 calories a day. One pound of body fat burns only 2 calories a day.

Everyone Is Different

The metabolism rate varies from person to person. People who are muscular have higher metabolism rates than people who have a high percentage of body fat. Men usually have higher metabolism rates than women. Age is a factor as well. Genetics, the characteristics you inherit from your parents, is also a factor. Some people just naturally burn food faster than other people.

Regular exercise helps change your metabolism rate. Aerobic exercises burn more calories as you are doing the exercise. They increase your heart rate and breathing rate. Other kinds of exercise, such as lifting weights, build muscles. Muscles burn more calories than fat. Therefore, the bigger and healthier your muscles, the higher your metabolism rate, even when you are just resting.

Swimming, cycling, playing tennis, and running are types of aerobic exercise.

A person's metabolism rate usually slows as he or she gets older.

GET YOUR HEART PUMPING

Your heart is a powerful muscle that pumps blood all around your body. Each time you feel your heart beat, it is because the heart muscle has contracted, pushing the blood forward. Your resting heart rate is the rate at which your heart beats when you are not active. Learn how to test your heart rate, then grab your sneakers and a stopwatch, and see what happens to your heart rate when you get up and get moving.

What Makes Your Heart Beat Faster?

YOU WILL NEED:

- Paper
- Pencil
- Volunteers
- Watch, clock, or stopwatch
- Thermometer
- Television or computer
- Soccer ball
- Jump rope
- Colored pencils

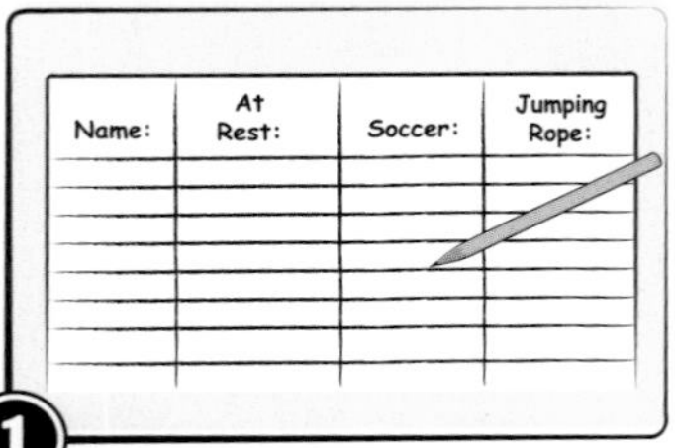

1. Make a chart with three columns labeled "At Rest," "Soccer," and "Jumping Rope."

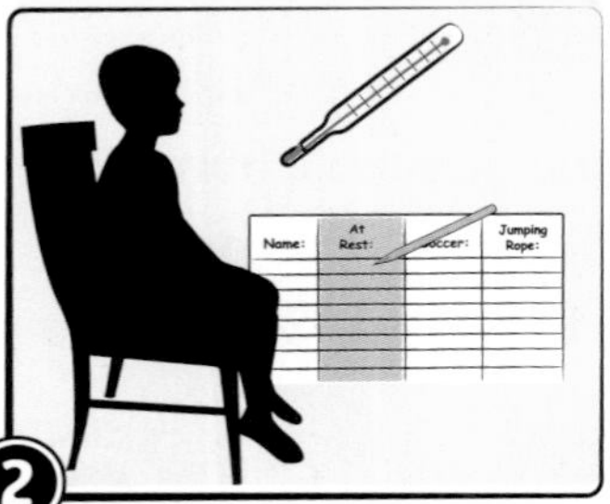

2. Have your volunteers watch television for 5 minutes. Use the thermometer to measure your volunteers' temperatures. Record these in the "At Rest" column.

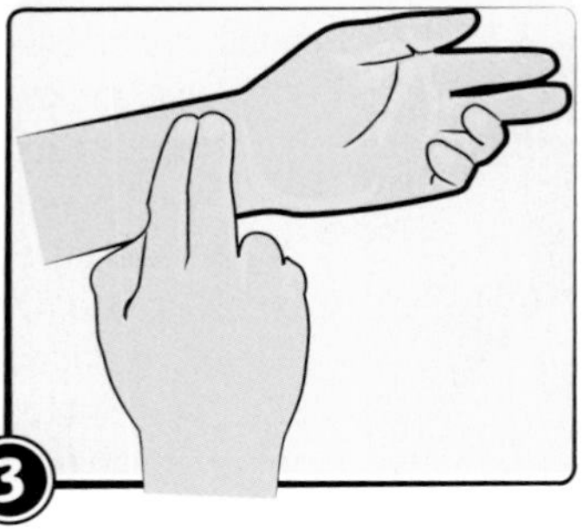

3. Measure your volunteers' heart rates and record them in the "At Rest" column as well. To find out a person's heart rate: Place the index and middle fingers of one hand on the inside of a volunteer's wrist. Your fingers should be about ½ inch (1 cm) down from the wrist joint, directly below the index finger. Feel for a pulse. Count the number of heartbeats you feel in 15 seconds, then multiply by 4.

4. Have your volunteers play soccer for 5 minutes.

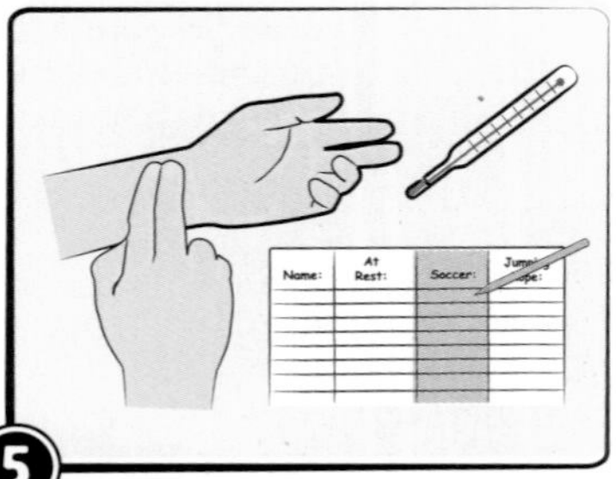

5. Measure your volunteers' temperatures and heart rates as soon as the 5 minutes are up. Record these in the "Soccer" column.

6 Have your volunteers rest for 5 minutes. Then, have your volunteers each jump rope for 5 minutes.

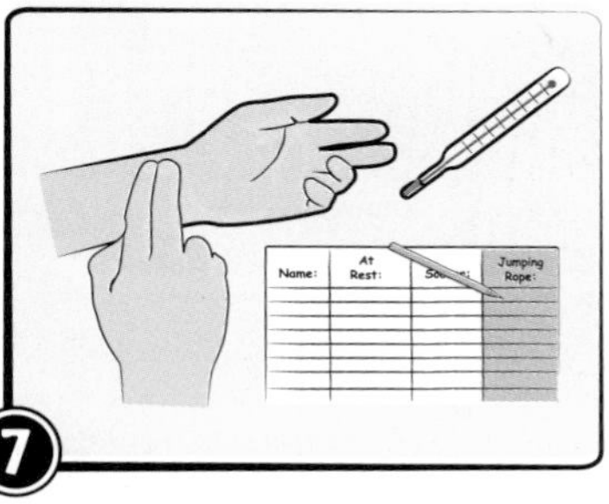

7 Measure your volunteers' temperatures and heart rates as soon as the 5 minutes are up. Record these in the "Jumping Rope" column.

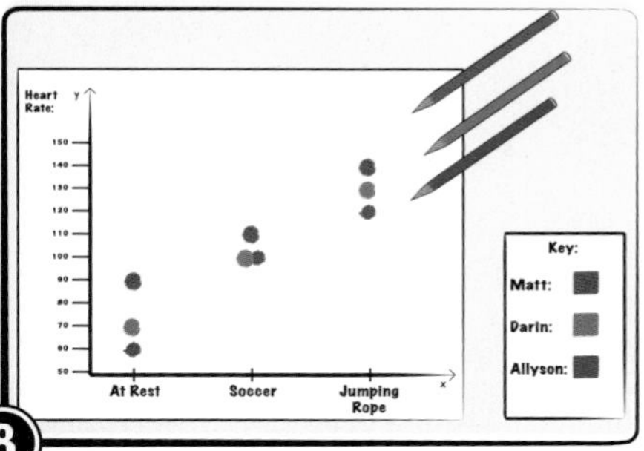

8 Observe your results. When were the heart rates and temperatures the highest? Using a different colored pencil for each volunteer, make a graph to show the heart rate results and a graph to show the temperature results. Make sure to include a key, showing which person's data is shown in which color.

KEEPING THE BEAT

Heart disease is the leading cause of death in the United States. Many of the factors that lead to heart disease are preventable. To keep your heart healthy, it is important to exercise several times a week, eat lots of vegetables, and get plenty of sleep.

There are many kinds of doctors and scientists who study the human heart and come up with new techniques to help people with heart trouble. Since 1967, doctors have been performing heart transplants. Now, doctors are developing procedures that would be less invasive, such as injecting muscle cells to repair weak sections of the heart.

☞ See how dodgeball, yoga, ballet, or baseball affect the heart rate of your volunteers.

☞ You can also test to see what affects your heart the least: try watching television, walking, or lying in bed.

☞ See if your resting heart rate changes throughout the day. Record it just when you wake up, after watching television in the afternoon, and just before bed.

Relaxing and having fun with friends and family is good for your heart!

The SCIENCE Behind It

Your heart rate and temperature go up when you exercise. This is because your body is burning energy, and your heart has to pump lots of blood to get oxygen to your muscles. Movement like soccer or jumping rope is called cardiovascular exercise because it keeps your heart and blood vessels healthy and strong. The more you move, the more oxygen your muscles need, and the harder your heart has to pump. It's healthy to increase your heart rate with exercise, so try to do some exercise every day.

GET MOVING!

Imagine life without bones. Could you stand up? Could you walk? Without your bones and muscles, these movements would be impossible. Your body would be like a bag of skin! Why do you have bones?

Bones Alive!

Bones do two things. Some bones protect your organs. Other bones give your body its structure. Your spine helps you stand up straight.

Your bones are living parts of your body. They grow, and they repair themselves when they break. Blood brings food and oxygen to bone cells. The blood also takes waste away.

Your bones move, but they don't move by themselves. The muscles in your body pull on the bones and make them move. Your muscles are attached to your bones. When your body is preparing to move, your brain sends a signal to the muscles. The muscles contract, or squeeze together. When the muscles squeeze together, the bones attached to them move, too.

Hurdlers use bones and muscles to jump.

When you were born, you had more than 300 bones. As you grew, some of the bones fused together. An adult has far fewer bones than a baby—206 in all!

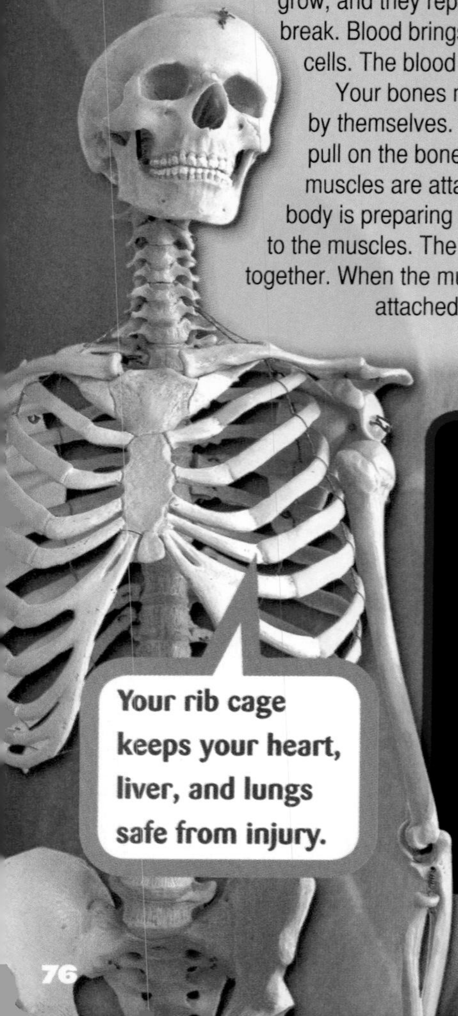

Your rib cage keeps your heart, liver, and lungs safe from injury.

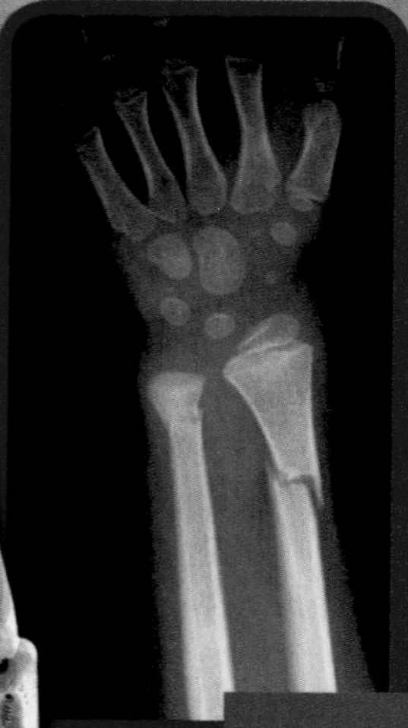

A doctor can see a broken bone in an X-ray.

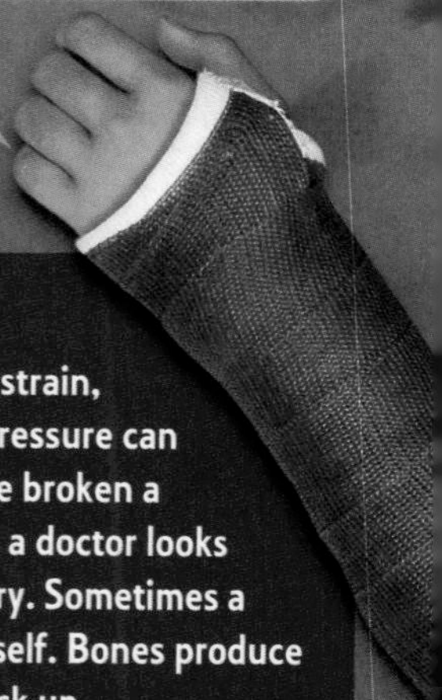

A BAD BREAK

Ouch! Breaking a bone hurts. Under a normal strain, bones will give a bit. But a sudden or strong pressure can snap a bone like a pencil. If you think you have broken a bone, be careful not to move it too much until a doctor looks at it. Some breaks have to be fixed with surgery. Sometimes a cast can keep a bone steady enough to heal itself. Bones produce new cells to heal the bones and build them back up.

Are Bones Brittle?

YOU WILL NEED:

- An adult helper
- 2 chicken bones (Save the drumstick from your dinner!)
- Jar with lid
- Vinegar
- Plate

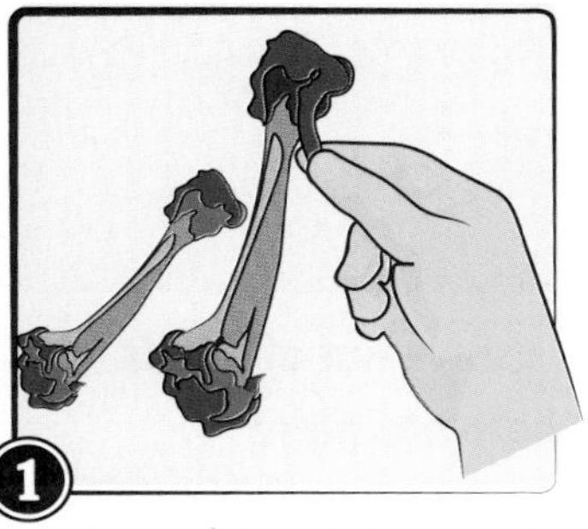

1. Ask an adult to help you take all the meat off the chicken bones.

2. Fill the jar three-quarters full with vinegar.

SAFETY NOTE

Do not drink the vinegar or eat the bones. Everything should be thrown in the garbage when your experiment is over.

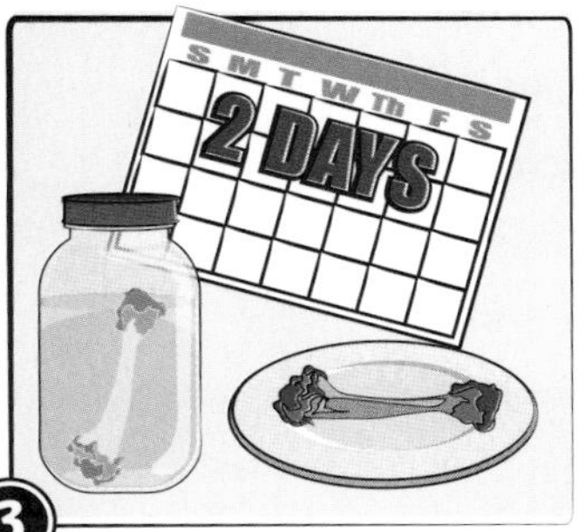

3. Place one bone in the jar. Put a lid on the jar and place it where it won't be disturbed. Place the other bone on a plate. Allow them to sit for 24 to 48 hours.

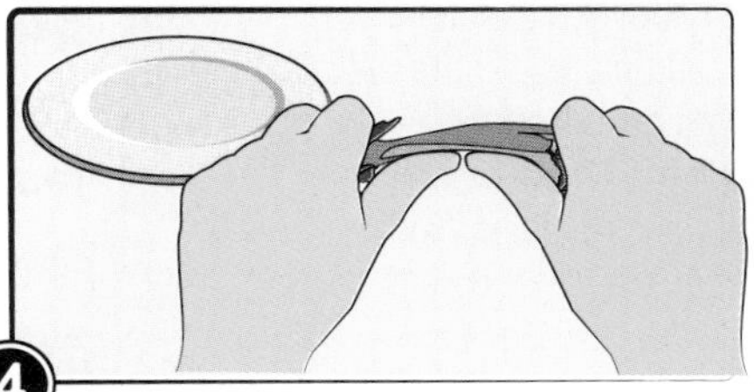

4. Pick up the bone from the plate. Try to break it. Is it easy to break? Look at the insides. Set it aside.

Change it UP!

☞ Compare and contrast a bone soaked in vinegar to bones soaked in orange juice, water, oil, or salt water.

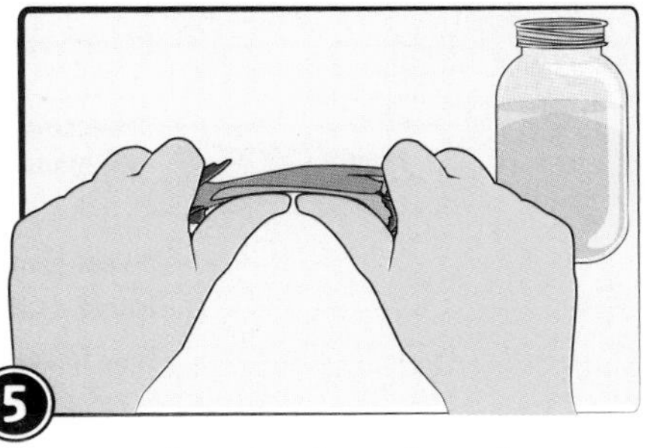

5. Remove the other bone from the jar of vinegar and examine it. Try to break it. How does it compare with the unsoaked bone?

The SCIENCE Behind It

If we do not get enough calcium from the foods we eat, our bones can become very weak. Calcium is a mineral that helps keep our bones strong. The chicken bone that was soaked in the vinegar lost some of its strength because an acid in vinegar broke down the calcium. The vinegar dissolved the calcium, and the bone structure changed.

Milk, cheese, yogurt, green leafy vegetables, broccoli, almonds, and sesame seeds are foods that are high in calcium.

SKIN: IT'S ALL OVER YOU

The skin is the biggest organ, or structure, of your body. It's also one of your most important organs. It keeps your insides in and helps to protect those insides. Your skin helps keep your body at the right temperature. It aids with removing waste from the body. And it provides you with lots of information about the world around you.

Is Skin Alive?

The skin has two main layers. The outer layer, or **epidermis,** is the layer you see. Its surface consists of tough, flat, dead cells. Underneath are living cells. The living cells divide rapidly, creating new cells. The new cells push upward, replacing the dead cells above them.

Under the epidermis is the **dermis.** It is much thicker than the epidermis. It contains tough, stretchy material that keeps the skin firm, yet flexible. It also contains many specialized cells and structures. There are glands that make sweat and oil, and hair follicles that produce hair.

The dermis contains millions of tiny nerve endings. These make the sense of touch possible. They respond to many kinds of things in the environment, including touch, pain, itchiness, pressure, heat, and cold. There are about 20 different kinds of nerve endings in your skin. Each one is sensitive to certain kinds of information. For example, some nerve endings detect heavy pressure and vibrations; others detect light touches or heat. This information is carried from the skin to the brain by stringlike nerve fibers.

Below the dermis is another important layer, called the **subcutaneous layer**. It consists mainly of fat. This helps insulate the body. It also acts as a cushion, helping to protect inner organs if you fall down or bump into something.

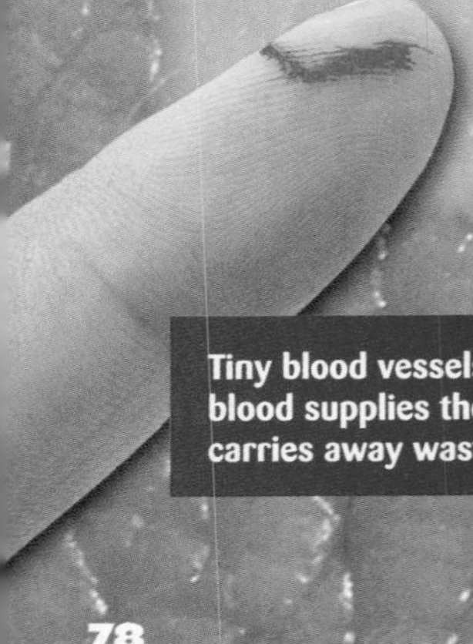

Each hair grows out of a hair follicle. There are more than 100,000 hair follicles on your head. Oil from a gland near the hair follicle coats the hair and makes it shine.

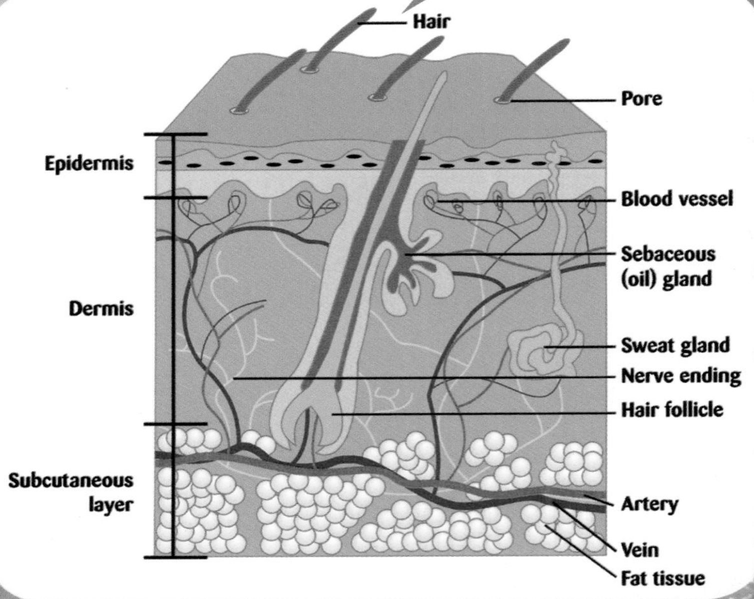

Tiny blood vessels bring blood to the dermis. The blood supplies the cells with food and oxygen and carries away waste products.

Thickest and Thinnest

Your skin isn't the same everywhere on your body. Its thickness varies. So does the number of special structures such as hair follicles and sweat glands. The eyelids and lips have the thinnest skin. The thickest skin is on the palms of your hands and the bottom of your feet.

There are no hair follicles on the palms of your hands and the soles of your feet. But follicles are found everywhere else, though there are more on the scalp than anywhere else. Sweat glands are found everywhere but they are most abundant on the palms and soles. They also are concentrated in your armpits. Oil glands and nerve endings are unevenly distributed, too.

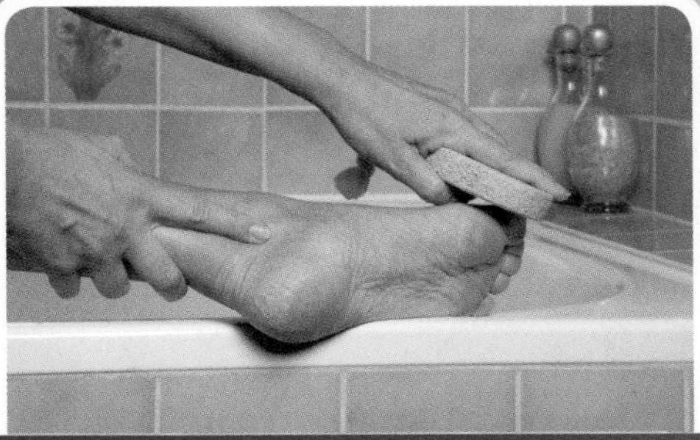

Thick skin can form on parts of the body, like hands and feet, that get a lot of pressure or abuse. Some people use pumice stones to rub off the hard, or calloused, skin.

Skin Changes as You Change

Skin changes when boys and girls are in their teens. The skin of males becomes thicker and hairier. Girls usually have less body hair than males.

Skin also changes as a person ages. It gets thinner and less elastic. The oil glands produce less oil, and the sweat glands produce less sweat. Aging is natural, but people's behavior can speed up skin aging. Spending time in the sun and smoking, for example, can cause wrinkles. In contrast, drinking plenty of water helps keep skin looking young, regardless of one's age.

Girls generally sweat less than boys.

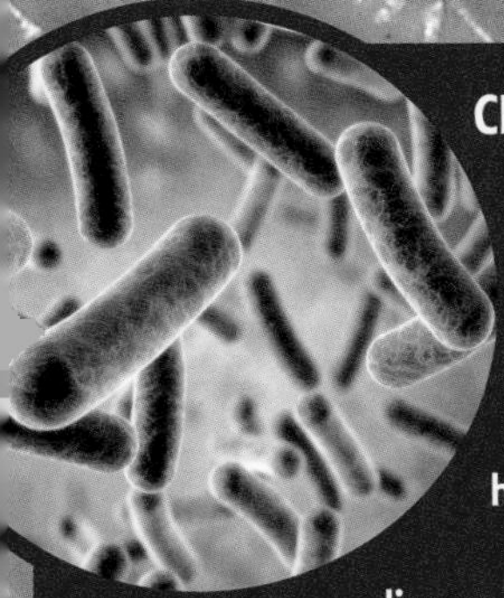

CREEPY, CRAWLY DANGER

It's a dangerous world out there. Billions of tiny bacteria crawl on the surface of your skin. Many of them want to get into your body, where there are warm places to live and plenty of food. But your skin helps to keep them out.

Hundreds of different kinds of bacteria live on the skin. Some are useful, actually helping to prevent disease. Some are harmless. Still others are harmless until they get into a cut. Then the bacteria can cause infections that make you very sick. To avoid this, use soap and water to clean cuts and scrapes. Watch closely for redness, swelling, or other signs of infection. If you think a wound is infected, see a doctor.

Dead cells on the surface of your skin are constantly flaking off. Every minute you lose about 30,000 to 40,000 dead skin cells. That's about 50 million cells a day!

MESSAGES FROM YOUR SKIN

Your skin is a huge sense organ, sending instant messages to the brain when something touches your body. Discover how people's sensitivity to touch varies from upper arm to lower arm to hands and fingertips.

Which Part of Your Arm Is the Most Sensitive?

YOU WILL NEED:

- 13 toothpicks
- 7 craft sticks
- Tape
- Ruler
- Pencil
- Sheet of paper
- Helpers (sensitivity testers)
- Chair

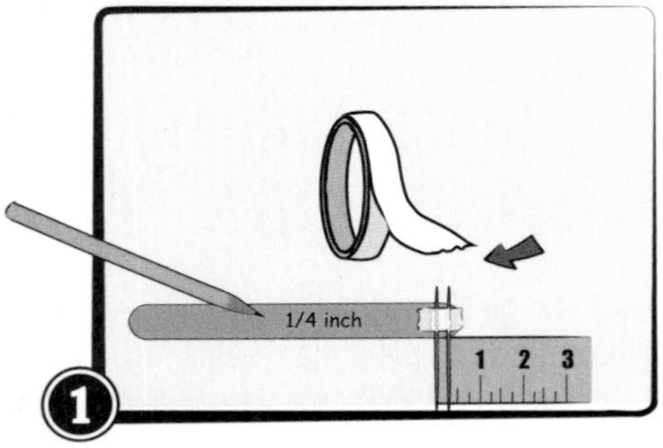

1 Create six sets of test sticks by taping the wide ends of two toothpicks to each of six craft sticks. The tips of the toothpicks should be at least 1 inch (2.5 cm) away from the stick. For the first test stick, tape the two toothpicks ¼ inch (0.5 cm) apart. Write ¼ on the bottom of the stick.

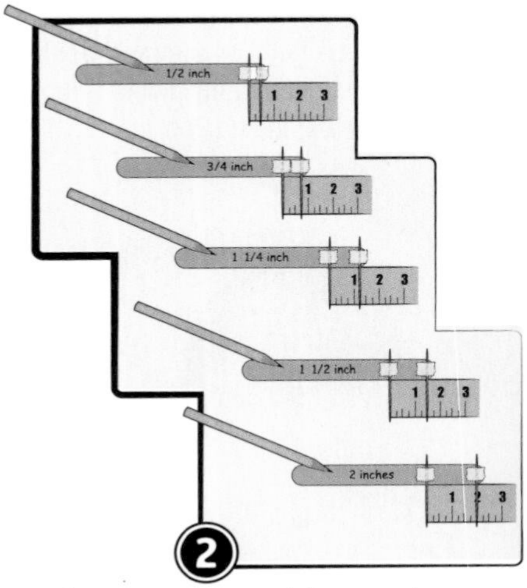

2 For the second test stick, tape the two toothpicks ½ inch (1 cm) apart. For the next four sticks, tape the toothpicks ¾ inch (2 cm) apart, 1¼ inches (3 cm) apart, 1½ inches (4 cm) apart, and 2 inches (5 cm) apart. Label each stick.

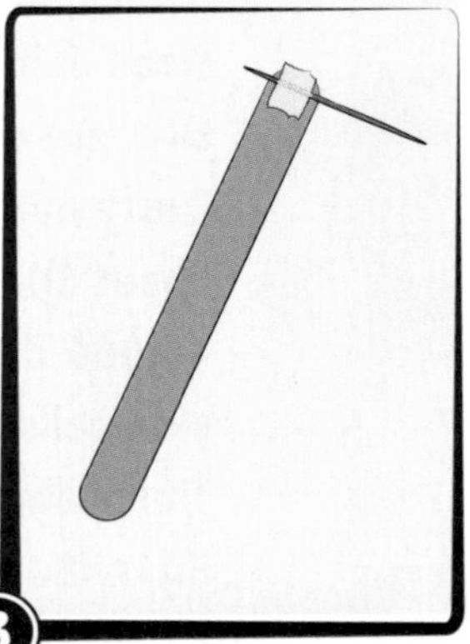

3 Create a spot-check stick by taping a single toothpick to a craft stick.

Skin Sensitivity Testing Chart 1

		Sensitivity Tester #1			
Test Sticks	Toothpick Distance	Upper Arm	Forearm	Back of Hand	Fingertip
1	1/4 inch (0.5 cm)				
2	1/2 inch (1 cm)				
3	3/4 inch (2 cm)				
4	1 1/4 inch (3 cm)				
5	1 1/2 inch (4 cm)				
6	2 inches (5 cm)				

4 For each sensitivity tester, create a chart like this.

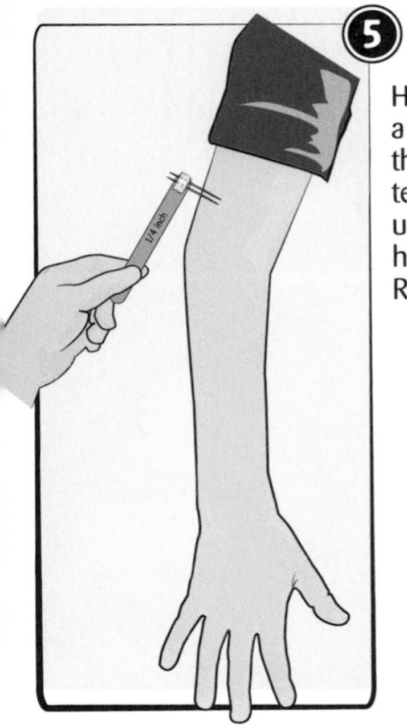

5 Have your sensitivity tester sit in a chair with eyes closed. Place the toothpicks attached to the test stick against your tester's upper arm. Ask your tester if he or she feels one or two tips. Record the answer.

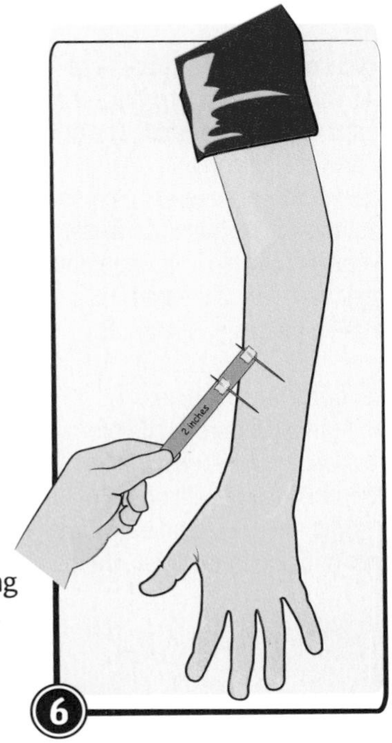

6 Repeat with the other test sticks and parts of the arm. Testing tip: Surprise your testers by switching the order of the test sticks. Also, use the spot-check stick to keep testers guessing about the number of tips they should feel.

READING WITH YOUR FINGERS

Your fingertips are sensitive enough to read! Visually impaired people use a reading system made up of bumps called Braille. You may notice Braille on bank machines and building signs. Some forms of currency, such as those in Mexico, Canada, and India, have raised areas that help blind people know which bills they are using.

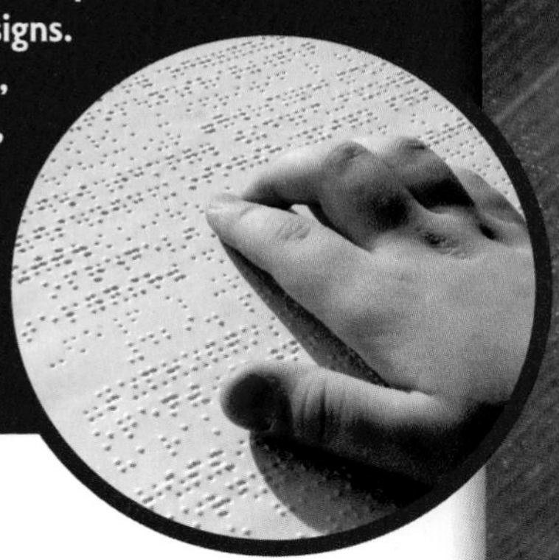

The least sensitive part of your body is the middle of your back.

☞ Test the sensitivity of spots on your face or leg, or on different areas of your back. Are any areas more sensitive than your fingertips?

The SCIENCE Behind It

You're testing the nerves in your arm! Your skin contains a lot of tiny parts for handling its many functions. It has a thick, tightly bonded layer of cells to keep out microbes. Skin also has small hairs to keep us warm, and it has nerves to tell us when it is touched and what objects feel like. Nerves are what let us feel temperature, pain, itches, tickles, pressure, or vibrations. The nerve endings are packed together in the skin and relay messages to your brain. Each nerve ending sends one message to the brain. An area of skin with more nerve endings can send more messages to the brain than an area with fewer nerve endings. The more nerve endings in one place, the more sensitive that area is. You have more nerve endings in areas that need to give the brain more information, like on your fingertips.

GENES AND HEREDITY

Why do you look like your mom? Or laugh like your dad? How can strangers tell by a glance that you are related to your brother or sister? It has to do with a combination of genes and your environment.

Whether or not a person has freckles is controlled by his or her genes.

What Makes You YOU?

You owe much of your looks and health to your biological parents. That's because they passed certain **traits,** or physical characteristics, on to you. This passing along of traits is known as **heredity.** Biological factors that control traits are called **genes.** The genes that you get from your parents control how your body grows and looks.

There are two or more variations of each gene, called **alleles** (a-leelz). Your mother and father each gave you one allele for each trait. This means you have two alleles for every trait. Alleles can be **dominant** or **recessive.** A dominant allele is stronger than a recessive allele. A dominant allele means you show that variation of the trait if it is one of the two alleles you have for that gene. A recessive allele means you show its variation of the trait only if both alleles are recessive.

For example, there is a gene that controls whether or not a person has freckles. Each person has two alleles for this trait (one from each parent). If both alleles are for having freckles, the person will have freckles. If both alleles are for being freckle-free, the person will not have freckles. But what happens if one allele is for freckles and one is for not having freckles? In this case, having freckles is the dominant allele, and being freckle-free is the recessive allele. So, if a person has one allele for freckles and one for being freckle-free, the person will have freckles.

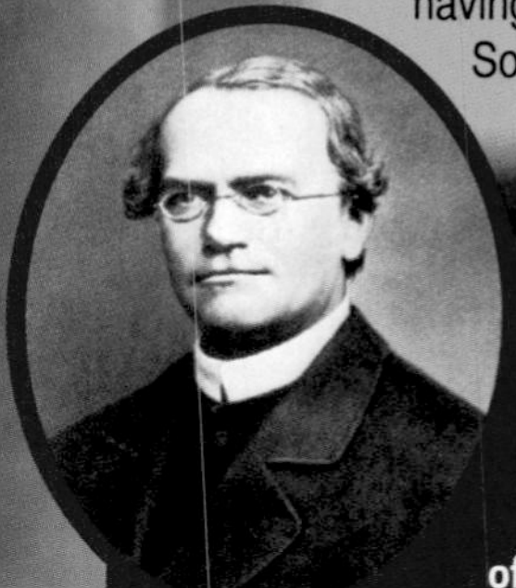

THE FATHER OF GENETICS

Gregor Mendel was a monk who lived in the 1800s. He is considered the founder of genetics, or the study of genes and heredity. He wanted to learn what would happen when two pea plants with different physical traits, such as a yellow pea plant and a green pea plant, were crossbred. What he discovered was that organisms inherit traits in pairs, one from each parent. He learned that the different forms of a gene, called alleles, can be either dominant or recessive. He also figured out a way to calculate the odds of passing on a gene and the likelihood that the gene would be displayed.

Picking Up the Cues

How you behave and how your body develops are not determined only by heredity. Environmental factors also play a role in what traits you display. The characteristics you exhibit as a result of heredity and your environment make up your **phenotype.** What physical characteristics do you share with your parents or siblings? If you are adopted, what characteristics do you share with your adoptive family? Those characteristics are likely driven by your environment, or how you were raised. Both your genes and your environment work together to make you who you are!

Determining Traits

A chart called a **Punnett square** can help determine the odds that an offspring will inherit a certain trait. One set of letters runs along the top of the chart and another set runs along its left-hand side. These letters represent each parent's alleles for a particular trait, like the color of a pea plant.

Let's look at one trait, the color of a pea plant, and see what happens if we cross a purebred yellow pea plant with a purebred green pea plant.

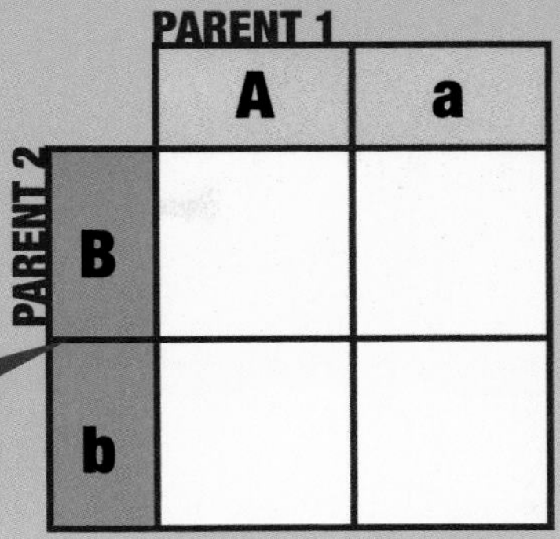

Here is an example of a Punnett square.

Parent 1 is the purebred yellow pea plant. Its alleles for color can be represented as **YY.** An uppercase letter represents a dominant allele.

Parent 2 is the purebred green pea plant. Its alleles for color can be represented as **yy.** A lowercase letter represents a recessive allele.

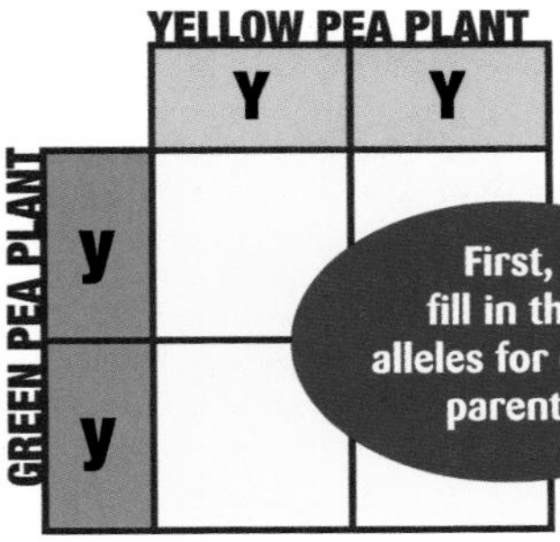

First, fill in the alleles for each parent.

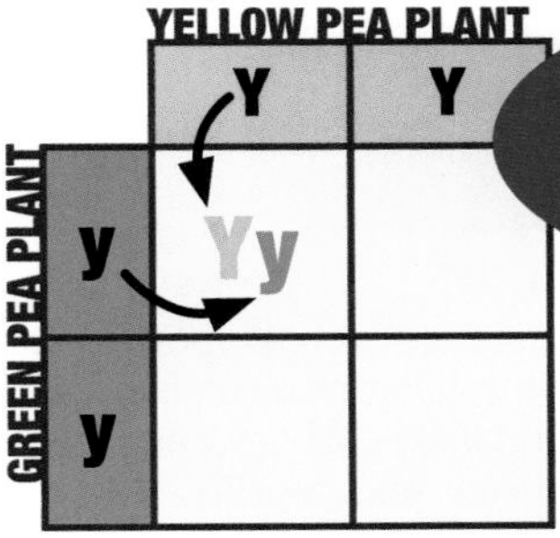

To fill in a Punnett square, you combine one allele from one parent with an allele of the other parent.

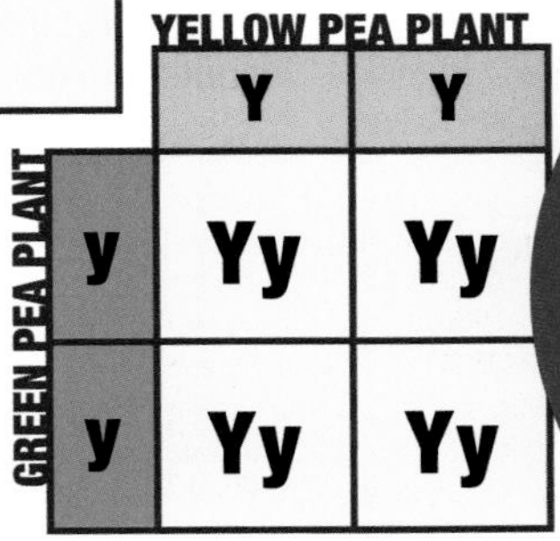

Once you have filled in the entire chart, the four inner squares represent all the possible offspring combinations.

Because the color yellow (Y) is dominant over the color green (y), a Yy pair would be a yellow plant. By looking at this Punnett square, you can see that if you were to cross a purebred yellow pea plant (YY) with a purebred green pea plant (yy), the odds of the pea plant appearing yellow would be 100%.

A COLORLESS LIFE

Albinism (*al*-buh-niz-um) is a trait in which a human or other animal lacks coloring. An albino zebra, for instance, lacks the typical black stripes. The odds of a human being born with the characteristics of albinism are only about one in 20,000. The odds of a wild animal being born with albinism are even lower! That's because predators easily spot the pale creatures and kill them before they are able to breed and pass along their genes to any offspring.

Albino alligators do not blend in to their surroundings like other alligators.

FAMILY RESEMBLANCE

Certain physical characteristics are passed from one generation to the next. By looking at your relatives, you can learn a lot about yourself—and which traits you might pass on to your own children one day!

Which Traits Do You Share With Your Family?

YOU WILL NEED:

- Camera
- Printer
- Paper, one sheet per family member
- Tape
- Pencil
- Family tree (page 192)

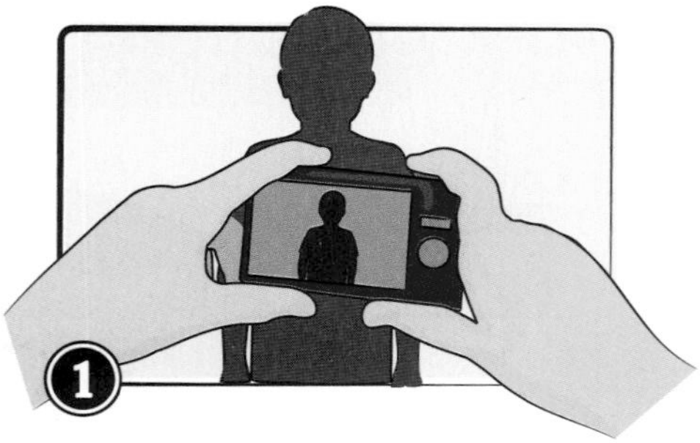

Take a photo of each of your family members smiling. You can include extended family such as grandparents, aunts, uncles, and cousins.

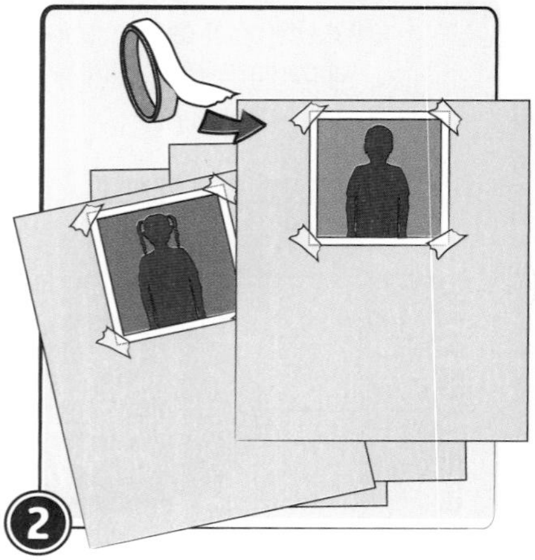

Print out each member's photo, and attach it to a sheet of paper.

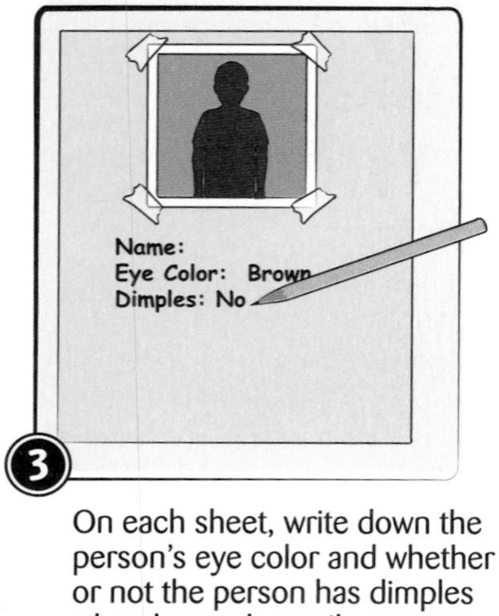

On each sheet, write down the person's eye color and whether or not the person has dimples when he or she smiles.

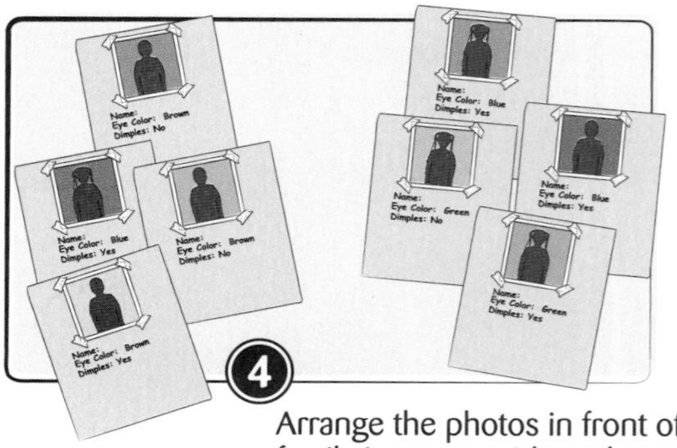

Arrange the photos in front of you so that your father's family is on one side and your mother's family is on the opposite side. Place each generation in a horizontal line. Place the older generations above the younger generations. Put married people side by side with their children underneath, also in a horizontal line. An older child should be to the left of the younger child.

GENETICS AND DISEASE

We study genetics to understand inheritance. Some traits are linked to only one gene. Many traits are linked to a complex combination of several genes. Some genes affect the likelihood that a person will have certain diseases or conditions like heart disease, asthma, or diabetes. Of course, diet, lifestyle, and environment also impact a person's health. By studying genetics and disease, scientists can develop new medicine and treatments and help people live healthier, longer lives. Experts can also study genes to trace how people's ancestors traveled around the globe and uncover how people are related to one another.

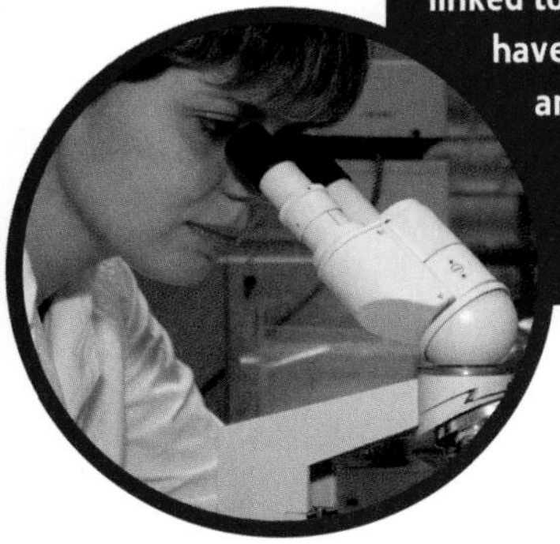

Cleft chin

Widow's peak hairline

Change it UP!

☞ Look through your family tree again and try to find another trait that may be controlled by a single gene. Here are some of the single-trait genes that scientists have identified.

DOMINANT	RECESSIVE
Big toe shorter than second toe	Big toe longer than second toe
Cleft chin	Smooth (noncleft) chin
Having freckles	No freckles
Widow's peak hairline	Straight hairline

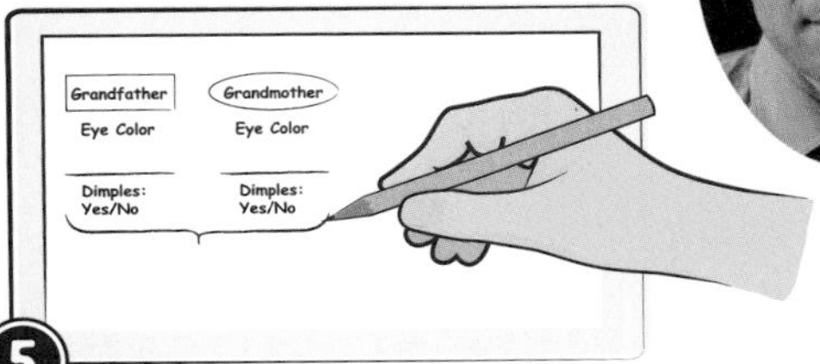

5 Using the family tree on page 192, draw your own family history chart. Add your family members' names according to your arranged photos. Add uncles, aunts, cousins, brothers, and sisters to your chart so that it matches your family photos. Use a square to mark men and boys, and a circle to mark women and girls in the chart.

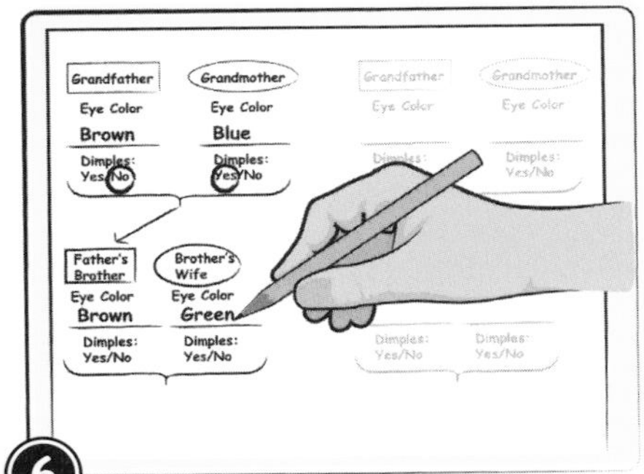

6 Fill in the family tree with the two traits for each member. Do you see a pattern in any of the traits?

The SCIENCE Behind It

You're following family traits in a generational tree! A generational or family tree shows how family members are related to you. You share genes with each member of your family. Showing dimples when you smile is a trait controlled by a dominant allele. You only need one of the two alleles for this trait to be dominant to have dimples when you smile. Certain traits are controlled by a set of two or more genes. There are at least three genes that combine to give you your eye color! There are more variations in eye color because there are more possible combinations than with a single gene. This means it is harder to figure out which alleles you have for your eye color.

GROWING UP

During late childhood and adolescence, the human body undergoes many changes. The period of time during which the body completes its growth is called puberty. Puberty begins at different ages for boys and girls. And the bodies of boys and girls change in different ways. But the end result is amazing: Boys have changed into young men and girls have changed into young women.

It's All About Chemistry

The changes that take place during puberty are triggered by chemicals called **hormones.** Hormones are produced by glands in the body. The body produces many different hormones, each with its own functions. Only certain hormones are involved in puberty. When you are young, your body produces these hormones in very small amounts. Production of certain hormones speeds up as puberty starts.

Boys develop larger voice boxes than girls. This creates a lump in the neck called an Adam's apple.

Some kids begin—and end—their growth spurt earlier than others. But by age 18, the kid who was shorter at age 12 may be much taller than his friend.

Changing Shapes

One dramatic change during puberty is a change in height. During a "growth spurt," kids shoot up. A boy who is a little more than 4 feet (122 cm) tall at age 8 may top 6 feet (183 cm) at age 16. Bones get longer, muscles change shape, and weight increases. During puberty, a person also becomes able to reproduce.

Differences between boys and girls become more obvious during puberty. Girls develop breasts. Their hips and thighs become rounder. Boys develop broader shoulders, and hair begins to grow on the upper lip, cheeks, and chin. Their voice boxes grow, and their voices become deeper.

Everyone's Different

Puberty starts and ends at different times in different kids. Each body goes through these changes at its own pace. One 12-year-old boy may grow 3 inches (7.6 cm) taller in a year. His friend may grow only 1 inch (2.5 cm) taller—but then grow 4 inches (10 cm) at age 15. Girls usually enter puberty between the ages of 8 and 13. Boys begin puberty later, between the ages of 10 and 15. Growth spurts usually start earlier for girls, and girls finish their growth spurts earlier than boys.

People are also different because of their **genes,** which are the characteristics they inherited from their parents (for more on genes, see page 82). Genes are the major factor determining how a person changes during puberty. If a woman entered puberty at an early age, her daughter is likely to do so, too. If parents are short, their children will probably be shorter than average as well.

Nutrition plays a role in the way people grow, especially for girls. Girls whose diets include a lot of meat tend to begin puberty early. Girls who eat less meat but a lot of fruits and vegetables usually start puberty later. Girls who are very overweight usually start puberty early.

During puberty, physical characteristics that you inherited from your parents generally become more obvious.

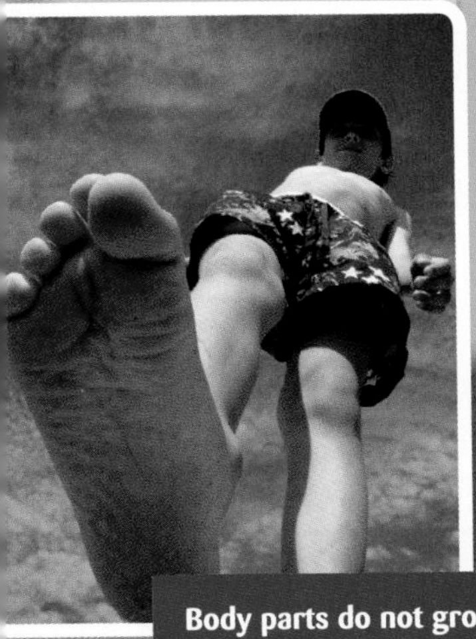

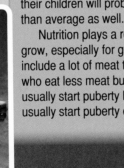

Body parts do not grow at the same pace. Hands and feet usually grow first. Then arms and legs get longer. Finally, the rest of the body catches up.

Teens going through puberty usually sweat more than they used to.

TALL, TALLER, TALLEST

You and your friends have grown a lot taller since you were born. You'll grow still more before you become an adult. Will everyone grow at the same rate? Will boys grow faster than girls? Or will girls start their growth spurt first?

Do Boys and Girls Grow Differently?

YOU WILL NEED:

- Graph paper
- Pencil
- Your classmates
- Measuring tape
- 2 different colored pencils or crayons

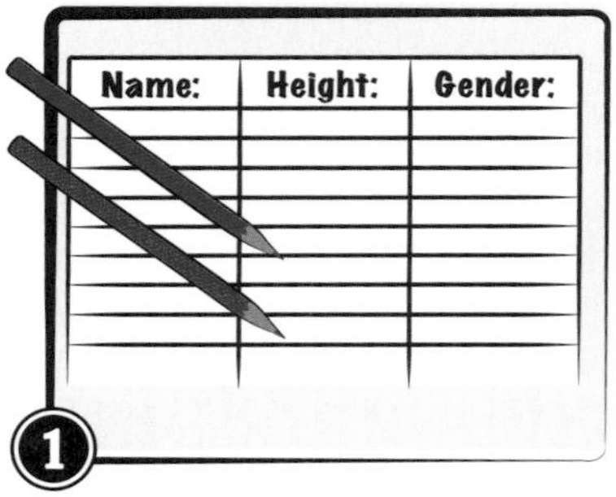

1

Create a chart with three columns and as many rows as there are kids in your class.

2

Measure the height of each person in your class. On the chart, write down each student's name and height. Write down "boy" or "girl" in the gender column.

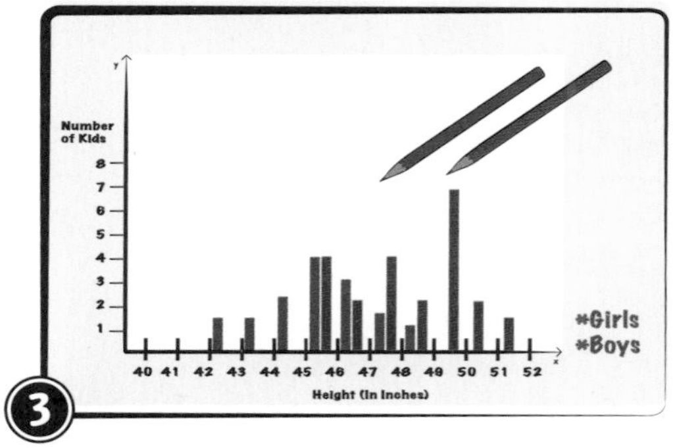

3

Create a bar graph, using a different-colored bar for each gender. Put the height in inches or centimeters on the x-axis. Put the number of children at that height on the y-axis. What do you notice? Does one group tend to be taller than the other?

Before you conduct your experiment, ask your classmates what they think will happen. Then interview them after you've graphed your results. Display some of the "before" and "after" quotations along with your project.

science fair tip

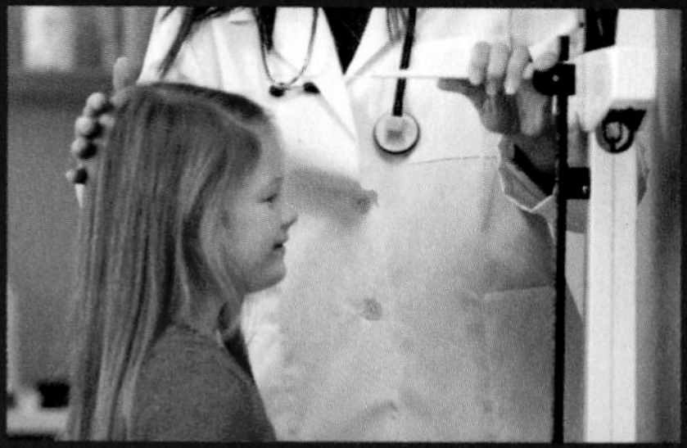

CHARTING HEIGHT

Some doctors study how boys and girls grow. They even come up with charts that show the average heights of girls and boys from year to year. These heights also change over time. For example, the average height of a 10-year-old boy in 1963 was 55.2 inches (140 cm). Forty years later, the average was about half an inch (1 cm) taller. Scientists may compare the height statistics to those of other countries. Doctors will also keep track of a patient's height over time. If a child isn't growing or if an adult is getting shorter, it may indicate that there is a health problem that needs to be checked out.

Change it UP!

☞ Perform this experiment at the beginning, middle, and end of the year, and compare the results.

☞ Try investigating some other traits of boys and girls. Test to see if there is a difference in resting heart rate (see page 74), reaction time, highest singable note, and how fast fingernails grow.

☞ You may not see such a big difference between the heights of boys and girls when they are 7 years old. And 11th graders may show something else entirely. Test several classes of different age groups, then create a graph to show how the classes compare. If you have an older brother, sister, or cousin, ask them to help you collect data.

The SCIENCE Behind It

When you are young, your skeleton tends to grow about 2 inches (5 cm) per year. This is the same for boys and girls, as long as they eat well, exercise, and are not unusually sick. A growth spurt happens for one or two years during puberty. But because boys and girls have different amounts of growth hormones at different times, growth spurts hit at different times for boys and girls. Girls tend to begin puberty one or two years before boys do, and girls also usually have their growth spurt earlier in puberty than boys. This means that girls tend to be taller than boys between the ages of about 11 and 13 years. After that point, boys grow faster.

When they are done growing, teenage boys tend to be about 5 inches (12.5 cm) taller than teenage girls. But height isn't determined by gender alone. Your adult height has a lot to do with your genes, and how tall the people in your family and ethnic group are.

The growth of facial hair usually begins late in a boy's puberty. At first, the hair is soft. Gradually it becomes coarse and wiry.

FORMS OF IDENTIFICATION

No matter how similar two people may look, there are ways to tell them apart. Find out how everything from fingerprints to a strand of hair can be used to identify a person.

You Are Unique

The typical person has two eyes, two ears, a nose, a mouth, two lungs, a heart . . . you get the idea. Most people are quite similar to one another. Despite those similarities, however, everyone—even identical twins—is unique. For example, fingerprints are completely unique to you. So is your DNA (though it is very difficult to see the differences in DNA between identical twins). **DNA,** short for deoxyribonucleic acid, is a complex molecule found in each cell of your body. Sections of DNA, called genes, guide your development and pass on characteristics from one generation to the next. (For more on genes, see page 82). If you've left behind a flake of skin or a strand of hair with the follicle attached, scientists could extract and analyze your DNA. They can prove that the skin or hair follicle belonged to you and you alone. Experts called forensic scientists use techniques like these to help solve crimes.

A fingerprint on paper can survive for more than 40 years!

A forensic scientist searches for evidence by dusting for fingerprints.

CRIME DETECTIVES

A forensic scientist might work for the FBI, a hospital, or even a university. Police call in these experts to study crime scenes for DNA or fingerprints and then ask them to explain the evidence to juries, lawyers, and judges. By looking at clear prints, experts can identify anywhere from 35 to 50 unique characteristics, called attributes. The tiniest of clues could nab a criminal!

What Are Fingerprints?

Fingerprints are the tiny ridges on the tips of your fingers. They give your fingertips texture. These ridges also contain sweat glands that moisten your fingertips. Together, these features increase the friction between your fingertips and various objects—giving you a better grip on things.

Types of Fingerprints

When you touch something, small amounts of oil from your skin rub off on the object and leave a fingerprint.

There are three types of fingerprints: arch, loop, and whorl. Look closely at the pattern of ridges on your fingertips: Which types of fingerprints do you have?

ARCH

Lines start on one side of the print, rise in the middle, and then exit on the other side.

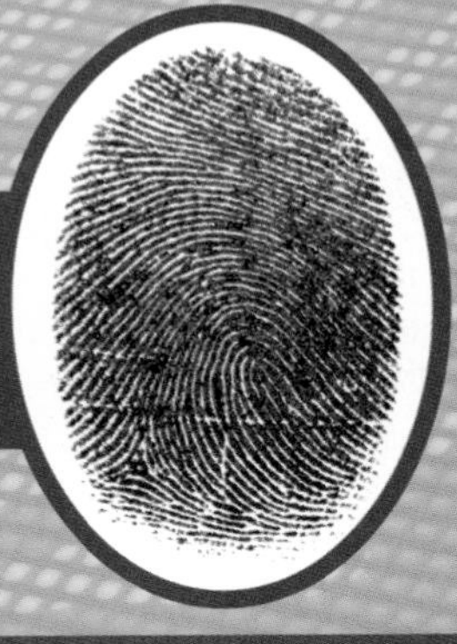

LOOP

Center lines enter and exit on the same side of the print.

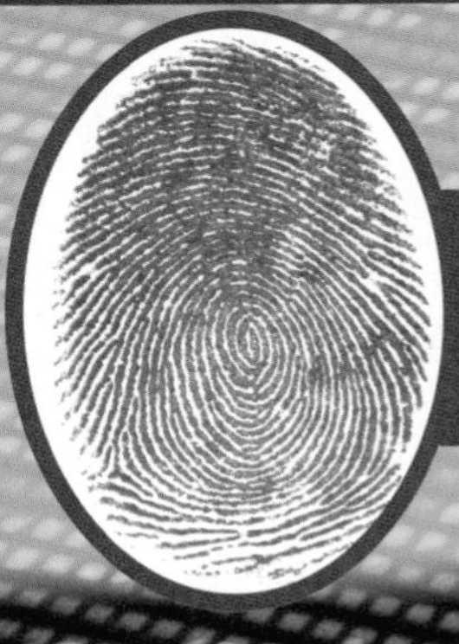

WHORL

Circles in the middle don't exit on either side of the print.

OTHER WAYS TO ID A PERSON

You're different from other people in many ways. For instance, the colored part of your eye, called the iris, has a pattern unique to you. In fact, your left iris is distinct from your right iris! A computerized eye scan can identify a person based on the amount and color of pigment in the iris as well as the iris's pattern of pitted depressions and raised ridges. There are 226 measurable characteristics of your iris—much more than the 35 to 50 characteristics of your fingerprints.

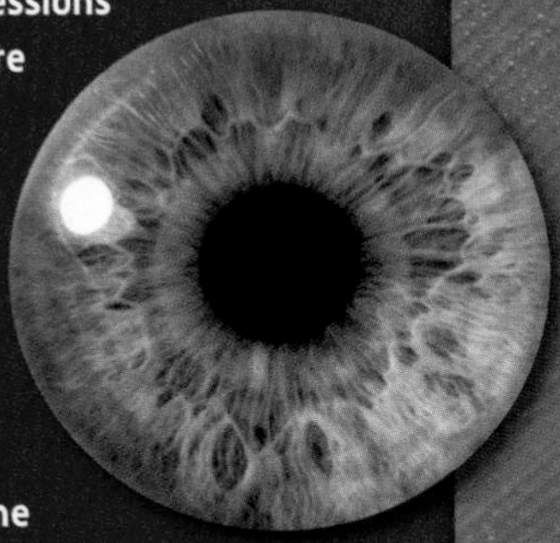

How else are you different from everyone else on Earth? The ridges and lines of your palm are unique to you too. In fact, palm prints are more commonly used to identify a suspect of a crime than fingerprints are. At least 30% of the prints lifted at crime scenes are of palms, not fingerprints!

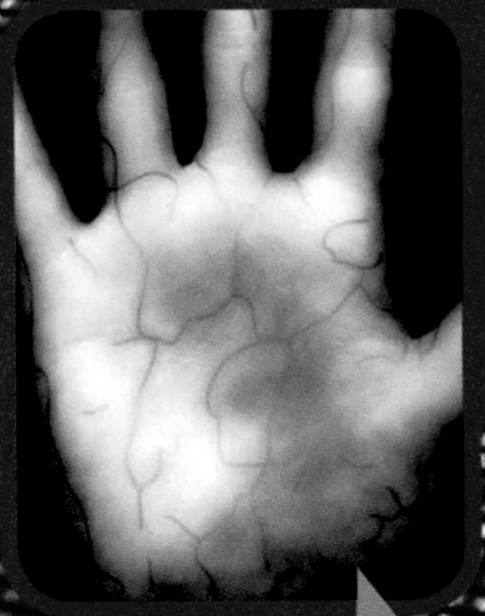

The use of characteristics of the human body to identify individuals is called biometrics.

COMPARING PATTERNS

You are unique from everyone else in the world in many ways. Try this experiment to compare your fingerprint patterns with those of your friends and family. How are they similar? How are they different?

What Is Similar About People's Fingerprints?

YOU WILL NEED:

- Epsom salt
- ½ cup (60 mL) measuring cup
- 1 cup (120 mL) measuring cup
- Bowl
- Warm water
- Spoon
- 3 paper towels
- 3 small sandwich containers
- Talcum powder
- 4 sheets of black construction paper
- Sandwich bag
- Petroleum jelly
- Towel
- Soft paintbrush
- Magnifier
- Marker

1 Dissolve ½ cup (60 mL) of Epsom salt in 1 cup (120 mL) of warm water.

2 Dip each paper towel in the mixture, and wring it out as much as possible. Unfold the paper towels without ripping them.

3 Crumple each paper towel into a sandwich container so it fills up the entire bottom of the container. Let the towels air-dry for at least one day or until they are hard.

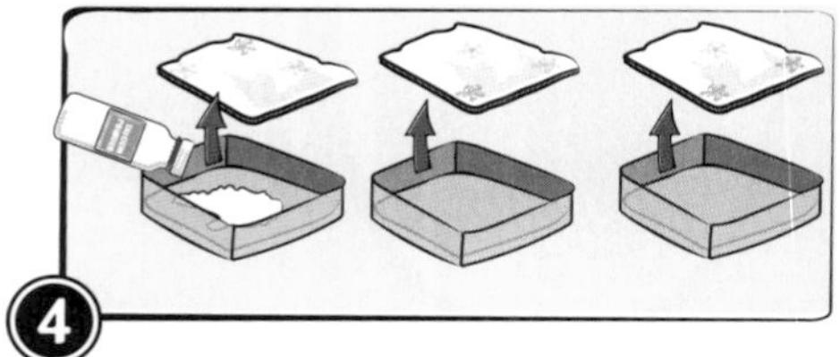

4 Remove the paper towels from the containers. Cover the bottom of one container with talcum powder.

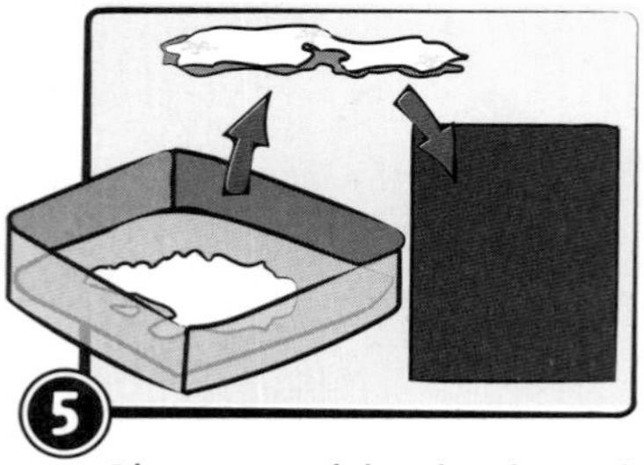

5 Place one of the dried towels in the powder and then stamp it onto a piece of black construction paper.

6 Repeat step 5 with the other towels. Compare the powder patterns each towel made. How are they different? How are they the same? Can you figure out which towel made which print?

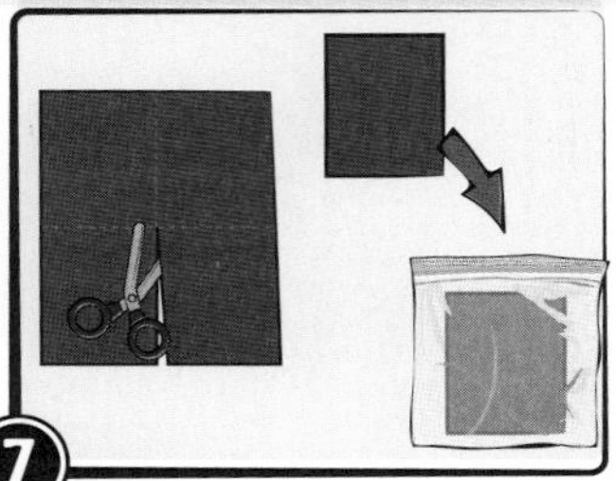

7 Cut a piece of black construction paper so it fits exactly inside the sandwich bag.

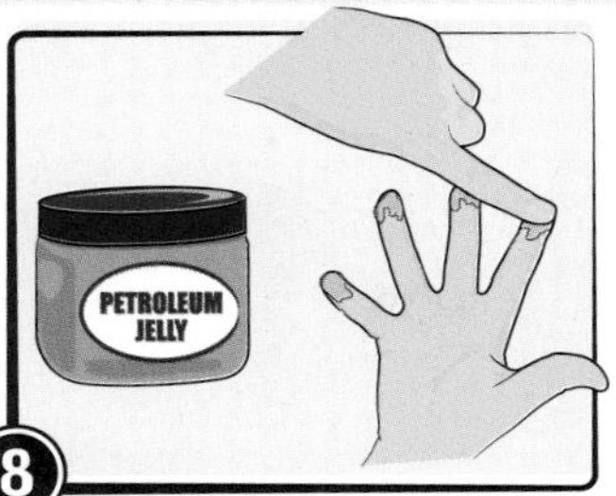

8 Rub petroleum jelly over your fingertips, and wipe off the excess with a towel.

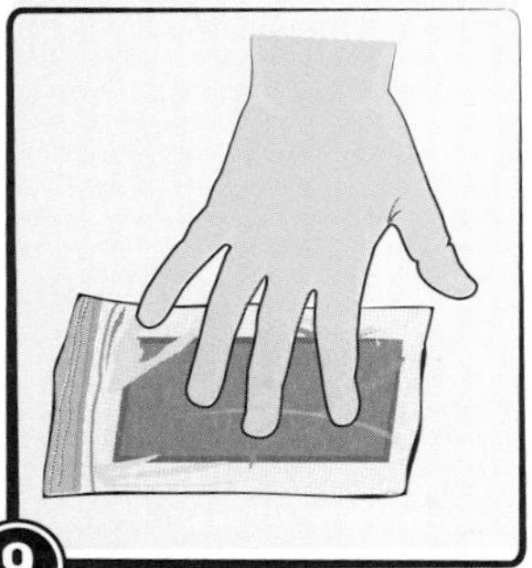

9 Press your fingertips against the sandwich bag.

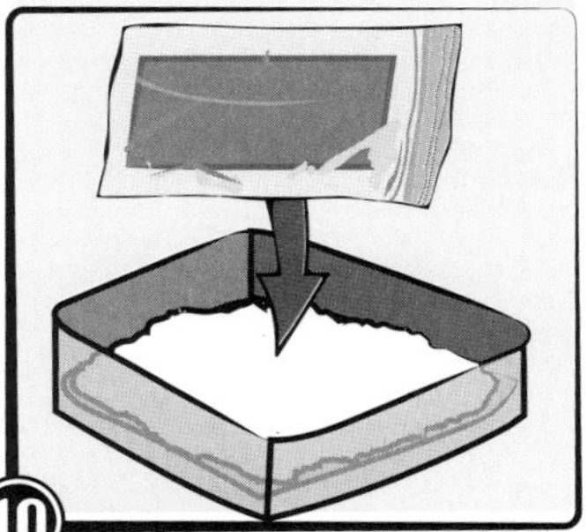

10 Flip the bag over, and push it against the talcum powder.

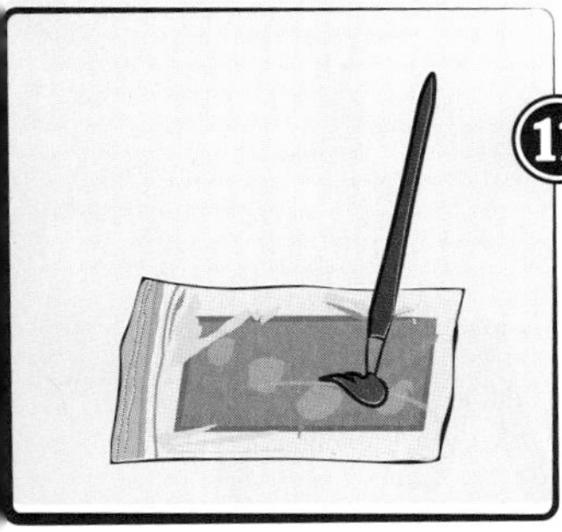

11 Use the paintbrush to brush off the excess powder. You will see your fingerprints!

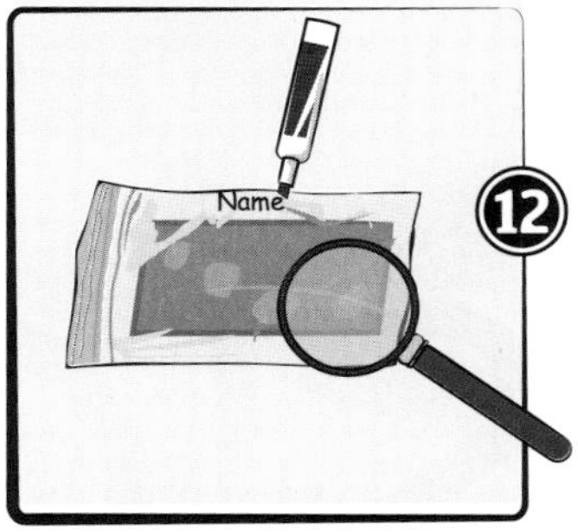

12 Label the bag with your name. Repeat the fingerprinting technique with friends and family. Use a magnifier to compare the patterns of the fingerprints.

IDENTIFICATION AND SECURITY

Security officers collect fingerprints and store them in a database to help them identify unknown individuals. Fingerprints are also used as pass codes by some people who want to safeguard computers. The person must place a finger or palm onto a pad to gain access to the computer's files. Some homes and cars no longer require keys, because they are outfitted to open or turn on when the owner places his or her hand on a pad. Other people may use iris scans or full-body scans as ways to foil thieves and protect high-security locations.

Change it UP!

☞ Collect prints from your classmates, family members, or sports team. Sort them by pattern. Then make a graph showing the most common types.

☞ Dog nose prints are also unique to each dog! Ask a veterinarian to help you collect dog nose prints. Compare them to find common patterns.

The SCIENCE Behind It

Our fingerprints are all made with the same stuff—skin! Skin is made up of many layers. The top layer is the epidermis (see page 78). This layer becomes folded at a baby's fingertips as the baby grows inside its mother's womb. Layers of skin below the epidermis stick to the folded epidermis and hold them in their pattern. This is how your fingerprint pattern formed, and you'll have the same pattern for life! Fingerprint patterns are unique for each finger, just like the pattern of each crumpled paper towel was different. The folds and ridges on the paper towel are much bigger than the ones at your fingertips, but they were created in a similar way.

Some people have no fingerprints at all! The extremely rare condition is called adermatoglyphia and is caused by a genetic mutation.

PHYSICAL SCIENCE

How do light and sound travel? What is gravity, and why do astronauts float in space? Why do things explode? Physical science is the study of nonliving things, such as energy, matter, and magnetism. There are many branches of physical science, including chemistry, which explores chemical reactions and how elements interact, and physics, which is the study of matter, energy, forces, and how they affect one another.

A SIMPLE REACTION

Chemical reactions can cause exploding fireworks, burn a match, and make your bread dough rise. Such reactions occur when two or more molecules interact and make something happen.

Chemical Reactions

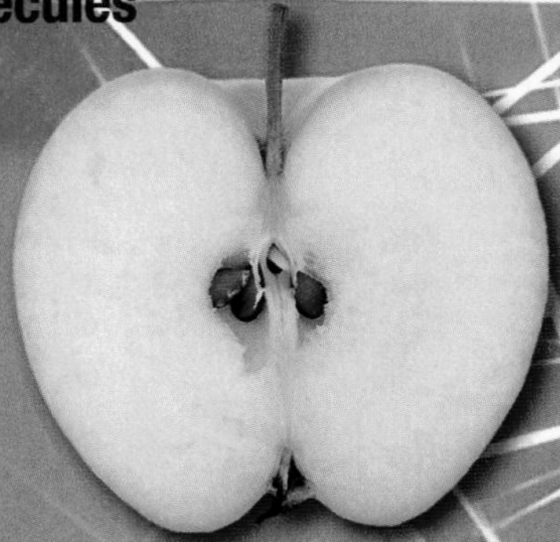

When you cut an apple in half, have you changed the apple? It looks different, but it's made of the same things. You've created a **physical change.** A physical change happens when the form of something changes.

What kind of change happens when a bicycle gets rusty? The iron in the bicycle mixes with oxygen in the air and makes a new substance: rust. During a **chemical change,** one substance is changed into a different substance.

The coating of the Statue of Liberty contains copper, which has oxidized, or combined with the oxygen in the air. That's why the statue looks green.

The bright flash of early flashbulbs resulted from magnesium igniting in carbon dioxide.

When you digest your food, chemical reactions give off heat that makes your body warm.

CHEMISTRY AT HOME

Chemical reactions occur all the time. When you chop onions and your eyes tear up, it is because of a chemical reaction. Onion cells contain the chemical sulfur. When you cut an onion, the cells are broken. A chemical reaction takes place when the sulfur compounds react with the moisture in your eyes to form sulfuric acid. Your brain doesn't want acid in your eyes. So it sends a signal to your tear ducts to make more tears to dilute the acid. You cry to protect your eyes.

Explosions are chemical reactions. When Alfred Nobel invented dynamite, he wanted to help miners. He didn't know it would be used as a weapon. He used money earned from this invention to fund the Nobel Peace Prize.

Can Vinegar Clean a Tarnished Penny?

YOU WILL NEED:

- Bowl
- Vinegar
- Salt
- Teaspoon
- A tarnished penny

1 Fill the bowl one-quarter full with vinegar.

2 Add 1 teaspoon (5 mL) of salt.

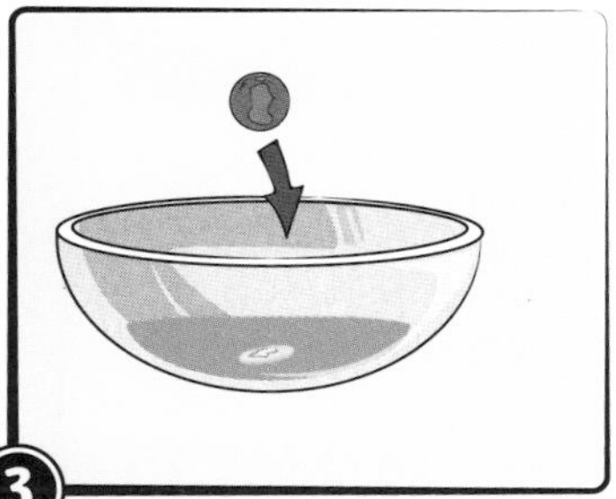

3 Add your penny.

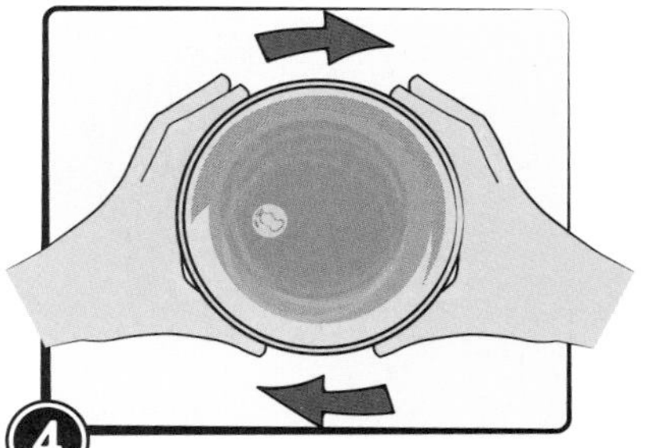

4 Swirl the bowl to mix.

5 Set the bowl aside for 5 minutes. What happens?

Change it UP!

☞ Gather several tarnished pennies and try to clean each one with a different substance. Try ketchup, lemon juice, dish detergent, and water. Compare and contrast the results.

The SCIENCE Behind It

A penny contains a metal called copper. (And U.S. pennies made before 1996 contain more copper than newer ones.) After a while, copper loses its shine and becomes tarnished. This tarnish is caused when the copper in the penny mixes with the oxygen in the air and makes a coating called an oxide. When you put the penny in an acid like vinegar (acetic acid) and add salt (sodium chloride), the acid and salt combine to form hydrochloric acid. The acid removes the oxide. You're left with a bright copper penny!

ACIDS AND BASES

Many substances can be classified as acids or bases. Lemon juice is one weak acid that you know from the kitchen. Like lemon juice, most acids taste sour. A base is the opposite of an acid.

What is pH?

The value of pH is simply a way to measure how acidic or basic a liquid is. You can use pH to describe everything from shampoo to the water in a swimming pool. The value ranges from 0 to 14. Acids have pH values between 0 and 7. What are the pH values of bases? You guessed it! From 7 to 14.

Some strong acids can attack your skin and ruin your clothes. Strong bases are just as dangerous as strong acids. That's why they might irritate your skin unless you wear rubber gloves.

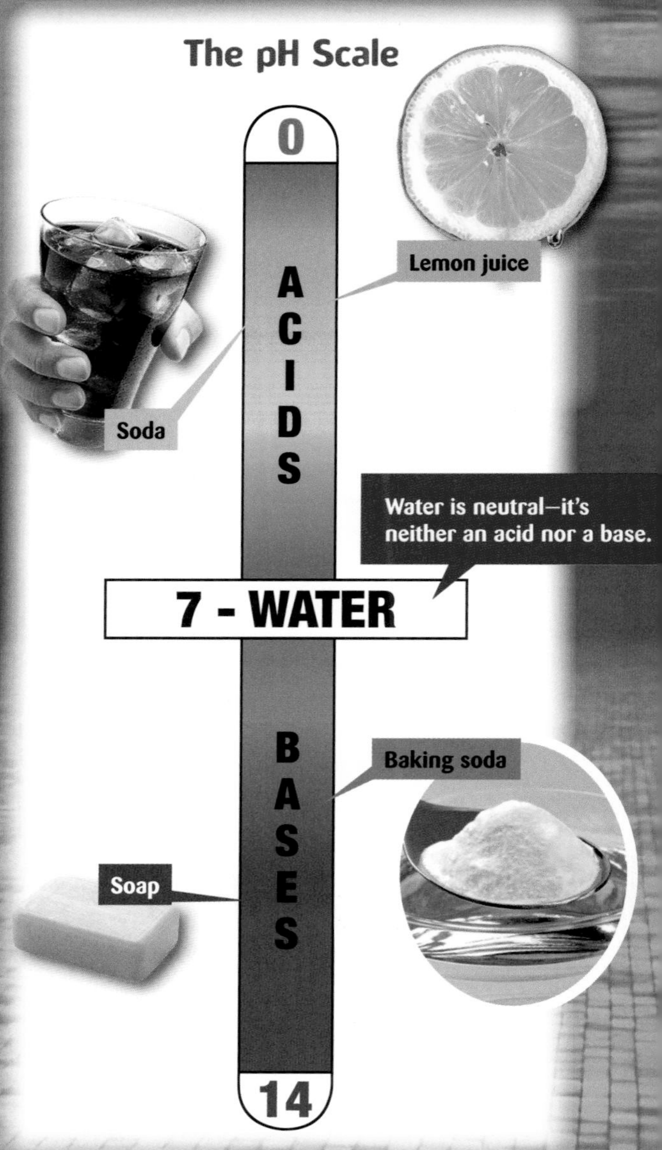

In the Swim of pH

The pH is important to keep a swimming pool clean and safe! The pH of our eyes is slightly basic, at 7.2. To keep a pool comfortable, the pH needs to be somewhere between 7.0–7.6. When the pool's pH is too low, acidic water can dissolve the cement or marble sides of the pool, creating places for algae to grow. Metals on the stairs and pumps could corrode, and it could make your eyes and nose burn. If the pH gets too high, you can still have problems with itchy eyes and dry skin. Swimming pool water starts to get murky.

Low pH may be the culprit if algae begin growing in a pool.

How Can You Tell an Acid From a Base?

1 Use the grater (with an adult's help) to grate some red cabbage into a medium-size bowl.

2 Cover the cabbage with cold water and let it sit for 45 minutes.

3 Strain the juice into a plastic container. Your cabbage juice indicator is ready to use.

4 Test for acids. Pour an equal amount of cabbage juice into each plastic cup.

5 Add 1 teaspoon (5 mL) of baking soda to all but one of your cups. What color does it turn? The cup without the baking soda is the "control" for this experiment.

6 Add other substances to each glass of cabbage juice with baking soda. What happens to the color? Can you change the juice back to its original color?

YOU WILL NEED:

- Head of red cabbage
- Medium-size bowl
- Grater
- Water
- Strainer
- Plastic container
- 4 clear plastic cups
- Baking soda
- Test liquids: lemon juice, vinegar, cola, milk

Change it UP!

☞ Repeat the experiment with Concord grape juice instead of cabbage juice. How do the cabbage and Concord grape juices compare as indicators?

The SCIENCE Behind It

The cup without the baking soda is your control. You'll want to get your mixtures to match that color. Red cabbage juice contains chemicals that change color when mixed with certain other chemicals. Add an acid to the cabbage juice, and the cabbage juice will turn different shades of red. If you add a liquid and the juice stays blue, the liquid is probably a base, not an acid. Baking soda is a base.

CRYSTALLINE GROWTH

Some minerals, metals, and snowflakes are made up of crystals. This means that the atoms of the mineral or the ice link up in a neat, repeating pattern.

Snowflakes are made up of ice crystals. Even though snowflakes have different patterns, snow crystals all have a six-sided, or hexagonal, structure.

What Is a Crystal?

In some solids, the way in which the molecules and atoms build on one another can be random. But crystals are different. The atoms and molecules of a crystal repeat in an exact pattern, or uniform arrangement, over and over throughout the entire material. These patterns are symmetrical, which means they look exactly the same on one side as on the other.

Because of this repetitive structure, crystals take on unique and often beautiful shapes naturally. Gemstones, such as diamonds, rubies, emeralds, and sapphires, are crystalline minerals found within and among rocks. Raw gemstones (before they are cut and polished) grow into interesting, geometric shapes with lots of angles and flat sides. Crystals' sizes vary, but if you could look at the tiniest part of the internal structure of a ruby or diamond, you would find that the mineral's atoms are connected in a neat, symmetrical, identical pattern.

See the difference between a raw diamond and one that has been cut and polished.

Quartz is the second most abundant mineral on Earth.

CRYSTALS IN NATURE . . . AND IN YOUR BATHTUB

Water can carry dissolved minerals into your home, too! Sometimes calcium and limestone particles will dissolve in water. Over time, these heavier minerals can get left behind on a sink or bathtub. They may look like a powdery or scummy film on the sink or tub.

Stalagmites grow from the ground up. Stalactites hang down like icicles. Sometimes they meet and form columns.

CAVE CRYSTALS

Stalactites and stalagmites form from the dripping water inside caves. Cave water has many dissolved minerals in it, because the water has seeped through the ground and picked up dissolved materials along the way. This mineral-rich water then drips into underground caves. As the water drips and runs off, these beautiful towers of minerals are left behind. The formation of stalactites and stalagmites is a slow process that takes place over thousands of years.

Solutions, Solvents, and Solutes

When some substances mix with liquid, they break down into very tiny clusters of molecules that cannot be seen with the naked eye. We call this process **dissolving** (see also page 108). Even certain metals like sodium and calcium can dissolve in water. In this process, we call the liquid a **solvent,** and the material being dissolved a **solute.** Once the solute has dissolved into the solvent, we have what is called a **solution.**

Solutions look like they are only a single liquid, but they have teeny bits of material floating around in them. One way to prove that a liquid is a solution is to allow all of the liquid to evaporate. Once the liquid has dried up, the solute will reappear because solids cannot evaporate. If the solute was a crystal, it may re-form differently. Sometimes the speed at which a crystal forms changes the way its molecules are arranged, giving it a different appearance.

For example, have you ever sprinkled sugar into your drink only to watch it disappear before your eyes? Those crystals are not disappearing, they are dissolving. In other words, they are breaking down into pieces too small to see. If the liquid dries out, or evaporates, those particles reconnect and will once again be big enough to see.

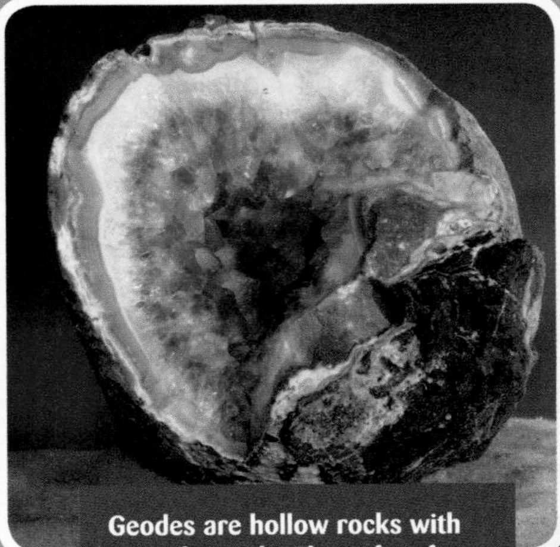

Geodes are hollow rocks with crystals inside. They often form near volcanoes. Water with dissolved minerals flows into cracks and holes in the rock. Crystals slowly form inside as the water evaporates.

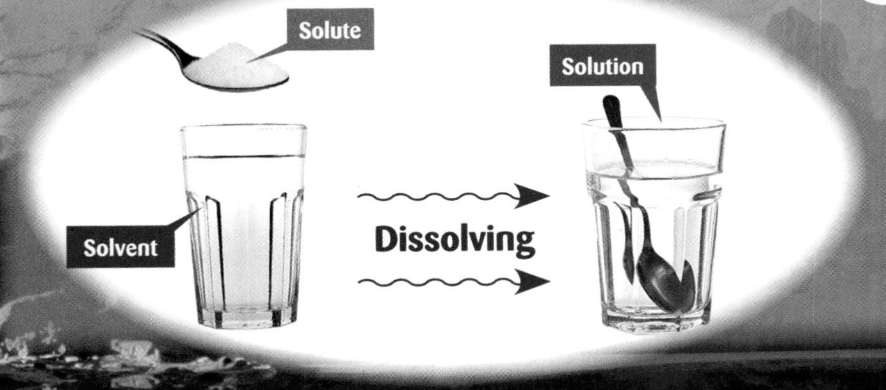

ROW YOUR OWN CRYSTALS

es and stalagmites are naturally occurring crystals. But not all crystals are formed in re. You can make your own solution and grow crystals at home.

ow Do Crystals Form?

OU WILL NEED:

- 2 cups of warm water
- Spoon
- Salt
- Sugar
- Paintbrush
- 2 pieces of black construction paper

Fill two cups with warm water.

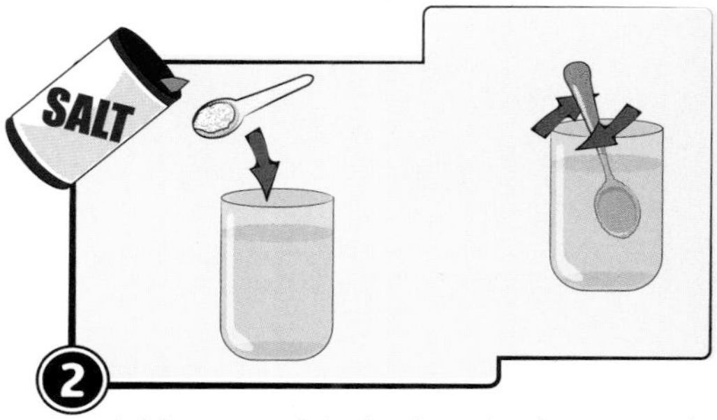

Add a spoonful of salt to the first cup of warm water, and stir until it dissolves.

Keep adding spoonfuls of salt to this cup and stirring until no more salt will dissolve. This is your salt solution.

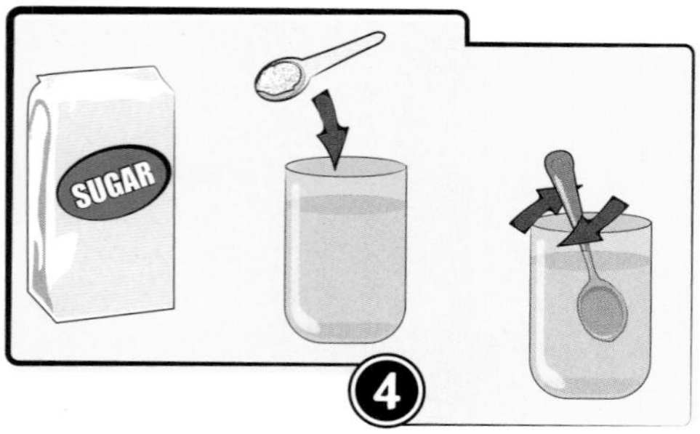

Add a spoonful of sugar to the second cup of warm water, and stir until it dissolves.

Keep adding spoonfuls of sugar to the second cup and stirring until no more sugar will dissolve. This is your sugar solution.

6 Use a paintbrush to draw thick lines with the salt solution on a piece of black construction paper.

7 Use a paintbrush to draw thick lines with the sugar solution on a second piece of black construction paper.

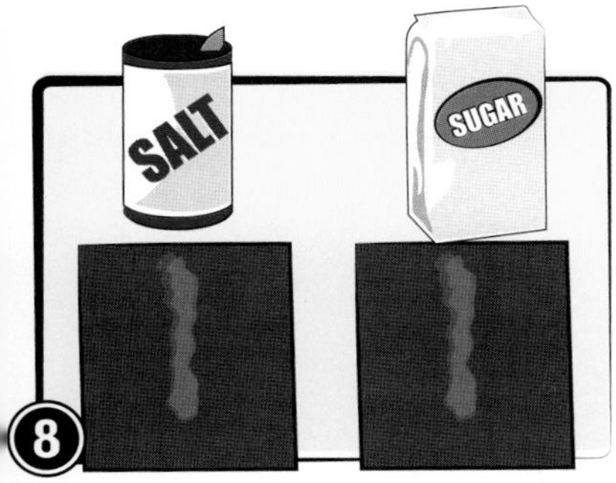

8 Allow the paper to dry, and compare the crystal formations. How are they similar or different?

INCREDIBLE EDIBLE CRYSTALS

If you've ever eaten rock candy, then you've already eaten food made from crystallized sugar. And rock candy is easy to make at home. Just ask your parents to help, find a recipe online, and a few days later, you'll have a homemade sugary sweet treat! Some high-end cake decorators use sugar crystals to make edible decorations that look just like diamonds and other glittery jewels.

Change it UP!

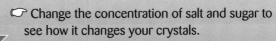

☞ Change the concentration of salt and sugar to see how it changes your crystals.

☞ With an adult's help, use boiling water instead of warm water. This will allow you to add even more of your solute.

☞ Compare and contrast the effects of different types of paper, such as white, colored, or glossy.

☞ What happens if you use different solutes, like baking soda, flour, or brown sugar? Do all powders create good crystals?

The SCIENCE Behind It

Crystals are made of repeating patterns of atoms or molecules. They grow best when each new crystal attaches itself to an existing crystal. When you dissolve a solid like salt in a liquid like water, the solid is called the solute and the liquid is called the solvent. You can add more solute to a hot solvent than to a cold one. As the solvent evaporates and cools, the solute comes out of the solution. The solute molecules slowly bind to each other to form crystal patterns.

Sugar comes from either sugar beets or sugarcane.

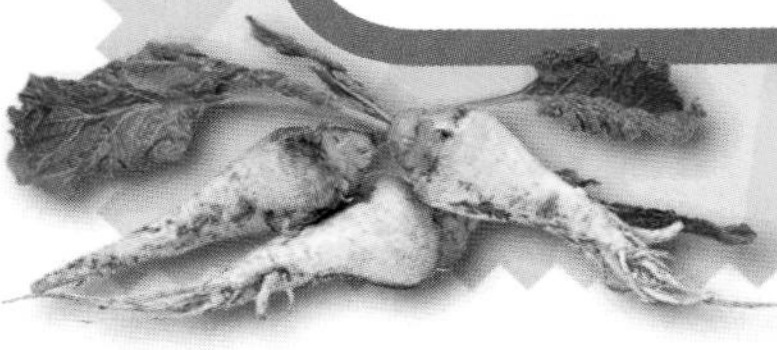

UN-MIXING IT UP

There is much more to the color of a pen or marker than it may seem. Almost all colors are the result of mixing pigments. Chromatography allows us to separate those pigments and see the "ingredients" of certain inks.

Combining Colors

Black and white appear very different. Which one absorbs more light?

Chromatography is the separation of mixtures. In science, this can be applied to many things, but it often refers to the separation of colors in ink.

Most colors are the result of blending two or more colors together. You may already know that blue and yellow make green, while red and blue make purple. The proportions of color used also make a big difference when blending colors together. Darker colors absorb more light, while brighter colors reflect more. This gives them the appearance of being darker and lighter.

Blending different colors of light will give you very different results from mixing paint or ink. Colored light does not blend in the same way, so you might be surprised by the color you get when you cross beams of different colored light.

Experimenting with color blending can be fun and beautiful. The possibilities are endless.

RADIANT RAINBOWS

Light is very different from pigment, which is used in inks, paints, food, fabric, and other materials. Light from the sun is called white light even though it seems more clear than white. That white light is actually a combination of all colors of light. Sometimes white light passes through a prism (or through raindrops which end up acting like a prism), and those colors appear to separate. That's when you see a rainbow.

Making Mixtures

A mixture is a combination of two or more substances that do not change one another's molecular structure. The molecules of the substances in the mixture stay the same. A good example of a mixture is trail mix. Even though there are many things in the trail mix—such as nuts, raisins, and seeds—each item stays the same and can be taken away or separated from the mixture. When the molecules of the substances in a mixture change, we call this a chemical reaction. (For more on chemical reactions, see page 96.)

Sometimes mixtures are sneaky and appear to be a single substance. In cases like this, scientists can perform experiments like chromatography to separate the ingredients in a mixture and see what it's really made of.

Separating Substances

There are many kinds of chromatography. Some types use liquids or gases to separate mixtures.

Part of the process usually includes putting the mixture into a liquid or solvent such as water. Then the mixture and the solvent must pass through a material such as paper, silica, or charcoal. Some substances dissolve more easily in the liquid. Those substances will be carried farther than components that do not mix well with the solvent. The result will show the components of the mixture separated and spread out on the material.

As the water from the dish travels up the paper strip, notice how the blue substance is carried farther than the red.

This experiment allows you to separate the color mixtures in ink. Use chromatography to uncover the many hues that actually make up the colors of your pens and markers.

What Color Marker Runs the Most?

YOU WILL NEED:

- Pipe cleaner (chenille stem)
- Paper coffee filter
- 3 different pens or markers
- Cup of water

1. Poke a pipe cleaner through the center of a coffee filter.

2. Use three different pens or markers to make a circle of dots around the center of the filter.

3. Place the pipe cleaner end in a cup of water, with the coffee filter at the top. Observe the coffee filter for about 5 minutes. Compare how the different inks traveled and separated. Which is made from the most different colors?

science fair tip

Grab a stopwatch, put your camera on a tripod (so it stays in the same position), and take a photo of the coffee filter every 10 seconds. A slide show of the images will show exactly how the inks moved.

FROM PERFUME TO PENS

Chromatography is used in many fields. Perfume makers use it when developing new scents and identifying the components of perfume mixtures. Pharmaceutical companies use the technique, both in developing drugs and testing to make sure the quality is the same from one batch to the next. And environmental scientists use it to assess the amount of pollution in air and water samples.

ou don't need
hromatography to
ee that this list has
een tampered with!

Because chromatography can often identify substances from very small samples, it is particularly helpful for police officers and forensic scientists, who use it to help solve crimes. They can even use a process similar to the one in this experiment to identify when and how ink has been used. Chromatography allows an officer to find out if more than one pen was used to write a note or a check. In this way, officers can prove that someone changed the amount on a check or changed the meaning of a message. The U.S. Secret Service stores more than 10,000 analyzed inks in the International Ink Library. By comparing ink from a crime scene or a suspect's home, experts can determine which pen was used to write a confidential spy communication or a note written by a bank robber.

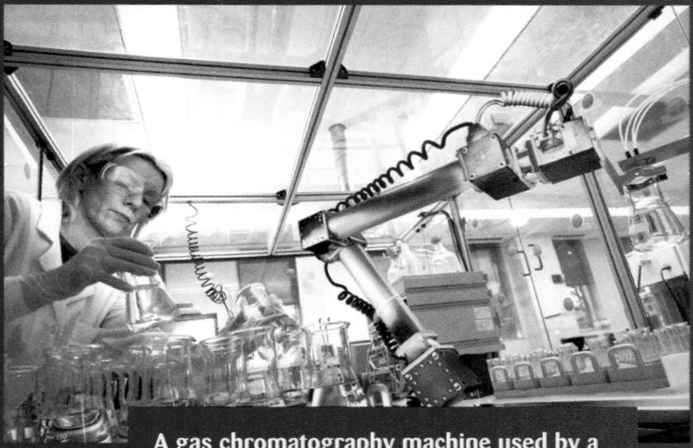

A gas chromatography machine used by a pharmaceutical company will test sample after sample to make sure certain medical mixtures all have the same ingredients in the same amounts.

Change it UP!

☞ Try testing different types of pens or markers.

☞ Do you get different patterns with different types of paper?

The SCIENCE Behind It

You just performed ink chromatography! Chromatography can separate inks into the different colors they are made of. In your experiment, the water travels up the stem, and the different inks get picked up by the water. Different inks travel in different ways, and some travel farther than others. Each ink has its own unique color bands.

MAKING BUBBLES

After you stir salt or sugar into a glass of water, you can no longer separate the grains from the water. These are solids that have dissolved into liquids. What about gases? Can a gas dissolve into liquid?

Oxygen in Water

You won't have to look far to come up with a great example of a gas dissolving in a liquid. Just look at the ocean. Oxygen is highly **soluble** in water. That means that it can be dissolved in water. If oxygen were not soluble, it would remain in large bubbles, float to the surface, and escape from the ocean. Because the oxygen has dissolved, it can be everywhere in the water and sustain marine life.

Oxygen is soluble in water, which is how animals with gills are able to breathe underwater. Gills pull the dissolved oxygen from the water so the animal can survive.

Escaping Gases

Have you ever dropped ice into a soda and watched the bubbles surround the ice, then bubble to the top? Science can explain the behavior of those bubbles.

Sodas are fizzy because of dissolved carbon dioxide (CO_2). The tiny bubbles of CO_2 in the drink bump into other bubbles and merge to become larger bubbles. Once a bubble is big enough, it becomes less dense than the liquid it is in and floats to the top, where it escapes from the liquid. This is why you always see bubbles rise to the surface.

Bubbles do not collect along perfectly smooth surfaces. Instead, they group together in little cracks and crevices. Known as **nucleation sites,** these are spots where gas can easily collect. One way to speed up this process and release dissolved gas faster is to introduce something with a pitted surface into the bubbly liquid, providing lots of nucleation sites.

The surface of the cherry provides tiny nucleation sites, where CO_2 bubbles can form.

THE SCIENCE OF FIZZ

Have you ever tried to open a warm soda only to find that it explodes all over you? That's because changing the temperature of a liquid changes its solubility. When soda gets warm, the CO_2 is less soluble and escapes easily, leaving soda tasting flat. The colder the soda, the more carbon dioxide dissolves in it. The bubbles stay in the soda instead of escaping into the air, and the drink stays fizzy.

What Makes the Bubbliest Soda?

YOU WILL NEED:

- Unopened bottle of diet cola
- Unopened bottle of cola
- Index card
- 2 packages of Mentos candy
- A friend

NOTE: This experiment is messy. Do it outside on the grass or pavement. Wear clothes that you don't mind getting a little dirty.

1 Outside, set the two cola bottles about five big steps apart.

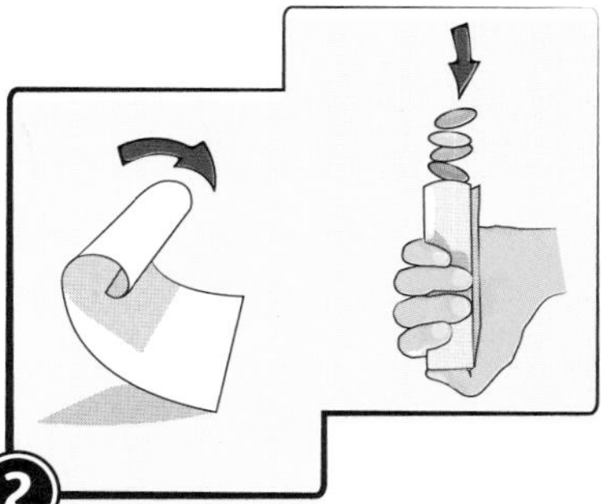

2 Roll an index card into the shape of a tube. Cover the bottom with your thumb, and fill the tube with Mentos candies.

3 Have your friend take the cap off the diet cola bottle. Get ready to step away quickly!

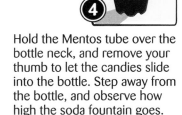

4 Hold the Mentos tube over the bottle neck, and remove your thumb to let the candies slide into the bottle. Step away from the bottle, and observe how high the soda fountain goes.

5 Repeat steps 2 through 4 with the regular soda bottle. Which soda fountain shot the highest?

Change it UP!

☞ Repeat the experiment using a room-temperature bottle of diet cola and a chilled one. What happens?

The SCIENCE Behind It

Mentos have tiny bumps and ridges on their surface, along with a coating made mostly of sugar. The ridges and cracks on the candy create nucleation sites, or perfect places for the carbon dioxide in soda to collect. This experiment shows you what happens when all of the gas in the soda rushes to nucleation sites and begins bubbling to the surface at the same time. The different ingredients affect how quickly the carbon dioxide is released from the soda. Diet soda contains aspartame, an artificial sweetener, and Mentos contains gum arabic. Both of these ingredients reduce the surface tension of water, which helps the bubbles escape faster.

TURN UP THE HEAT

If you rub your palm back and forth along a carpet, what happens? Your palm warms up, because you are creating heat. But what exactly is heat? Where does it come from?

Heat Moves

Heat is another name for thermal energy. It's the energy stored inside a substance. When two substances with different amounts of internal energy are near each other, heat transfers from one substance to another.

Heat moves in three ways: radiation, convection, and conduction.

Radiation is heat from invisible rays, like radio waves or ultraviolet light. The sun's heat comes to Earth by radiation.

Convection is the transfer of heat from one area to another when matter moves. When you heat a pot of water on the stove, the hot water rises to the top of the pot and gives off energy. The air is heated by convection.

Conduction is the direct transfer of heat from one object to another. If you have walked across sand on a hot day, you've experienced conduction. Some materials, like metals, are good at conducting heat. Wood is not a good conductor.

Temperature Scales

You measure your body temperature with a thermometer.

Temperature indicates how fast molecules are moving. Thermometers measure temperature. Have you noticed that there's a thermometer on your oven? Scientists use thermometers in the lab, too.

Scale	Water Freezes	Water Boils	Quick Facts
Fahrenheit	32°	212°	This scale divides the difference between the freezing and boiling points of water into 180 equal degrees.
Celsius	0°	100°	This is the Celsius scale, with 100 degrees between the freezing point and boiling point of water.
Kelvin	273.15	373.13	This scale starts with absolute zero, the temperature at which no molecules move. Instead of saying "one degree Kelvin," you just say "one Kelvin."

What Makes a Good Conductor?

YOU WILL NEED:

- Scissors
- Paper
- 3 toothpicks
- Tape
- Plastic knife
- Butter, margarine, or shortening
- Metal jar lid
- Plastic margarine or yogurt lid
- Small piece of wood
- Large bowl or bucket
- Hot tap water
- Watch or clock

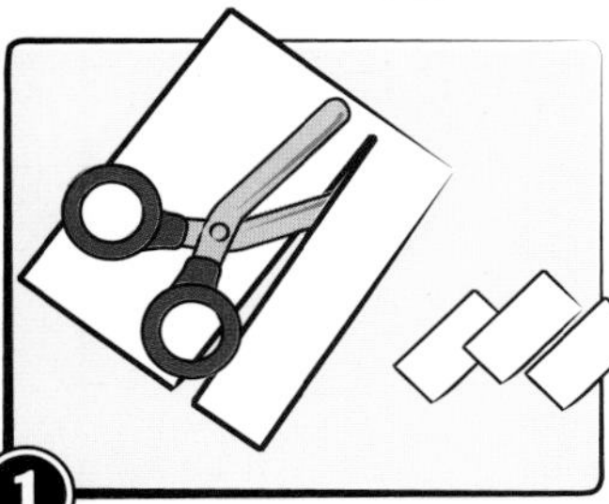

1. Cut out three pieces of paper all the same size, about 1½ inches by ¾ inch (4 cm x 2 cm).

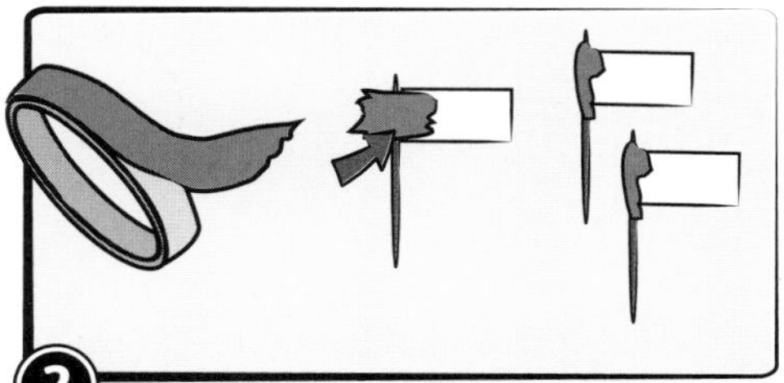

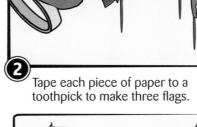

2. Tape each piece of paper to a toothpick to make three flags.

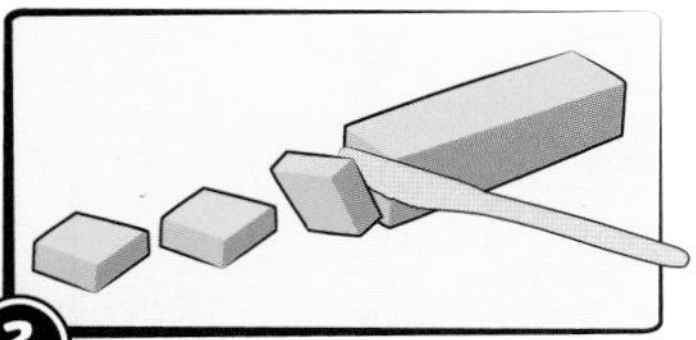

3. Cut three pieces of butter, margarine, or shortening with the plastic knife, making sure they are all about the same size.

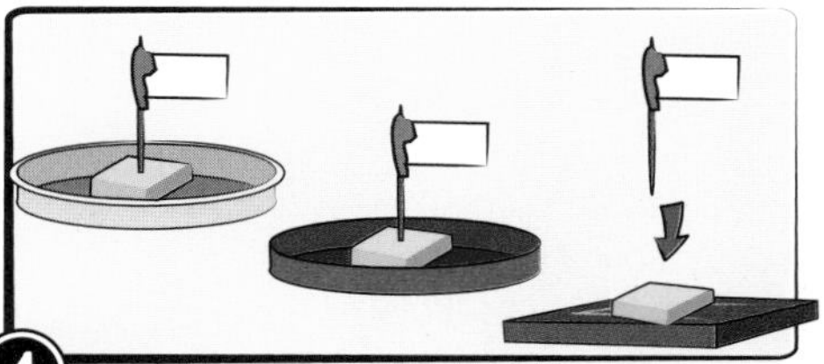

4. Place one piece on the metal lid, one on the plastic lid, and one on the small piece of wood. Put a flag into each piece.

5. Ask an adult to help you put hot water into the large bowl or bucket. Place the lids and piece of wood gently in the water so they float.

6. Time how long it takes each piece of butter to melt and each flag to fall over. Which piece melts the fastest? Which takes the longest to melt? How is this related to conduction of heat?

Change it UP!

☞ Try testing different materials such as Styrofoam, cardboard, aluminum foil, and clay to see how well they conduct heat.

The SCIENCE Behind It

The flag on the metal lid drops first, because the tiny molecules that make up the lid conduct heat very well. Heat energy moves quickly from water molecules to the molecules of a conductor and from there to the butter, causing it to melt. The flag on the piece of wood is the last to fall. Why? Because molecules of wood are poor heat conductors.

HEAT RISES

Have you ever wondered how a hot-air balloon can rise and fall without the assistance of jets, propellers, or wings? Have you noticed that the top floor of a house is always the warmest? These two scenarios are different, but the cause is the same. When air heats up, it does two things: It expands and it rises.

Expanding and Rising

Think of **molecules** as the teeny-tiny building blocks of the universe. Everything is made of molecules. Different types of molecules fit together in different ways to make up everything from a hamburger to a block of wood, a cloud in the sky to a glass of juice. Even though air is invisible, it is also made of molecules. The molecules that make up air are in a group we call gases. Gases are invisible and have no definite shape. When heated, air molecules start to move and bounce around like crazy. This movement results in the air taking up more space. When the air takes up more space, it becomes lighter and floats upward.

Hot-air balloons were first created in 1783.

In the case of a hot-air balloon, burners or heaters are used to make the air molecules inside the balloon start to dance around quickly.

The air molecules spread out, making the air lighter. As the air rises, it pushes up against the balloon and carries it higher.

To descend, the pilot stops heating the air and releases some of the hot air from the top of the balloon. When that is done correctly, the balloon gracefully floats back down to the ground.

Home Heating Troubles

The fact that hot air rises makes heating a big house in the winter a special challenge. Because all of the hot air rises to the top floors of a building, it's not uncommon for a person to be chilly on the ground floor while the people on the top floor are sweltering. How do you think you could use this information to heat your home more effectively?

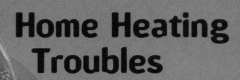

BALLOON MAGIC

One quick and easy way to see how air temperature affects the amount of space air takes up involves a simple balloon. Blow up a regular balloon (or use one of those shiny Mylar balloons). Make sure it's tied off, so no air is getting in or out. Place that balloon in the freezer for 30 minutes. What happens? Leave the balloon out on the counter for another 30 minutes. What happens now? What happens if you heat the balloon very carefully with a hair dryer on low?

During a fire, it is important to remember that, just as heat rises, so does smoke. That's why you should stay close to the ground as you make your way out of a building.

Some tornadoes exist for only a few seconds and others can go on for more than an hour, but most do not last longer than 10 minutes.

Extreme Weather

Just as warm air expands and rises, cold air compresses (gets smaller and more dense) and sinks. We see dramatic displays of this in certain kinds of extreme weather. Violent storms called tornadoes are created when warm, moist air crashes into lots of cold, dry air. When these two walls of air, or fronts, collide, the warm air traps the cold air underneath it. With nowhere to go, the cold, dry air starts spinning with the warm, moist air. If the conditions are just right, a funnel cloud forms and a tornado with winds blowing up to 300 miles (483 km) per hour may be created in an instant.

HEAT IT UP AND WATCH IT GO!

This experiment demonstrates the effect of microwaves on water and air molecules. As the waves agitate these molecules, they vibrate and start to heat up. How does this affect bars of soap?

What's So Weird About Ivory Soap?

YOU WILL NEED:

- Ivory bar soap
- Microwave
- Paper towels
- Another brand of bar soap

1. Place a bar of Ivory soap on a paper towel.

2. With an adult's help, put the soap and the paper towel in a microwave, and microwave it on high for up to 2 minutes.

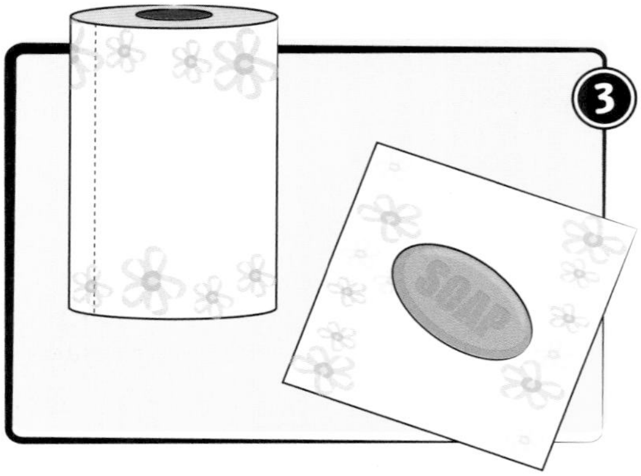

3. Place your other bar of soap on a paper towel.

science fair tip

Write down your observations, and photograph your results. Display your pictures and observations as part of your presentation.

SAFETY NOTE

Adult supervision is required for any microwave use. Cooking times may vary depending on the wattage of the microwave.

HEAT EXPANSION IN THE KITCHEN

We can see the effects of heat expansion all around us. Popcorn expands when it is exposed to heat, just like Ivory soap does. Each kernel of corn contains water that turns to vapor when it gets hot. As this vapor expands, the pressure mounts until the kernel bursts open, and you've got a hot, tasty snack.

Using what you now know about hot air, why do you think it's important to remove lids from plastic containers before placing them in the microwave? Why should you poke holes in a hot dog or a potato before cooking it?

4

Microwave this other brand of bar soap on the paper towel for the same amount of time as in step 2.

5

Place your two microwaved bars side by side. What differences and similarities do you observe?

Change it UP!

☞ Try placing different bars of soap in a container of water to test their density. Denser bars will sink.

☞ Get an adult's permission, and try microwaving different brands of marshmallows or different brands of microwave popcorn. Which brands puff up the best?

The SCIENCE Behind It

Ivory soap is marketed as the soap that floats in the bath. Why does it float? Because it has a lot of air whipped into it. This makes it less dense than other bar soaps.

When you microwave a bar of Ivory, the bar softens, and the air and water trapped inside heat up and expand. They bubble out of the soap, causing it to puff and froth. Other bar soaps have less air whipped into them, so they do not puff up as much in the microwave.

ALL WATER IS NOT EQUAL

Have you ever noticed that even in the middle of the coldest winters, when the ground is covered with snow and lakes have become skating rinks, that the ocean doesn't turn into an enormous ice cube? That's because salt water and fresh water freeze at different temperatures.

Freezing Points and Melting Points

When a liquid gets cold enough, it goes through a phase change and becomes solid. Conversely, when a solid or frozen object gets warm enough, it will melt. Not all liquids freeze and melt at the same temperature. We call these temperatures the **freezing point** and the **melting point.** The freezing point for water is 32°F (0°C), but dissolving other materials into water can change its freezing and melting points.

The reason that the water in the oceans does not freeze in winter is because of the salt. Salt water has a freezing point that is much lower than fresh water. In fact, the more salt there is in the water, the lower the freezing point of that water.

Notice how the salt water has not frozen in this wintry scene.

Icebergs are not frozen salt water, but broken pieces of glaciers that form from compacted layers of snow.

ONE-OF-A-KIND WATER

Water is unique in that it expands when it freezes. Most materials contract, or get smaller, when they freeze. Have you ever noticed that windows and doors are easier to open when it's cold outside? This is because the materials contract in winter and expand in the summer. This is also why placing a can of soda in the freezer for too long is a bad idea. Chances are, the can will explode and leave quite a mess to clean up. Want to test this safely? Put a sealed plastic water bottle in the freezer. The plastic will stretch instead of exploding.

Adding salt and other materials to water can make them boil at a higher temperature. Want your pasta to cook faster? Sprinkle a little salt in the water.

Feeling Hot, Hot, Hot

Once they reach a certain temperature, some materials go through yet another phase change and become a gas. We call this temperature a **boiling point.** Air pressure can change a substance's boiling point. This is why cooking at high altitudes requires some changes to ingredients and cooking temperature.

ALTITUDE MATTERS

When making brownies from a mix, you may notice that the recipe calls for extra water, added flour, and/or less oil if you are cooking at elevations higher than 5,000 feet (1,524 m). That's because water boils at a lower temperature in high altitudes. If the water boils off the dessert mix too early, it may mess up the chemical reactions that take place in the oven.

When Will It Boil?

Here are the boiling points of some common liquids.

LIQUID	BOILING POINT FAHRENHEIT	BOILING POINT CELSIUS
◀ Acetone (nail polish remover)	133°F	56.5°C
Alcohol (rubbing alcohol)	180°F	82°C
Butane	31.1°F	-0.5°C
Iodine	363.8°F	184.3°C
Linseed oil	649.4°F	343°C
Olive oil ▶	570°F	300°C
Gasoline	212–752°F	100–400°C
Propane	-44°F	-42°C
Turpentine	300–356°F	149–180°C
Water	212°F	100°C

CHANGING FREEZING POINTS

Can we slow down the freezing process or even keep water from freezing altogether? This experiment allows you to test the effects of salt, sugar, and other materials on water's freezing and melting points.

Can You Keep Water From Freezing?

YOU WILL NEED:

- 2 cups
- Water
- Tape
- Marker
- Teaspoon
- Salt
- Sugar
- 6 toothpicks
- Ice cube tray
- Freezer
- Clock
- Pencil
- Paper

1 Fill two cups with water.

2 Label one cup "salt," and stir in two spoonfuls of salt.

3 Label the second cup "sugar," and stir in two spoonfuls of sugar.

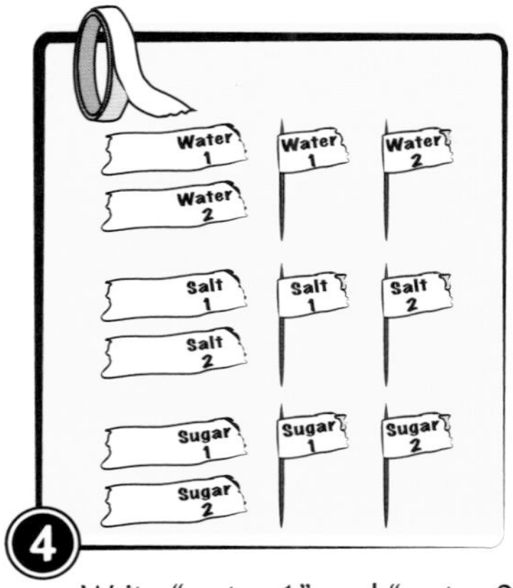

4 Write "water 1" and "water 2" on two small pieces of tape, and wrap each one around a toothpick, like a flag. Write "salt 1" and "salt 2" on two small pieces of tape, and wrap each one around a toothpick. Then write "sugar 1" and "sugar 2" on two small pieces of tape, and wrap each one around a toothpick.

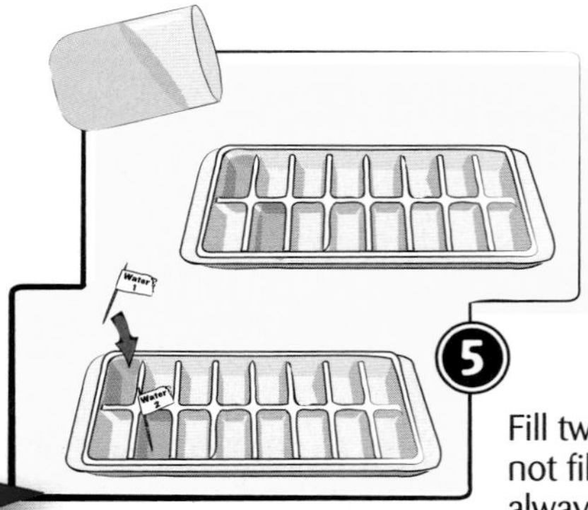

5 Fill two of the ice cube tray's wells with water. Do not fill two wells next to one another. Instead, always leave an empty well between the ones you fill up. Put a "water" toothpick in each well.

science fair tip

Use tape to mark a place on your counter where you will set your ice cube trays. Set up a camera on a tripod so you can take photos of the trays at the same angle each time. On your computer, create slides showing the time. Then create a slide show.

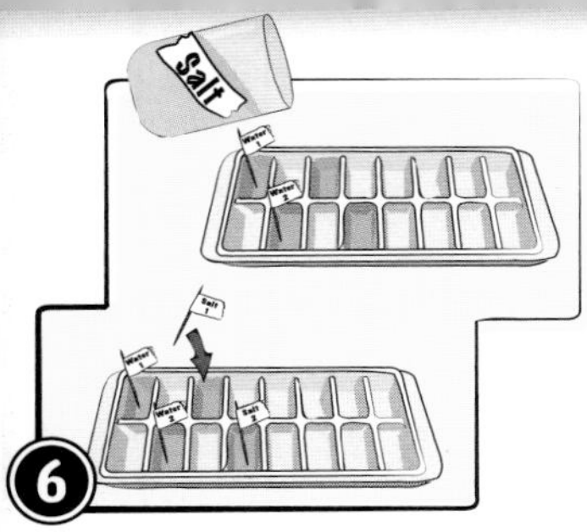

6 Fill two of the tray's wells with salt water. Put a "salt" toothpick in each well.

7 Fill two of the tray's wells with sugar water. Put a "sugar" toothpick in each well.

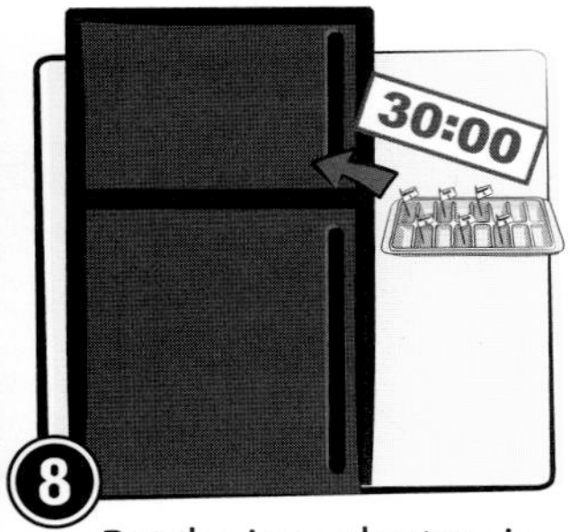

8 Put the ice cube tray in the freezer.

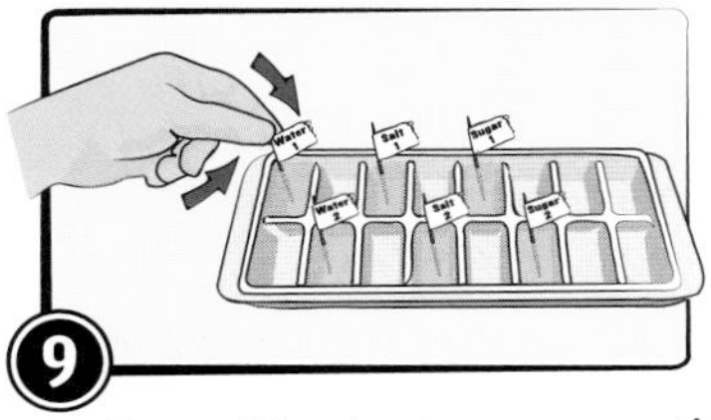

9 Every 30 minutes, remove the ice cube tray. Check to see which wells are frozen, by trying to move the toothpicks.

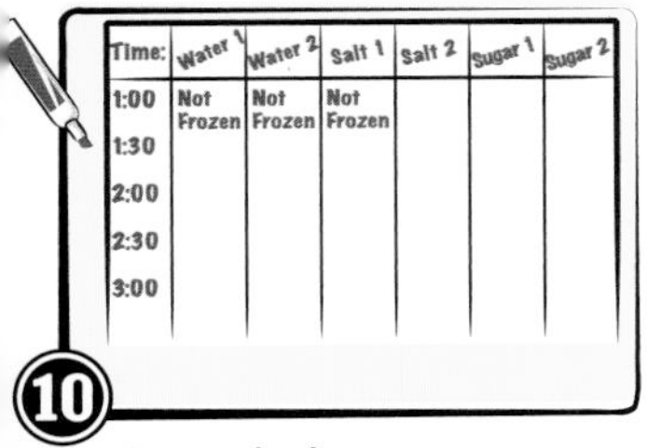

10 Record what you see on paper. Put the tray back into the freezer, and continue checking every 30 minutes until all the ice cubes are frozen.

11 Put the ice cube tray on the kitchen counter. Check it every 30 minutes to see which wells have thawed. Record what you see on your paper.

AMAZING ANTIFREEZE

We also use chemicals like salt to change the freezing-point temperature of snow and ice on the roads in countries that have cold winters. On snowy days, people sprinkle salt on roads and sidewalks to keep them from getting icy. Being able to change the freezing point of a liquid comes in handy in other places as well. For example, your car wouldn't be able to run if the fluid in the engine froze.

Change it UP!

☞ How would other materials affect water's freezing temperature? Try your ice cube freeze-thaw test with other materials such as:

dirt	flour
vinegar	milk
juice	pepper
baking powder	food coloring

☞ Which melts ice faster, a cup of fresh water or a cup of salt water? Thaw ice cubes to test your hypothesis.

The SCIENCE Behind It

You made antifreeze! Antifreeze is a mix of water and chemicals with very low freezing points. Water placed in a freezer loses its heat and drops in temperature. Water freezes at 32°F (0°C), but you've lowered the water's freezing point by adding salt or sugar. This means it takes the salty or sugary water longer to freeze than regular tap water. The salt or sugar also keeps the water colder, so these ice cubes thaw more slowly than the cubes made from fresh water.

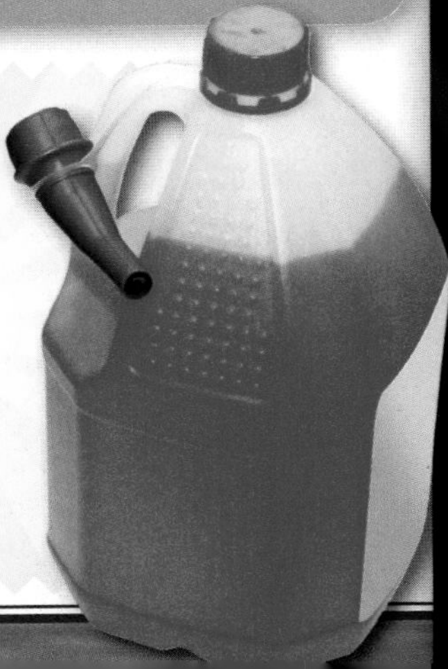

CHEMISTRY OF CLEAN

Cleaning can be a complicated business. Have you ever gotten something greasy on your hands and tried to get it off without using soap? The water just runs over the grease and doesn't clean you up at all. This is because water and oil don't mix. People have been experimenting with chemicals and cleaning methods for hundreds of years in order to remove grease, oil, and food stains.

Getting Between Oil and Water

You can see how water drops behave by putting a little bit of water on a nonstick pan.

If you leave small drops of water on a smooth surface they tend to "roll" toward each other making one big drop. This is a property unique to water, because of its molecules. Water molecules are like mini magnets with positive and negative poles. Just like any magnet, opposite poles attract, so water molecules within a drop are actually drawn to one another like a ball of magnets. This attraction allows water molecules to hold their position next to one another, and yet still remain separate.

This attraction also creates something called **surface tension.** The molecules at the top of a liquid tend to stay together to resist external forces. Surface tension is what allows small insects to walk on water without breaking through the surface of the liquid. It is almost as if a thin film forms at the top of a liquid. Surface tension also allows you to fill a glass higher than its sides without spilling. (Go ahead, try it! Just add the water very slowly). Most detergents have what is called a **surfactant.** A surfactant breaks the bond between water molecules and allows the water to get between the oil and whatever you are trying to clean, so the greasy mess can be rinsed away.

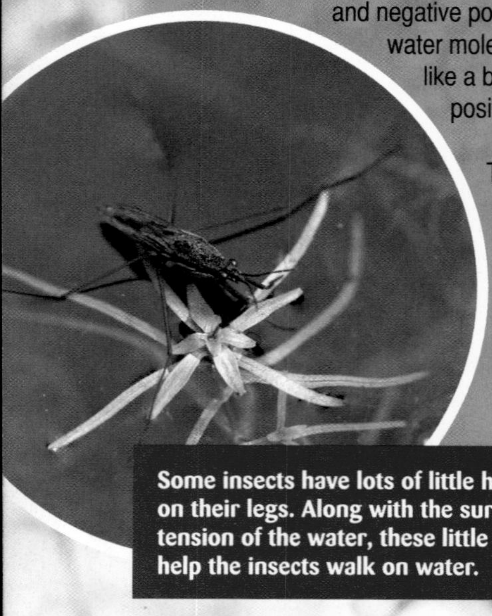

Some insects have lots of little hairs on their legs. Along with the surface tension of the water, these little hairs help the insects walk on water.

SOAP VS. DETERGENT

The main difference between soap and detergent is that soap is made from natural products and detergents are man-made (though some ingredients in detergent are natural). Soap is made by combining vegetable or animal fat with a strongly alkaline solution. An alkaline solution is a base, with a pH of more than 7. (For more on acids, bases, and pH, see page 98). Oil and grease attract dirt. Soap basically traps grease and oil while mixing with water, so the dirt that is stuck to grease and oil can be rinsed away.

Cleaning With Enzymes

Enzymes are proteins that help to break molecules apart. Though they are not living things, they are made up of cells. In fact, we have enzymes in our saliva and digestive systems to help break down our food. Enzymes are also used in cleaning agents. Enzymes can do the same job as man-made chemicals, only better. Enzymes are natural. They work in low-temperature water (many chemicals need to be mixed with warm or hot water to be effective) and are fully biodegradable.

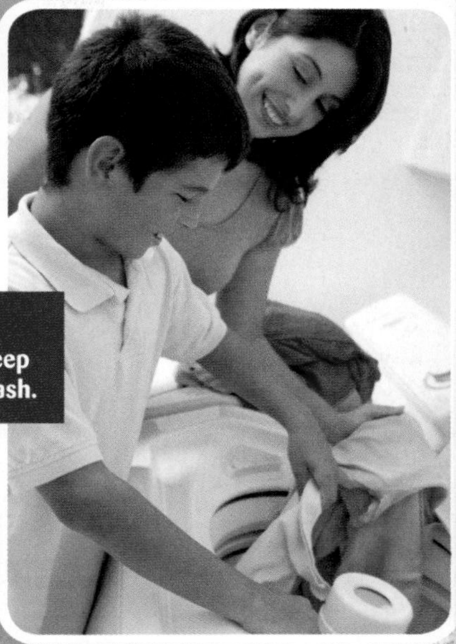

Some enzymes can even help fabrics keep their color in the wash.

Cooking With Enzymes

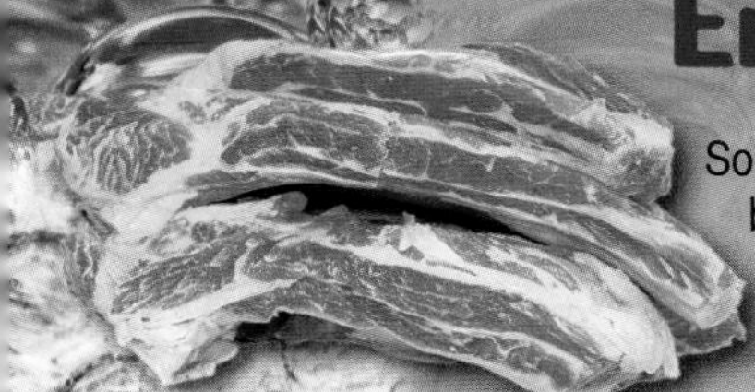

Some cooks will use meat tenderizer to make it taste better and easier to chew. The tenderizer powder contains enzymes that help break down the tough parts of the meat before it is cooked.

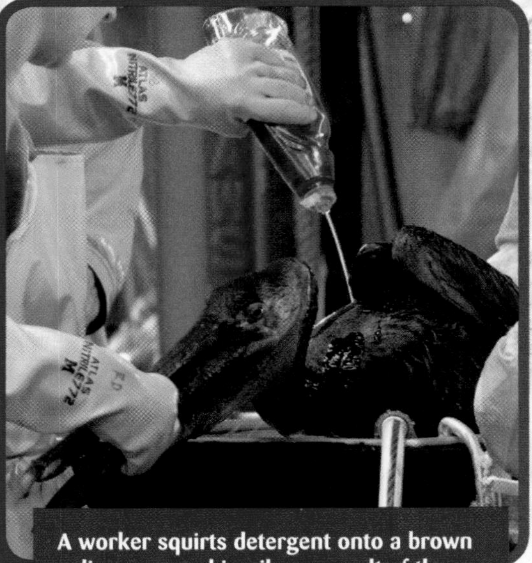

A worker squirts detergent onto a brown pelican covered in oil as a result of the Deepwater Horizon oil spill in 2010.

DETERGENTS SAVE WILDLIFE

Because detergents are so effective at removing oil, they have also been used to help clean up after oil spills in the ocean. Oil spills can be catastrophic to a marine environment and its ecology. When the feathers of marine birds are covered in oil, they can no longer fly or maintain their body temperature. Oil can also be devastating to otters, seals, and other marine life. Animal conservationists use mild detergents to clean marine animals after major oil spills. It can be a very difficult and time-consuming process, but it's the only way to help these critters once they get oil on them.

STAINS BEGONE!

In the following experiment, you can explore the strengths and weaknesses of different cleaning agents. Do they all work the same? Is one better than the other? Do you think there is a reason to have so many different types of cleaners?

What's the Best Stain Remover?

SAFETY NOTE

Have an adult help you with the laundry detergent and stain remover. These can contain harsh chemicals.

YOU WILL NEED:

- Coffee or grape juice
- Large bowl
- Cloth
- Plate
- Marker (or pen and paper)
- 4 clothespins (or safety pins)
- Teaspoon
- Water
- Dishwashing liquid
- Liquid laundry detergent
- Stain remover (Resolve or similar)

1. Pour coffee or grape juice into a large bowl.

2. Place the cloth in the bowl, and let it soak for 30 minutes. Remove the cloth and let it dry.

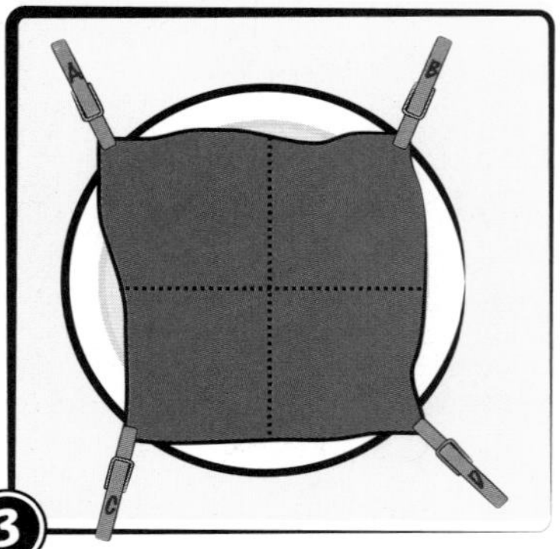

3. Place the cloth on a plate and divide it into four sections. Use a marker to label the clothespins A, B, C, or D. Affix one clothespin to each section of the cloth. (Or write A, B, C, or D on four paper scraps and use the safety pins to attach the scraps to the cloth.)

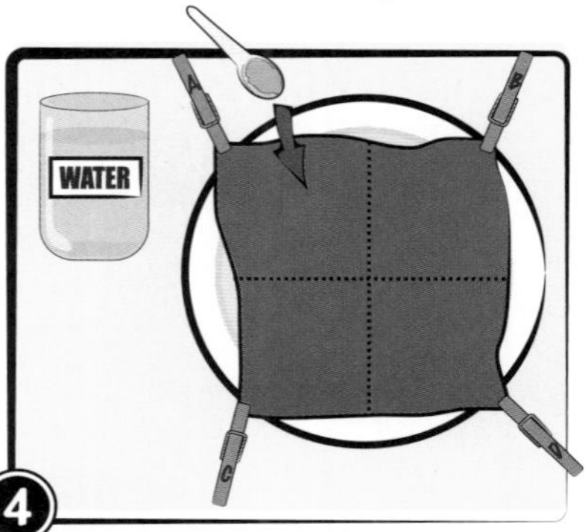

4. Pour a teaspoon (5 mL) of water onto the center of the "A" section of the cloth.

NOTE: Ask an adult's permission before staining a tea towel or washcloth for this experiment.

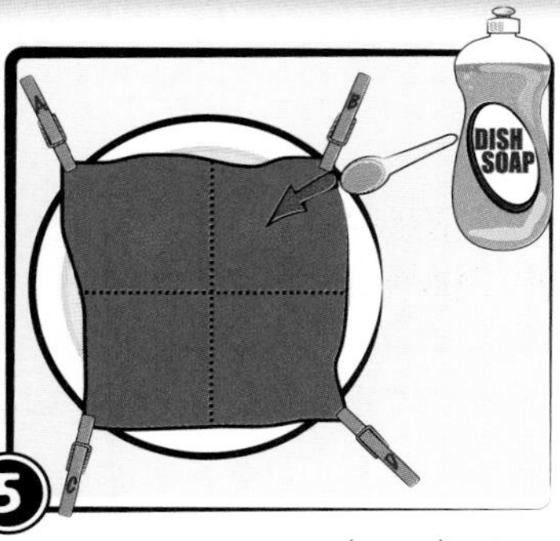

5 Pour a teaspoon (5 mL) of dishwashing liquid onto the center of the "B" section of the cloth.

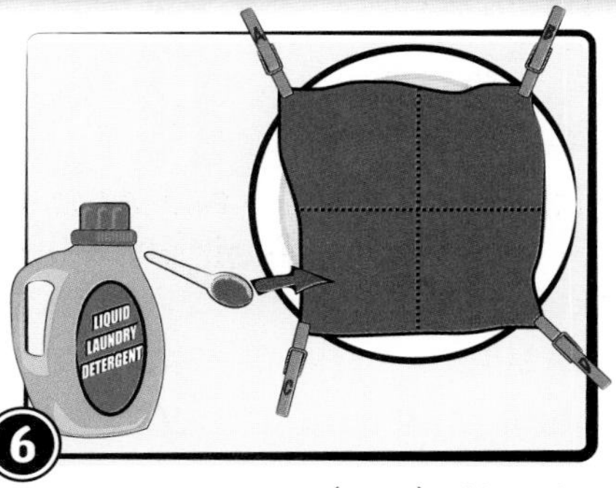

6 Pour a teaspoon (5 mL) of liquid laundry detergent onto the center of the "C" section of the cloth.

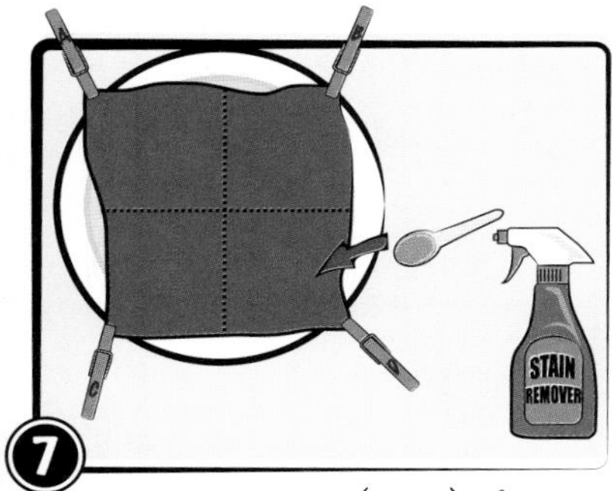

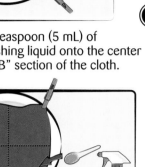

7 Pour a teaspoon (5 mL) of stain remover onto the center of the "D" section of the cloth.

8 Leave the cloth for 5 minutes, and then wash each section of the cloth in a bowl of water. Which liquid removed the stain best?

Change it UP!

☞ You can extend your research by testing other soaps, such as bar soap, hand soap, or Tide to Go.

☞ You can also test different stains, such as dirt, mustard, marker, mascara, or tomato sauce.

☞ Do your stain removers work better on some stains than others? Use a dish glove to test whether rubbing the soap into the stain makes a difference.

One of the earliest records of soap making dates back to 2800 B.C. The ancient Egyptians used soap to prepare wool for weaving.

MAKE YOUR OWN ENZYME

Your own saliva works great on food stains. The same enzymes that start to break down food in your mouth will also break down the juice, ketchup, ice cream, or whatever else you've spilled on yourself.

The SCIENCE Behind It

Soaps, detergents, and stain removers all have a similar objective: to clean up messes and make stains disappear. They can all be effective, but they do not attack a stain in the same way. Water doesn't normally mix with oil or dirt. Soaps and detergents help them mix so the oil and dirt washes away with the water. Soaps are made of particles with two ends. One of these ends sticks to water, and the other end sticks to dirt or grease. Most detergents also contain surfactants, which reduce surface tension and help greasy stains mix with water to make cleaning easier. Stain removers like Resolve or Tide to Go may contain enzymes, special proteins that help start the breakdown of stains.

MASS MATTERS

Cruise ships are enormous and they float, and yet a penny sinks immediately when tossed into a fountain. What is it that allows a big, heavy object to float, while a tiny thing drops straight down into the water? The magic behind this particular phenomena is density. Density describes how much "stuff" is in an object, or how closely packed together its molecules are.

Density Is Not Weight

Imagine you have two boxes. They are exactly the same size, but one is made of iron and the other is made of wood. Which do you think would be lighter? Iron is very dense, meaning the molecules are packed really closely together. The wood box would weigh less because there is a lot of space between the molecules in wood. Even though the two boxes are the same size, they have different densities.

Many people get density and weight confused. Density and weight are related to each other, but they are not the same thing at all. Objects have weight because gravity is pulling on them. Jupiter is a massive planet, and it has more gravity than Earth. If you were to travel to Jupiter, you would weigh almost two and a half times more than you weigh on Earth. Your density on Jupiter is the same as it is on Earth, but your weight would be different.

An object's **mass** is a measurement of its density, and the mass of an object does not change even if it is floating in zero gravity.

Aboard the International Space Station, both this astronaut and the fruit float. The mass of the apple, orange, and the astronaut is the same in space as it is on Earth.

Ice is less dense than liquid water. If it wasn't, ponds would freeze from the bottom up, and your ice cubes would sink to the bottom of your glass.

Liquid Density

Different liquids have different densities. One simple example is oil and water. Because oil and water don't mix, you can easily experiment with them to see which is less dense. If you pour a half a teaspoon of cooking oil into half a cup of water, what do you notice? Can you tell which is less dense from what you see?

What about the mystery of items that float for a bit and then sink? Have you ever watched something absorbent float and then slowly sink? This is because the density of the object changes when it starts to absorb water. Once the density of the object is greater than the density of the water, it sinks.

A sponge is not very dense and will float in water. But when all of its airholes fill with water, it becomes more dense and can no longer float.

There are special rocks that often float. Volcanic rocks called pumice can have so many airholes in them that they can float.

SALT CHANGES DENSITY

Salt water is more dense than fresh water, so objects float more easily in salt water. The Dead Sea has so much salt in it that people float with little or no effort.

DON'T BE DENSE!

This experiment allows you to explore density and an object's ability to float or sink. Using similarly sized and shaped objects can help demonstrate the relationship between density and floating.

Which Objects Float in Water?

YOU WILL NEED:

- Sink or pail
- Water
- Plastic spoon
- Metal spoon
- Wooden spoon

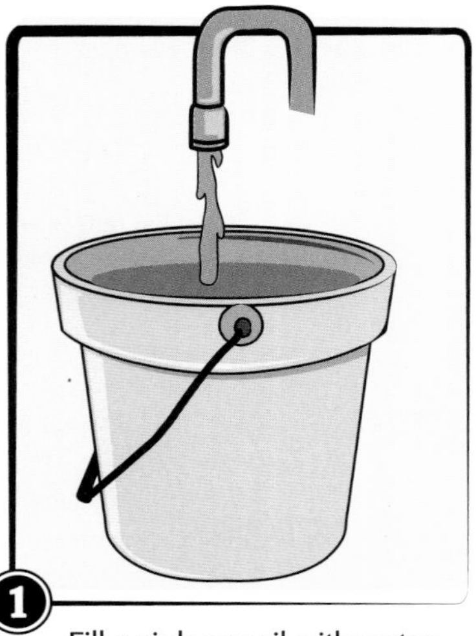

1. Fill a sink or pail with water.

2. Place the plastic spoon in the water. Does it float or sink? Record your results.

3. Place the metal spoon in the water, and record what happens.

FLOATING TREES, SINKING ROCKS

Knowing why certain materials float is very helpful for people who design everything from pool toys to boats. It can also be helpful for certain industries. For example, loggers use density to their advantage when transporting heavy lumber.

People use lots of paper products, and most of that paper comes from trees. Before lumber can be converted into paper, the trees have to be cut down and transported to paper-processing plants. A pine tree that is 200 feet (61 m) tall can weigh around 11,200 pounds (5,080 kg), so powerful trucks and trains are often needed to carry them overland. What about moving logs in water? Felled trees are often floated down rivers as a more efficient way of getting them out of the forest and closer to processing plants. The loggers don't even need to load the logs onto boats! Trees have lots of air in their wood, so they are much less dense than rocks and pebbles. The density of the wood in comparison to the water is what is most important. If something is less dense than water, it will float!

4 Place the wooden spoon in the water, and record what happens.

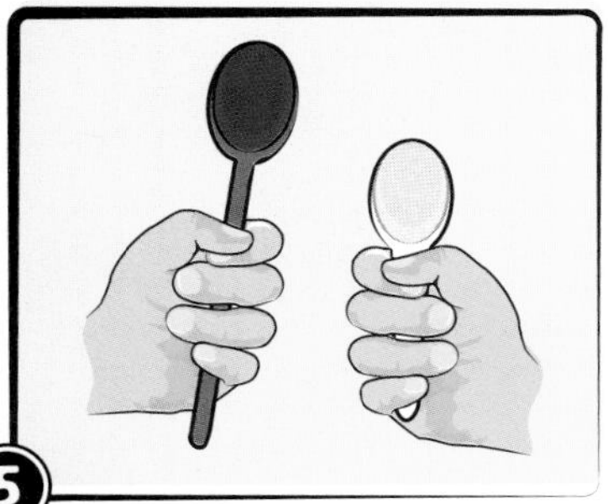

5 Hold the spoons in your hands, one by one. Which one feels the heaviest? Which one is the lightest?

Change it UP!

☞ Try testing other materials, such as: a tennis ball, a golf ball, a ball of foil, an empty bottle, a dime, an eraser, a potato, and some peas. Which items are more dense than water? Which are less dense than water?

☞ Do your results change if you use salty water? Can you find a way to make dense materials float?

The SCIENCE Behind It

Density is the amount of matter in a given space. Some materials are less dense than water, such as wood, oil, and some plastics. These materials float on water. Other materials are denser than water, such as steel and rock. These materials sink in water.

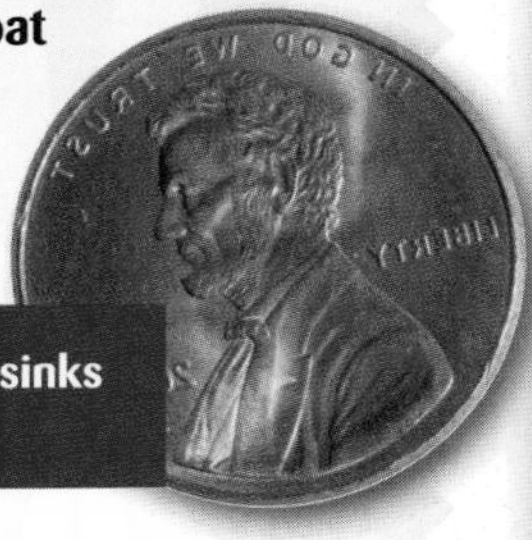

A penny is denser than water, so it sinks when you throw it in a fountain.

THE PRESSURE'S ON

When walking on a warm, sunny day, you can feel the sunshine on your skin. Maybe you also feel a light breeze. But can you feel pressure pushing on you? Believe it or not, a huge amount of air is pressing on you! Why don't you get crushed from the pressure? Because our bodies have pressure that pushes outward. It all balances out.

How Much Pressure?

Air pressure is the force that is exerted on you (and other objects) by the weight of air molecules. You can't see the molecules, but they take up space and have weight. Air molecules don't naturally stay packed together: there's space between them. So, they can be pressed together to fit in a smaller space. Weather forecasters measure the pressure of large masses of air. If a lot of air is packed in a small space, that's a **high-pressure system.** High-pressure systems bring clear skies and cooler temperatures. **Low-pressure systems** bring warmer weather, but they can also bring rain and storms.

You can't feel air pressure, but it's around you all the time!

The deeper a person goes into the water, the more pressure is exerted on the body.

Water Pressure

Water pressure is the force that is exerted on an object by the weight of water. Water is heavier than air. So, water pressure is much greater than air pressure. Water pressure is measured in units called atmospheres. For every 30 feet (9.1 m) or so that we dive down in the water, another atmosphere presses down on our bodies. We can only travel down to three or four atmospheres of pressure before we need the protection of a craft like a submarine.

HOW DO THEY DO IT?

The deepest place in the ocean is almost seven miles (11 km) deep! The water pressure there is more than 1,000 times greater than at sea level. How do the fish there keep from getting crushed? Their body tissue pushes back at the same pressure of the deep water. If these fish suddenly swam up thousands of feet, they could explode!

Can You Trap Air Underwater?

YOU WILL NEED:

- Rock or other large weight
- String
- Plastic soda bottle
- Masking tape
- 8 drinking straws (large milk-shake straws will work best)
- Bucket

1. Tie a string around your rock. Then tie the other end of the string to the mouth of the bottle so that the rock hangs about an inch (2.5 cm) below the center of the bottle opening. Secure with tape.

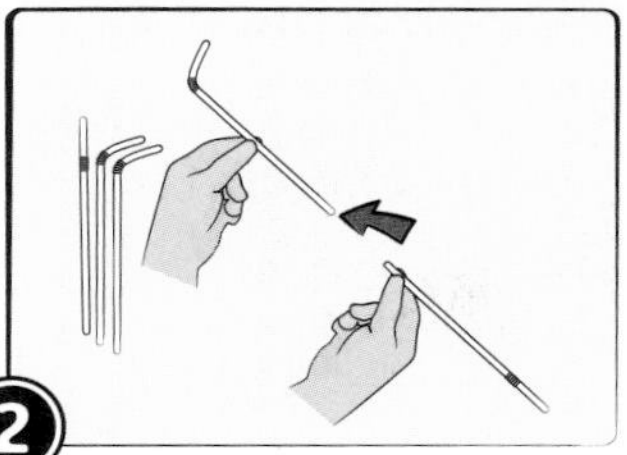

2. Create a long tube with your drinking straws by slipping them into the ends of each other.

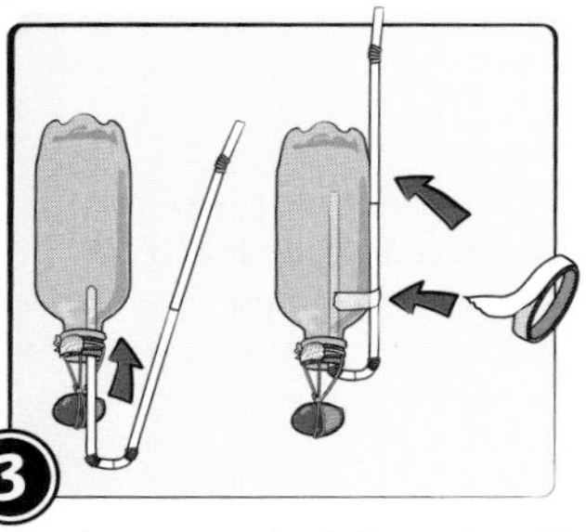

3. Push one end of the tube all the way into the bottle. Bend the tube gently where it exits the bottle, so the tube does not break or close off. Tape it to the outside of the bottle in two places: near the top and near the bottom.

4. Fill your bucket or sink with water.

5. Block the end of the tube with your thumb and put the bottle in the bucket or sink. The bottle should float with the weight hanging down.

6. Take your thumb off the end of the tube. The bottle should sink. When the weight hits bottom, blow into the tube. What happens? Can you get the bottle to hover in mid-water?

Change it UP!

☞ Re-create the experiments using a lighter weight and a heavier one. What else changes?

The SCIENCE Behind It

When you are scuba diving, the deeper you dive, the more water you have pushing against your body. Divers need to get air if they are going to work underwater for any length of time. One of the earliest inventions to do this was the diving bell, which trapped a supply of air for divers. You just created your very own diving bell! A diving bell is connected to the surface by an air hose and cable, and is weighted so it can overcome the pressure of the water to travel to the ocean bottom.

In 1939, the submarine U.S.S. *Squalus* flooded partially and sank. To rescue the survivors of the disaster, the Navy lowered a rescue chamber that was a version of a diving bell.

A PUSH FOR A PUSH

A space shuttle weighs more than 4.4 million pounds (1,996,000 kg) when it takes off. How do the flames shooting out of its engines make something so massive fly all the way into space? It's because of something Sir Isaac Newton discovered about 350 years ago.

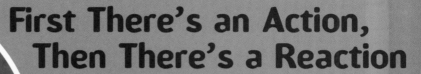

First There's an Action, Then There's a Reaction

In his lifetime, Sir Isaac Newton made many important observations about gravity, light, and the interaction of forces. He also devised three laws of motion that are part of the basis for modern science. Newton's third law of motion helps to explain how the space shuttle's engines are able to launch the enormous spacecraft into orbit.

Newton's third law of motion states: for every action, there is an equal and opposite reaction. (For more on the laws of motion, see page 141.) In the case of the shuttle taking off, the downward push from the engines has to be strong enough to push the spacecraft up and out of our atmosphere. That's a really big push!

Another good example of Newton's third law involves a deflating balloon. If you fill a balloon with air and then let go of it, you'll probably see it fly around the room. (You might also hear a very silly sound). The air being forced out of the opening in the balloon is called the **action.** The balloon flying in the opposite direction of the escaping air is the **reaction.** The speed and force of the balloon's flight depends on the speed and amount of air leaving the balloon's opening. The faster the air escapes in one direction, the faster the balloon will fly in the opposite direction. This is because the reaction is both equal and opposite of the action.

PLAYGROUND PHYSICS

A bouncing ball also demonstrates the relationship between action and reaction. When the ball hits the ground, the downward energy is transferred back to the ball in the opposite direction, and the ball bounces up again.

Brace Yourself!

You might be wondering if Newton's third law applies to all actions. And the answer is yes. For example, when someone pushes you forward on a swing, that person must plant his feet firmly on the ground to avoid falling over. Just as he pushes against your back, you push against his hands. If he's not ready, he might push himself right over and land on the ground.

Collision!

If two objects with the same mass crash into each other, they will bounce off of one another with equal force. If the objects have different mass, the object with less mass will take most of the energy and bounce farther. Imagine running into an elephant's leg. It's safe to say that you'll bounce farther. This is also why it hurts more to crash into a wall than to crash into something that moves when you hit it. When you hit a wall, you feel the force of the wall, as well as the force from the impact pushing you back.

PLAYING WITH REACTIONS

Poking holes in a soda can is one simple way to explore Newton's third law of motion: For every action, there is an equal and opposite reaction. See how various actions and reactions can create movement.

How Can I Make a Soda Can Spin?

YOU WILL NEED:

- Nail
- Empty soda can
- String
- Water
- Sink

SAFETY NOTE

Nails and cans can be sharp. Have an adult help you make the holes in the can.

1. With an adult's help, use a nail to poke a hole in one side of an empty soda can, near the bottom.

2. Push up the can's tab and tie a string to it.

3. Cover the hole you made with your thumb, and fill the can with water.

4. Hold it over a sink by the string and uncover the hole. What do you observe?

When a horse gallops, it pushes its hooves backward against the ground. As a reaction, the horse is propelled forward. When you want to jump into the air, you push down with your feet and legs in order to shoot upward. You know that when you push harder, you go higher. Jets and rockets also propel themselves with an action-reaction pair. They release gas, which creates thrust. Thrust is the force that pushes flying objects forward. As the gas exits in one direction, the rocket is propelled in the opposite direction.

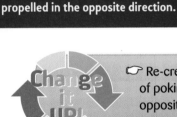

Jet propulsion is based on Newton's third law, too. As air is blasted out the back of the engine, the plane is thrust forward through the sky.

Change it UP!

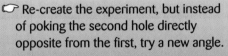

- Re-create the experiment, but instead of poking the second hole directly opposite from the first, try a new angle.
- What happens if you add more holes to the can?
- Compare several cans with different-size holes.
- Redo the experiment with three different cans: one with the hole near the bottom, one a little bit higher up, and one with the hole in the middle.

5 Make a second hole on the opposite side of the can and repeat the experiment. What happens now?

The SCIENCE Behind It

This type of device is called a "Hero's Engine," and it is named after the ancient Greek scientist who first invented it. These devices move by shooting steam or water from holes. The "Hero's Engine" perfectly demonstrates Newton's third law. When the fluid exits in one direction (the action), the device is pushed in the opposite direction (the reaction).

Light moves faster than anything known to man. It bounces off some materials and goes right through others. Light bouncing off a highly reflective material can cook an egg. When passing through plasma and focused into a very small beam, light can become a laser and burn a hole through a piece of metal. Light can be seen in many colors or be invisible to us. Ultraviolet light is visible to some insects and birds but invisible to the human eye.

Light reflects off the smooth surface of the stones, making them appear shiny.

Big Waves, Little Waves

Light travels in waves. All light travels at approximately 186,282 miles (299,792 km) per second. Higher energy light, like gamma rays, travels in shorter waves, and lower energy light, like the colors of a rainbow, travels in longer waves. Regardless of how much energy the light has, it follows a straight path until it hits something. If it bounces off something rough or bumpy, the light scatters in many different directions at once. Think of carpet. Light hits the uneven surface of a carpet and then bounces in many different directions, giving the carpet the appearance of being dull. But when light bounces off something smooth like a mirror or a polished stone, the light is redirected all together, so the object looks shiny or reflective.

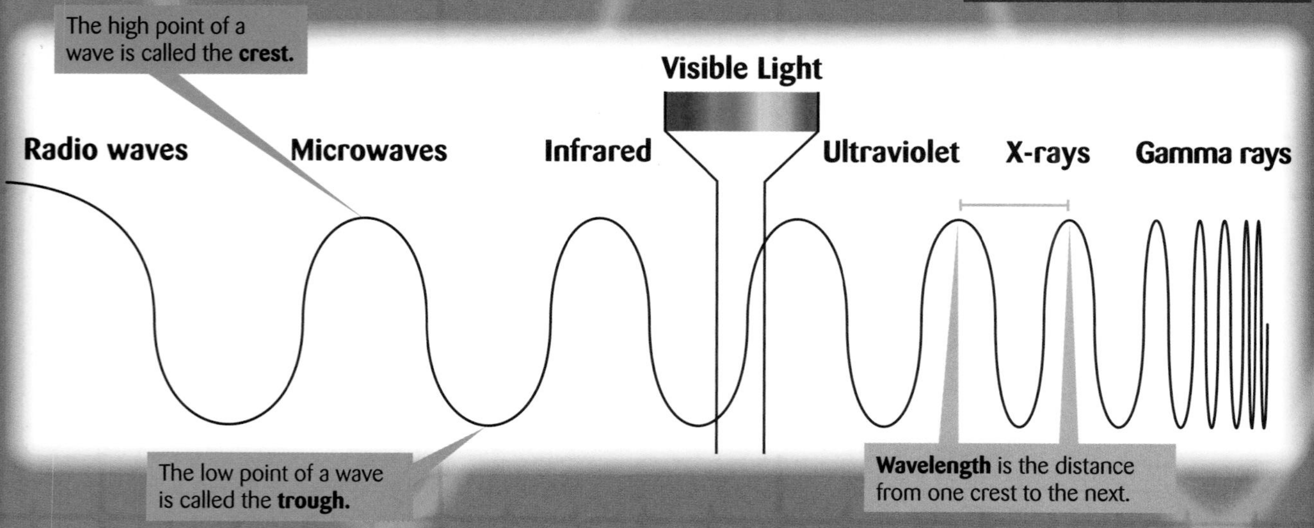

The high point of a wave is called the **crest.**
Visible Light
Radio waves
Microwaves
Infrared
Ultraviolet
X-rays
Gamma rays
The low point of a wave is called the **trough.**
Wavelength is the distance from one crest to the next.

The wavelength of a radio wave can be as big as a football field or as short as a water bottle. The wavelength of a microwave

Playing With Light

Light can also pass through clear materials, like glass or water, and be redirected in such a way that an object appears bigger, smaller, distorted, or even upside down. This is the function of a lens. Convex lenses are thicker in the middle, and concave lenses are thicker toward the edges.

Lenses are used in many different ways. Microscopes use lenses to magnify objects, or make them much bigger. The lens in a telescope can make something far away look much closer.

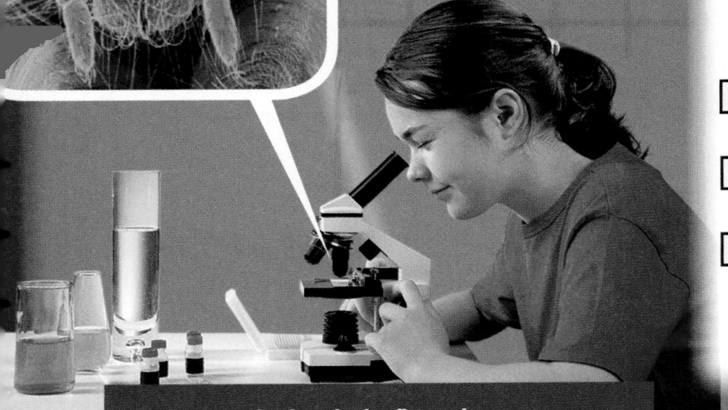

Looking at the head of a fly under a microscope allows a person to see detail that he or she could not see with eyes alone.

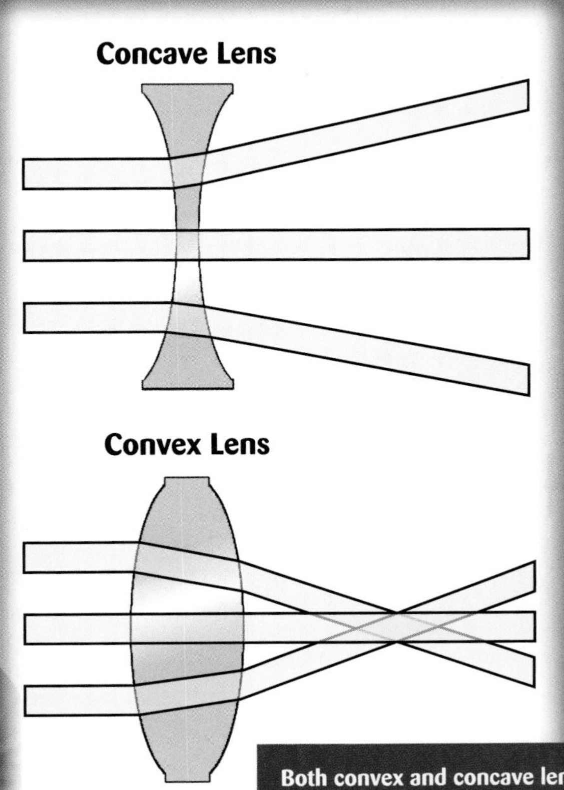

Both convex and concave lenses bend light rays and change the point at which they focus. Lenses are used in eyeglasses, contacts, cameras, and many other things.

LENSES HELP US EVERYDAY

Lenses can be many shapes and sizes. Humans have biconvex lenses in each of our eyes. These lenses allow us to focus on images both close to us and far away, but they also bend light in such a way that they send upside-down images to our brain. Our brain must take the information sent from our eyes and turn it right side up so that we can understand what we're looking at.

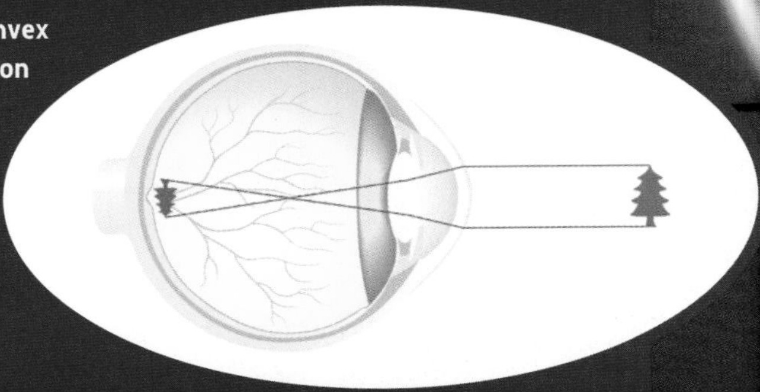

LENSES AND LIGHT

Use a drinking glass filled with water to create a homemade lens. What happens as light travels through the lens?

Can Water Affect How Light Moves?

YOU WILL NEED:

- 2 sheets of card stock
- Marker
- 2 tall clear drinking glasses with straight sides
- Water

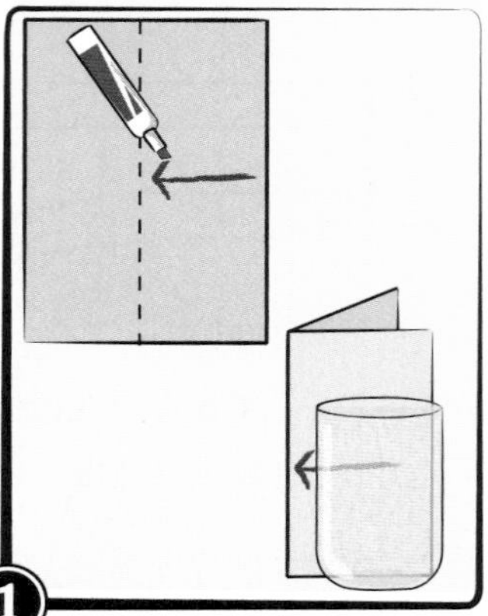

1 Fold the first sheet of card stock so that it can stand up. Draw an arrow pointing to the left, and place the card behind the first drinking glass.

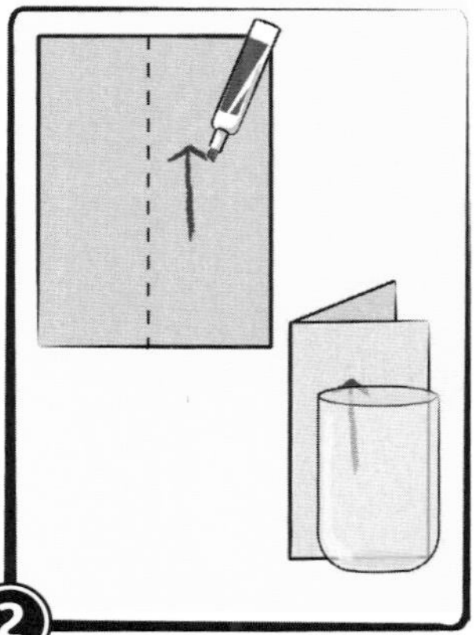

2 Fold the second sheet of card stock. Draw an arrow pointing up, and place the card behind the second drinking glass.

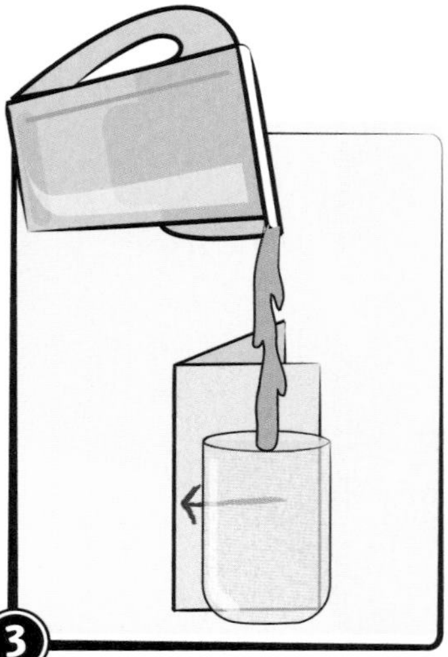

3 Pour water into the first glass so that it fills above the arrow.

4 Look through the first glass. Which way does the arrow point?

There are lenses in binoculars, car headlights, magnifying glasses, movie projectors, and telescopes.

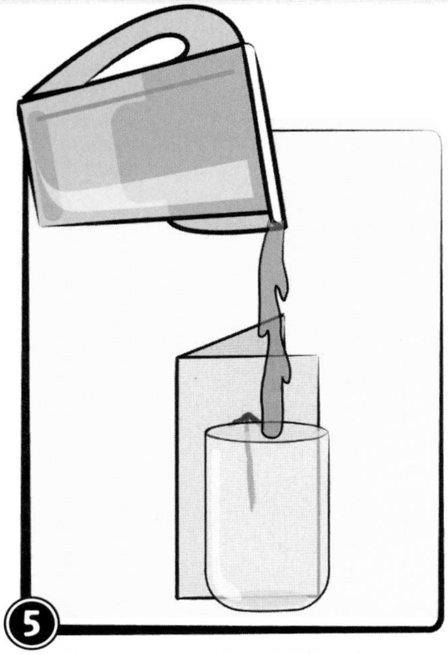

Repeat steps 3 and 4 for the second glass. Which way does the second arrow point?

There are many ways to alter this experiment to learn more about lenses and refraction.

☞ Change the medium inside the glass. Use vinegar, honey, or soda water. Does it change the refraction?

☞ Pour your medium into a glass of a different shape. How does this change the experiment's result?

☞ Try new angles for the arrow on the paper. Which directions get flipped?

The SCIENCE Behind It

You made a watery lens! Light travels in straight lines. Lenses refract, or change the direction of, a ray of light. The lens is a different medium than the air around us, which means that the lenses are made up of different material than air. Light slows down as it passes through the lens, and the direction of the light changes. Most lenses are spherical—they are rounded on one side. Because of their shapes, they bend the light even more than a flat shape would.

In the experiment, the glass gave your medium, the water, its shape. The water in the glass acts as a cylindrical lens. It bends the light so much that light coming in from the left bends to the right and vice versa. The result is a flipped image when you look through the glass. The second arrow does not flip, because this lens only bends horizontal light.

LENSES OF THE FUTURE

A farsighted person suffers from hyperopia, an eye condition that makes it difficult to see objects close to the person. A nearsighted person has a condition called myopia. Things in the distance appear blurry to a nearsighted person. Scientists have created glasses and contact lenses to help people with eye conditions see more clearly.

As people age, they sometimes have trouble seeing things that are both close up and far away. They wear bifocals, glasses that contain two different kinds of lenses in different parts of the glasses. Bifocals can be difficult to get used to and can cause headaches.

Recently, several companies have begun working with fluid-filled lenses for eyeglasses. The shape of the lenses can be changed by quickly shifting the fluid around. This would enable people to alter the focus of their glasses. They could see, no matter where they were looking—all with a single pair of lenses. Another company has created a less-expensive version of these glasses, which include dials that can be turned to adjust the level of fluid by hand. Adjustable lenses may soon be common.

TECHNOLOGY AND ENGINEERING

How do cables hold up huge bridges? Why do the patterns on the bottom of your shoes keep you from slipping? How does energy get from a power plant to your home? Technology and engineering are branches of science concerned with the practical application of scientific knowledge. Engineers use what they know about physical and Earth science to design and build objects and machines.

GRAVITY AND MOTION

In space, loose objects float. Here on Earth, they fall to the ground. Why do objects fall and crash, and what forces are involved when they do?

The Force of Gravity

A **force** is a push or a pull. Hold an object above the ground. Let go, and the object will fall toward the ground. The main force acting on it is the pull of gravity. **Gravity** is the force of attraction between objects—such as Earth and anything on or near it. Earth's gravity pulls objects toward the planet's center. It allows us to keep our feet on the ground, and it makes things fall downward. When a coconut falls from a tree, gravity sends it tumbling toward the ground.

Picking Up Speed

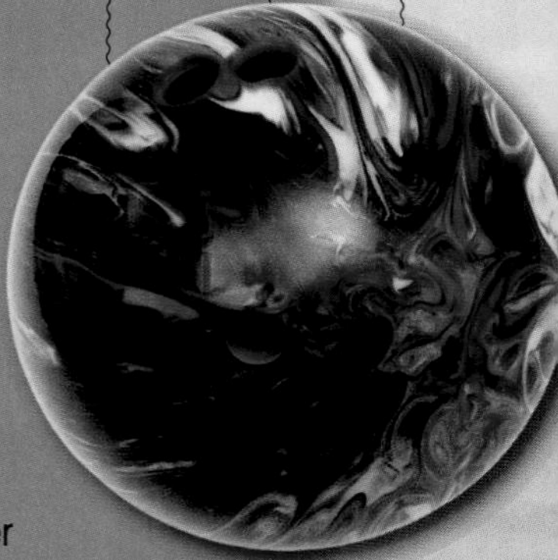

Objects have different masses. A plastic pen is much lighter than a metal one because the molecules that make up plastic are not as tightly packed as the molecules that make up metal. (To learn more about mass, see page 124.) Even though the metal pen has a greater mass than the plastic one, if you were to drop them both at the same time, they would **accelerate,** or change velocity, at the same rate. **Velocity** is a lot like speed, but it also takes into account the direction of motion.

Earth's gravity is constantly pulling, so falling objects are constantly speeding up. If it weren't for any other forces (like air resistance or drag) acting on the falling object, the object's speed would increase about 32.2 feet (9.8 m) per second every second.

A coconut, a bowling ball, and an apple have different sizes and different masses. But if you dropped them, they would all accelerate at the same speed.

Astronauts living in space grow 2 to 3 inches (5 to 8 cm) taller than they are back home on Earth. Without the pull of gravity on them, their spines lengthen and straighten out.

Motion, Inertia, and Impact

The movement of the falling pen or coconut is explained by Isaac Newton's **first law of motion,** which says that objects tend to resist changes in motion. An object in motion will continue to move at the same speed and in the same direction until another force slows it down or stops it cold (like when the falling coconut hits a tree branch, is pushed sideways by the wind, or lands on the ground.) This concept is also called **inertia.**

Still, inertia can't keep an object moving forever. Sooner or later, the falling coconut will hit something—another tree, a beach chair, or the ground. At that point, a second force comes into play. The gravitational force is still pulling the coconut downward. But now the force of the ground or the chair is also pushing upward. That upward force, if strong enough, will cause the coconut to bounce, crumple, or crack open.

The law of inertia says that a ball on the grass will stay put unless the wind begins to blow or someone kicks it.

NEWTON'S LAWS

Born in 1642, Sir Isaac Newton made many contributions to the fields of science and mathematics. His three laws of motion are:

- Objects at rest tend to stay at rest, and objects in motion tend to stay in motion.
- Force is required to make something move, or accelerate. You have to work harder to move something heavy than to move something light.
- For every action, there is an equal and opposite reaction. A rocket is a good example of this law. When a rocket is lifting off, hot gas and exhaust shoot downward. That downward force creates an equal reaction in the opposite direction: the rocket shoots upward!

NEWTON'S CRADLE

There is a toy named after Newton. Made up of a group of balls of the same size and weight hanging from a frame, a Newton's cradle illustrates the law of conservation of energy. When one ball is pulled up and allowed to fall, it bangs into the other balls and comes to a full stop. But its energy is transferred to the ball on the opposite end, which immediately swings out.

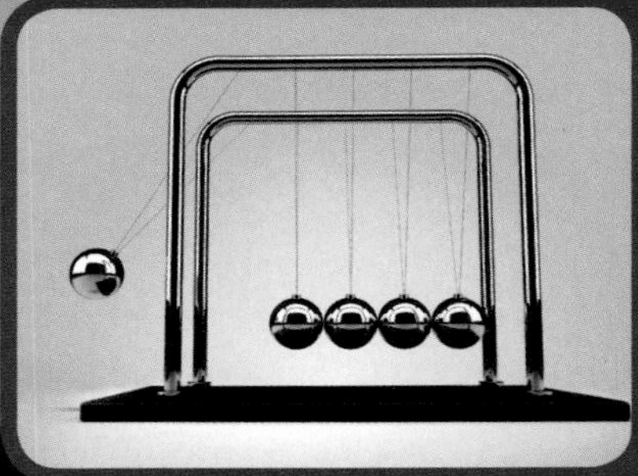

WHAT GOES UP MUST COME DOWN

When you drop an egg, you can see gravity at work as it pulls the egg toward the ground. If the egg falls onto a hard surface, it usually breaks. But does it have to? Can you make a cushion that will keep an object from going splat in a fall?

What Makes the Best Cushion for a Falling Egg?

YOU WILL NEED:

- 1 large garbage bag
- 2 resealable plastic sandwich bags
- Pitcher of tap water
- 2 eggs

1. Spread the garbage bag on the ground. This is your landing site—the place where the eggs you drop will land.

2. Half fill one plastic bag with water.

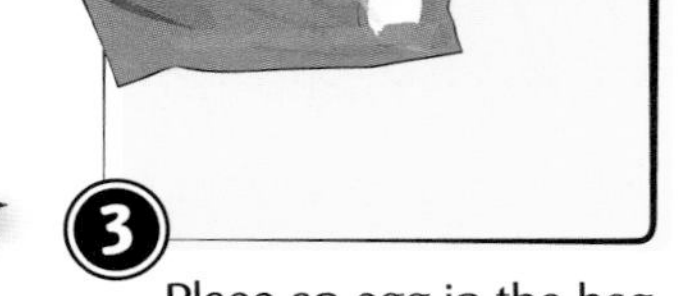

3. Place an egg in the bag with the water and seal it completely.

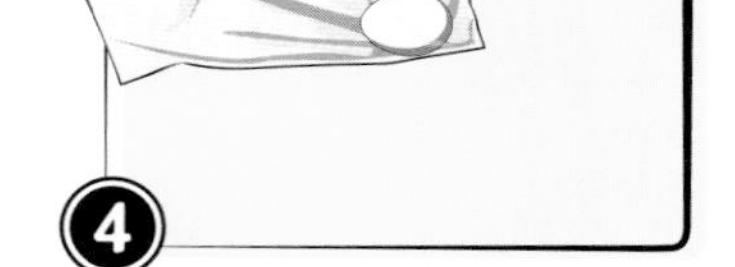

4. Place the other egg in the empty bag, and seal it completely.

science fair tip

Choose three or four different materials or devices to protect your eggs. Complete six trials for each type of cushion and graph the results. Determine how effective each material is as a cushion by comparing the number of trials in which the egg breaks to the number in which it does not.

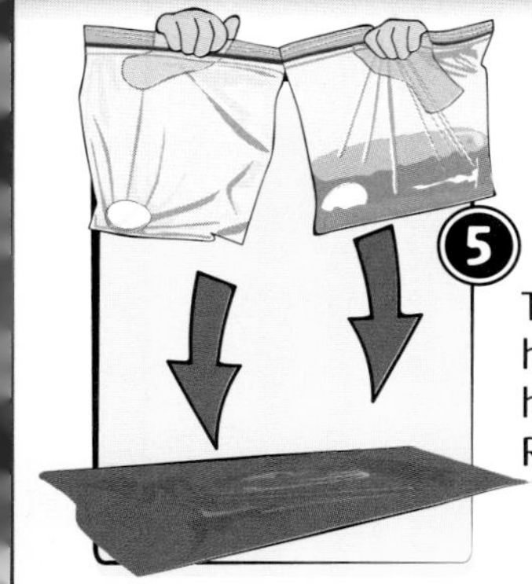

Take one bag in each hand. Then hold both egg-filled bags at shoulder height above the garbage bag. Release them at the same time.

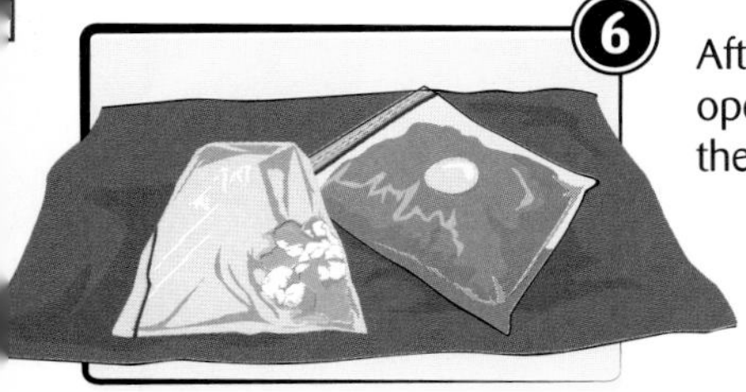

After the bags hit the ground, open both bags to examine the eggs. What do you see?

Change it UP!

☞ Does sand protect an egg better than water? Try the experiment with other materials:

- sand
- tissue paper
- cornflakes
- Jell-O
- Bubble Wrap

☞ Repeat the experiment, filling several baggies with different amounts of water.

☞ Create five bags filled with the same material, but drop them from different heights.

☞ Drop the egg onto different surfaces, such as pavement or grass, or into a bathtub filled with water.

☞ Be creative. Change variables and compare your results.

The SCIENCE Behind It

When you drop the egg, it gains speed and energy as it falls. With no protection, the egg hits the ground fast and hard—at one small point on its shell. Whack! The egg smashes. When you protect the egg—by packaging it in water or something else—two things happen. First, the material around the egg decreases the speed at which the egg hits the ground. Second, the cushioning material spreads out the impact from just one point on the eggshell to a larger area of the shell's surface. This reduces the force of the egg's impact with the ground. There is less damage to the egg with the watery cushion than to the egg that is dropped without a cushion. Whether the egg breaks—and how hard it splats if it does—depends on the amount of energy that your padding system absorbs.

Eggshells look solid, but each one contains up to 17,000 microscopic holes.

PROTECTING THE GOODS

The same principles that you applied to protecting the egg are applied by engineers who design other types of protective equipment—from car bumpers and air bags to Bubble Wrap and bike helmets. Today, helmets are made with a layer of foam to help absorb an impact. Scientists and students have recently conducted experiments that show a gel layer may be more effective.

GET ENERGIZED!

Energy can be found in many different forms: in light, heat, motion, and more. There is energy in everything, even an apple sitting on a table. All energy can be lumped into one of two categories: potential energy and kinetic energy.

When a car sits at the top of a roller coaster, it has a lot of potential energy derived from its location. When the car goes over and rushes downward, it has lots of kinetic energy.

It's Got Potential

Potential energy is stored energy. There are many types of potential energy.

- The food we eat has lots of potential energy. As soon as we eat it, it is converted into chemical energy. Humans get the energy we need to run, jump, laugh, and breathe from the chemical energy in food.
- Natural gas and coal have lots of potential energy. When we burn them, they are converted to thermal, or heat, energy.
- There is a great deal of nuclear energy stored in the nucleus of an atom. When atoms are split at a nuclear power plant, huge amounts of energy are released.
- Some potential energy depends on the position of an object. The higher up an object goes, the more potential gravitational energy it has. When you let the object go, its potential energy will immediately be converted to kinetic, or motion, energy.
- Like gravitational energy, mechanical energy depends on position. If you stretch a rubber band as far as it can go, it has the potential to fly farther than if you'd barely stretched it at all.

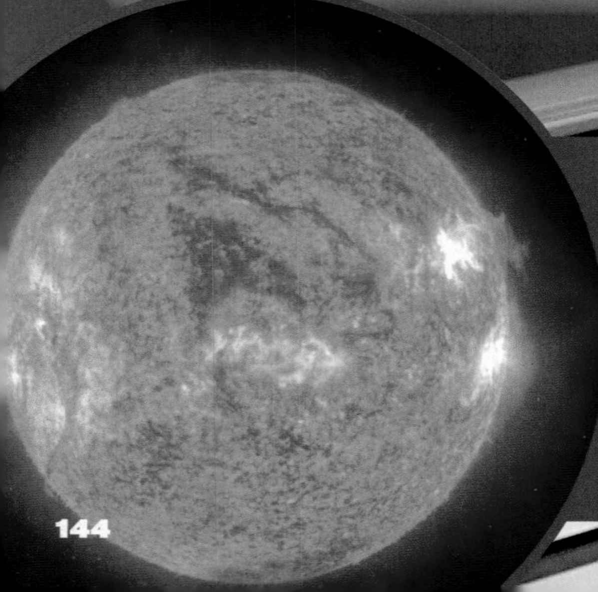

EXPLOSIONS OF ENERGY

The sun constantly produces energy through a process called fusion. Unlike fission, which is the process that nuclear power plants use to split atoms and produce energy, fusion brings atoms together. On the sun and other stars, hydrogen atoms combine with one another, creating huge amounts of nuclear energy. This energy is transferred into radiant energy in the form of sunshine. Today, we collect solar energy in special solar cells and use that solar energy to generate the electrical energy that powers your hair dryer and computer. Solar energy is also converted into thermal, or heat, energy to keep your home warm in the winter or to make water hot enough for a warm shower.

Energy in Motion

Kinetic energy is the energy of motion. Moving people or objects have kinetic energy. Heat, light, sound, and electrical energy are types of kinetic energy.

- The electrical energy that flows from power plants, through wires, and into outlets in your home is kinetic energy.
- To understand why heat is kinetic energy, remember that as something heats up, its atoms and molecules begin to move faster and faster. There is motion there, even if it is microscopic and you can't see it.
- Sound travels as vibrations in the air. When a musician plucks the strings of a guitar, the strings vibrate and send vibrations through the air. Your eardrum picks up these vibrations and detects the sounds. Here again, there is motion in the air, even though you cannot see it.

Lightning is a type of electrical energy.

Energy Transfers

According to the **law of conservation of energy,** energy cannot be created or destroyed. Instead, it changes form. When an object is held above the ground, it has potential energy. The second the object starts to fall or roll, potential energy starts to change to kinetic energy. As the object speeds up, its kinetic energy increases and its potential energy decreases. Upon impact, kinetic energy suddenly drops to zero. The energy in the object is converted to other forms of energy, such as heat energy or sound energy. And some of the kinetic energy transfers to other objects in the impact.

When a person holds a bowling ball or gets ready to roll it, the bowling ball has potential energy.

A bowling ball in motion has kinetic energy.

When the bowling ball collides with the pins, it transfers some of its energy to the pins, which scatter and fall.

READY, AIM, FIRE!

Slingshots, coiled springs, and catapults all get their potential energy from their position. Build a catapult, and learn more about transferring potential energy into kinetic energy.

Can You Launch a Ball Farther With a Catapult?

SAFETY NOTE
Do not aim your catapult at people.

YOU WILL NEED:

- Craft stick
- Plastic spoon
- 2 thick rubber bands
- Pencil
- Aluminum foil
- Ruler
- Pen and paper

1. Place the craft stick against the back of the spoon. Use a rubber band to attach the end of the stick to the bottom of the spoon.

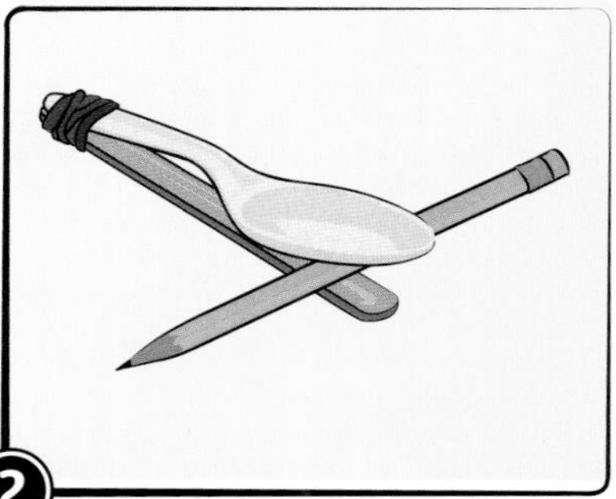

2. Lift the bowl of the spoon. Slide the pencil in between the spoon and the stick to make a T shape.

3. Push the center of the pencil down toward the rubber band, forcing the spoon upward.

4. Secure the pencil by looping another rubber band around it and the spoon and the stick several times. This is your catapult!

science fair tip

Include a model of your catapult as part of your presentation. If you have made adjustments to the catapult to make it more effective, show a "before" version and an "after" version.

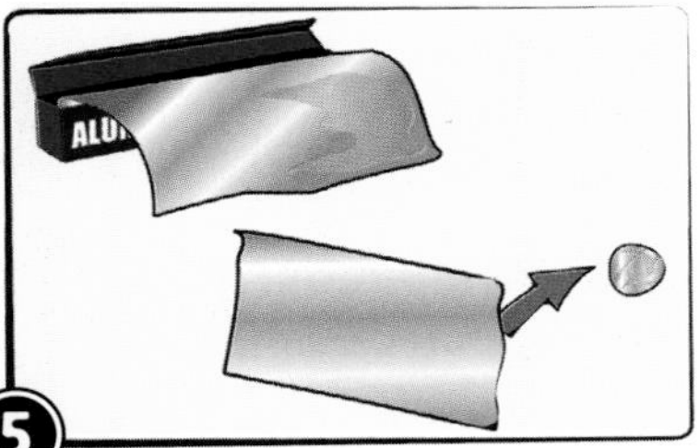

5 Crumple a piece of aluminum foil to make a marble-size ball.

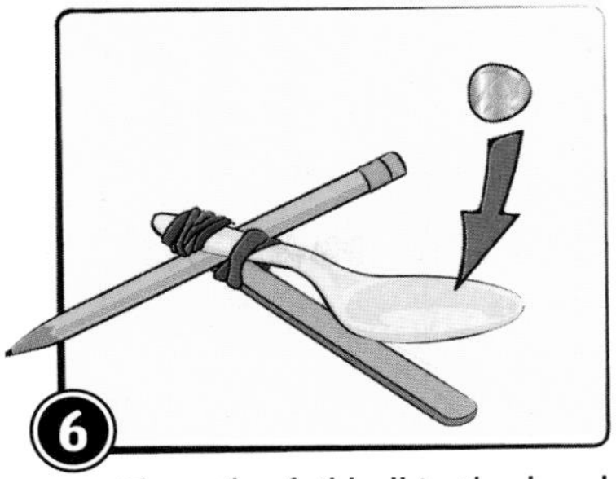

6 Place the foil ball in the bowl of the spoon.

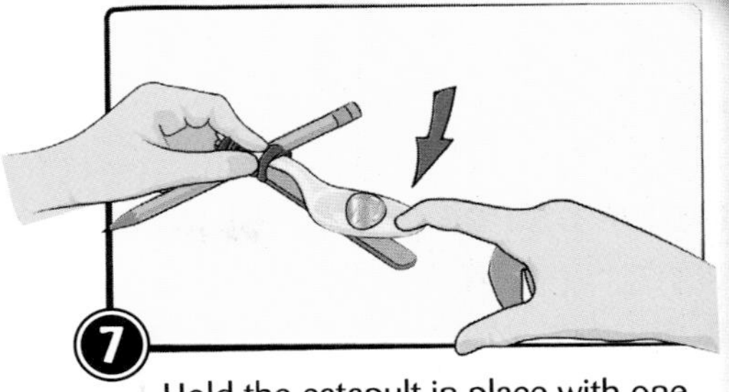

7 Hold the catapult in place with one hand, and push the bowl of the spoon down with the other hand.

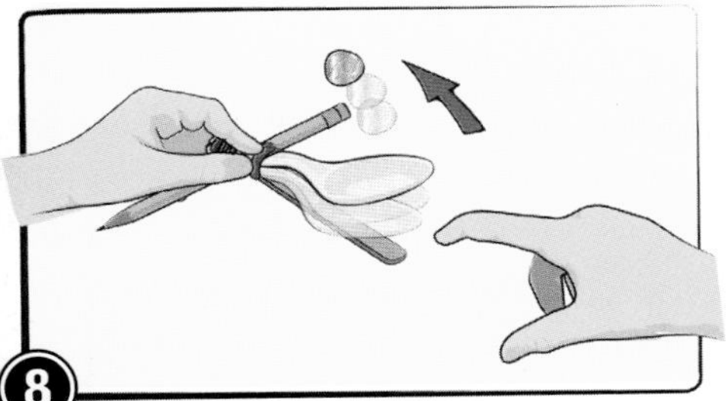

8 Release the spoon to launch your foil ball. Measure how far it travels with the ruler. Launch the ball several times, and push down less and less each time. Use a ruler to measure how far the ball travels each time, and record your results.

Change it UP!

☞ What makes a projectile fly farther? Launch two different objects and compare the results. Try a foil ball and a marshmallow. Compare an eraser to a Ping-Pong ball. Remember that a scientist likes to observe the same results over and over again, so make sure to launch each of them several times. Measure and record the distances your projectiles travel.

☞ Try pushing down on different parts of the spoon to launch the ball. Which area gives you the best launch?

☞ You can also change the angle of the spoon by replacing the catapult pencil with a thick marker or stick. How does this change the way the ball launches?

ENERGY AND YOU

Potential and kinetic energy transfer is important in sports. When you swing a baseball bat, you transfer energy to the bat and then to the baseball. When you land on a trampoline, the trampoline builds up potential energy, and transfers it into kinetic energy when it pushes you back up.

The SCIENCE Behind It

You transfer energy to the spoon when you push down on it. This is called potential energy, because it has the potential to make things happen! The bent spoon starts to move when you let go. The potential energy changes into kinetic energy. Some kinetic energy transfers to the foil ball, launching it across the room. The more you push down on the spoon, the more energy it has. And more energy makes the ball travel farther.

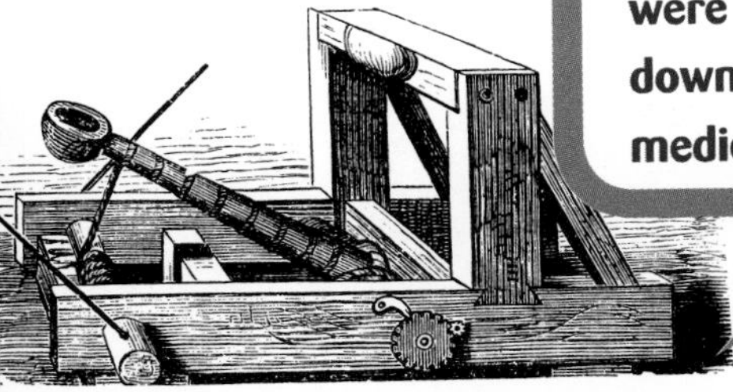

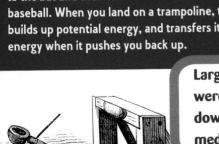

Large catapults were used to break down castle walls in medieval times.

MAKIN' IT STICK

Friction can be great, but it can also be a real drag. Get it? Friction can really slow you down. Have you ever slid across carpet or grass on bare skin? Maybe you've tried to go down a slide on a hot summer day while wearing shorts? You may have had the misfortune of a friction burn. If there is too much friction between your skin and another surface, you can easily irritate or even tear off the top layers of skin and, boy, does it hurt.

Friction Working Against You

Friction is the opposing force created from two objects rubbing against each other. It slows things down and heats things up. If there is enough friction, an object will stop moving completely. This is the principle behind the brakes on your bicycle. As the brake pads squeeze the wheel, they create friction and the rotating wheel slows down. Squeeze the brake slightly, and the bike slows down a little. If you squeeze the brake very hard and very quickly, the bike will stop suddenly. (Stopping very suddenly could also send you flying over the handlebars, so be careful!)

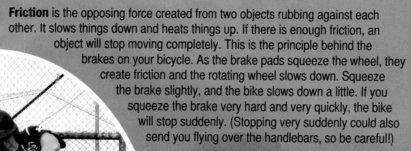

Friction between a baseball and a bat are necessary for a player to hit a ball. If there were no friction, the ball would just slide off the bat.

The perfect amount of friction is necessary for this champion boarder to tear up the slopes. Snowboarders wax the bottom of their boards to reduce friction. This allows them to shoot down a slope even faster.

Ice skates are designed to create very little friction, so a skater can glide along the surface of the ice.

A tire or shoe with good traction "grips" the ground.

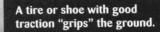

Friction Is Everywhere

One particular kind of friction is called **traction.** It refers to the friction between something and the surface on which it moves, such as a tire and the road, or a shoe and the floor.

If it weren't for friction, we wouldn't be able to walk. The friction created between your foot and the ground allows you to push off the ground and take a step. If there were no friction, your foot would slide out from under you and you'd probably wind up falling down. Understanding friction can help you choose the right footwear for a given activity.

If you're playing basketball, you'll want to be able to stop quickly and change direction, so a shoe capable of creating more friction will be useful.

Ballet dancers wear shoes that allow them to spin easily on the toe, but grip the floor on the sole.

LUBRICANTS REDUCE FRICTION

Push the palms of your hands together as hard as you can, and then try to slide them in opposite directions. What happens when you only touch your palms together lightly and try the same thing? You probably noticed that the harder you press your hands together, the harder it is to slide them. More pressure between two objects creates more friction, which slows things down more. What if you put a bunch of lotion or soap on your hands and try again?

Engineers are constantly working with and against friction. When designing an engine with moving parts, they must find ways to reduce friction. Adding lubricants like motor oil reduces rubbing and decreases the amount of heat created by all of the moving parts. If an engine is not well lubricated, the parts can wear out and overheat quickly.

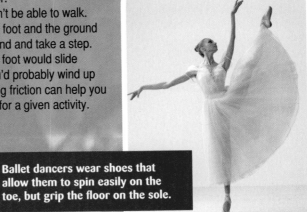

BEST TREADS

Use your shoes to explore ways of creating more and less friction. How could the information from this experiment be useful to you?

Which Shoe Is Best for a Big Hike?

YOU WILL NEED:

- Running shoe
- Non-running shoe
- Three-ring binder
- Magazines
- Ruler
- Protractor
- Pencil
- Paper

1. Inspect the soles of both shoes. Which do you think would slide down a hill first?

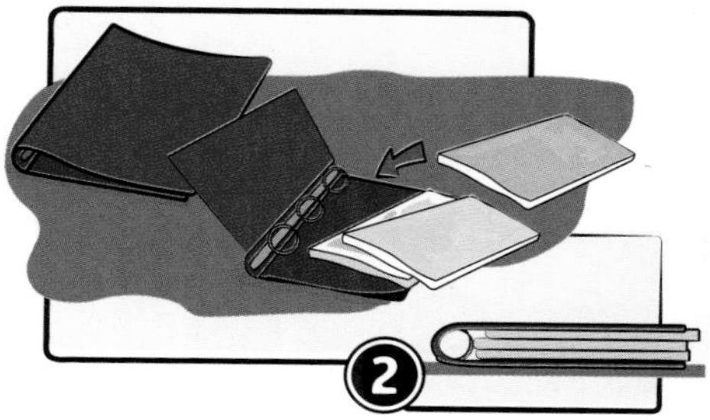

2. Place the binder on the floor. Put magazines between the covers so the binder top is level with the floor.

3. Place your two types of shoes on top of the binder. Arrange them side by side with the toes pointing toward the spine.

4. Slide another magazine under the binder cover. This will give a little incline to the binder top. Does either shoe slide off?

Use florist's foam to create a print of the bottom of each shoe. You also can make shoeprints using cocoa powder. Place each shoe in a tray covered with cocoa powder. Then press the shoe onto a sheet of white paper. Talcum powder on black paper works well, too.

science fair tip

5 Continue adding one magazine at a time until one of the shoes slides off the binder. Place a ruler on top of the binder so that it rests on the bottom edge of the binder and touches the work surface.

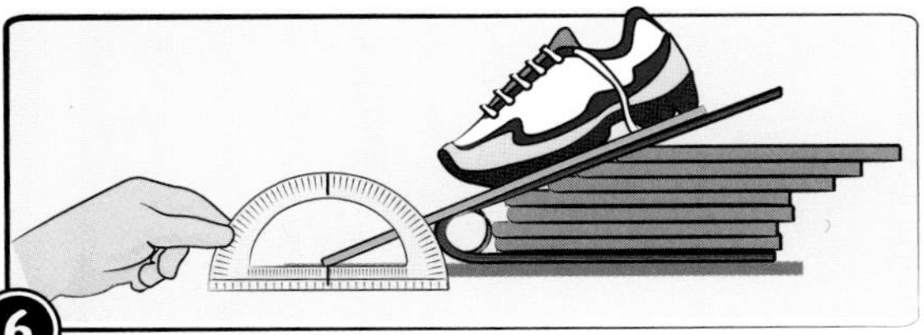

6 Place the protractor against the side of the binder so the spot where the ruler touches your work surface lines up with the center of the protractor. Measure the angle of the binder top. Record the angle and the number of magazines used.

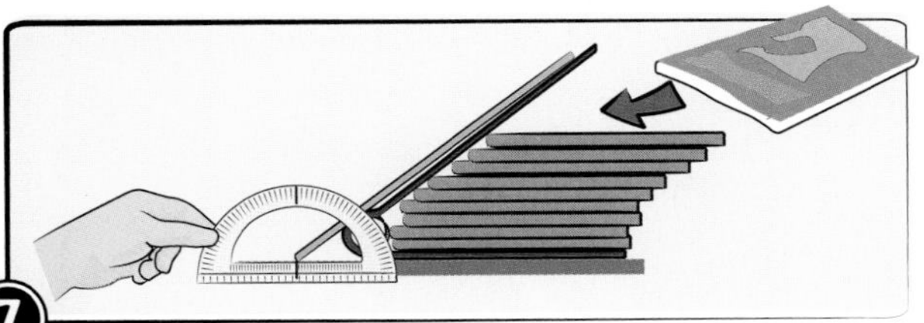

7 Continue adding magazines until the other shoe slides off the binder. Measure the angle of the binder top with the protractor. Record the angle and the number of magazines used. Was your prediction correct?

The SCIENCE Behind It

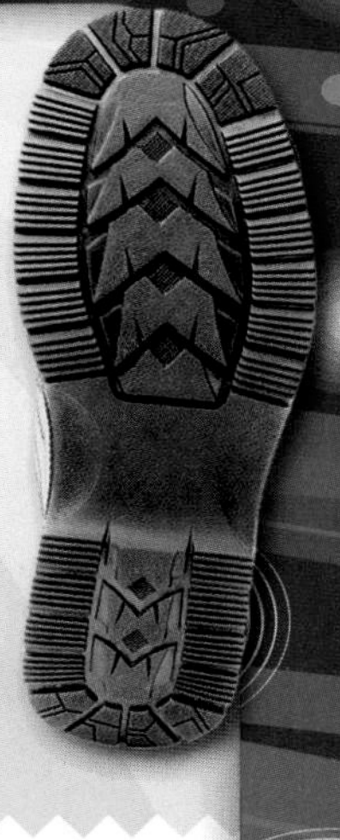

Some shoes are designed to have good traction. This means that they have friction with the floor to keep you from slipping. Traction is related to the pattern on the sole and what the sole is made of. Running shoes and hiking boots are made with rubbery soles that provide lots of friction. They also have ridged and bumpy designs on the bottom to grip the ground. Dress shoes and dance shoes have smoother soles that slip more easily.

Change it UP!

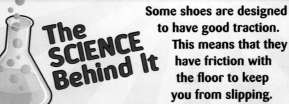

☞ Learn more about shoe treads, traction, and friction by changing the surface of the binder and seeing how the shoes perform. You could compare three binder surfaces:

- a regular binder cover
- a surface wet with a spray bottle
- a binder covered with sandpaper

☞ You can also test two different pairs of the same kind of shoe. For example, you can test your friend's running shoes versus your own. Which shoes have better traction?

☞ Use a board propped up on other boards and actually stand on it in the shoes. This lets you test how the shoes grip the ground when your weight is pushing down on them.

STRAIGHT AND SLIP-FREE

Some engineers work to develop polymers for shoe soles, and to create the best sole designs for traction. Running shoes are designed to help you run smoothly in a straight line. Hiking boots are designed to give you good grip on uneven, rocky paths. Some hiking supply stores have slant boards to let you test out their boots the same way you just did in the experiment.

GOING WITH THE FLOW

Electricity is one of those things people use every day, but few of us can really explain what it is. Simply put, electricity is the flow of electrons.

Energetic Electrons

Atoms are the building blocks of all matter. Whether something is living, nonliving, organic, or man-made, it is made of atoms. What makes one atom different from another is the number of particles in its center, or **nucleus. Protons** and **neutrons** are tiny particles that make up an atom's nucleus. Orbiting around the nucleus, in every possible direction, are **electrons.** Electrons are always in motion. Unlike protons and neutrons, electrons can easily jump from one atom to another. Sometimes they travel alone and sometimes in groups. If enough electrons move together at the same time, in the same direction, there is electricity. Electricity is the collective energy of lots of electrons moving, or flowing together.

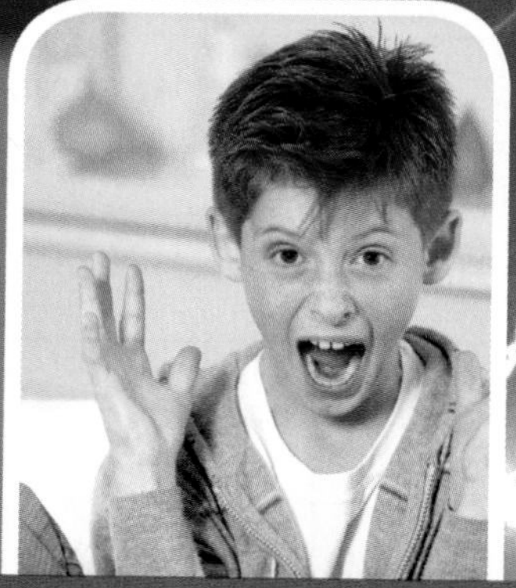

You know that kid in class who has tons of energy and just can't sit still? Well, electrons are kind of like that kid.

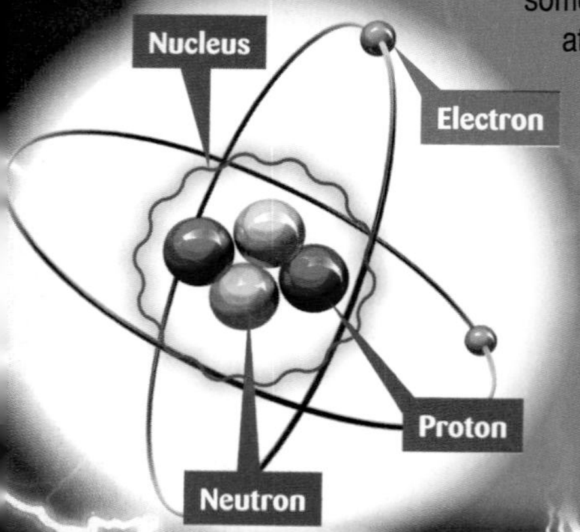

Opposites Attract

Protons and electrons have a charge, while neutrons are neutral, or without a charge. Protons are positive (+) and electrons are negative (–). Because they have opposite charges, protons and electrons are attracted to one another just like opposite ends of magnets. The negative charge of an electron also plays an important role in electricity.

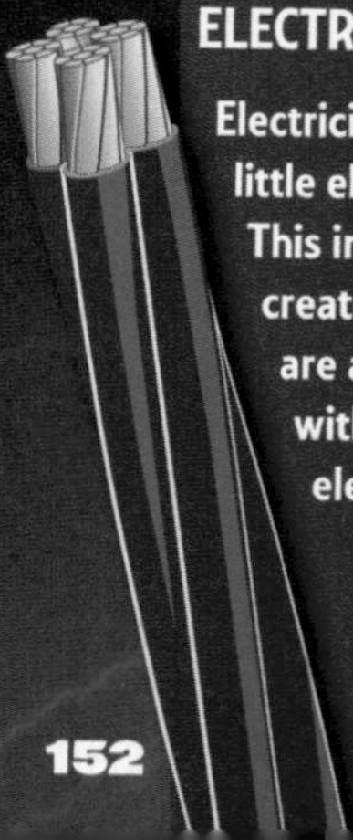

ELECTRICITY IS HOT STUFF

Electricity moves at the speed of light (which is really fast). Not only are all of those little electrons moving fast, but they're also doing a lot of rubbing as they move. This interaction is called friction (for more on friction, see page 148), and friction creates heat. Because the electrons in electricity are doing so much rubbing, they are also creating a lot of heat. This is one reason why it's important to cover wires with an insulator. Insulators hold in electricity and heat to help prevent accidental electrocution or fire.

Do you know why your palms heat up when you rub your hands together? Because the rubbing causes friction, which creates heat.

Making a Circuit

In order for electricity to do work, or turn something on, it must travel in a **circuit,** or a circular path. The electricity must leave an energy source (like a battery), travel along a path (such as a wire), and then return to the original source. The electricity must continue to flow in order to power something. If there is a break or opening anywhere along the path, the electricity will stop moving.

One side of a battery has a + sign and the other has a – sign. These symbols indicate which direction the negatively charged electrons flow out of a battery. The electricity always exits the battery from the negative side and returns on the positive side.

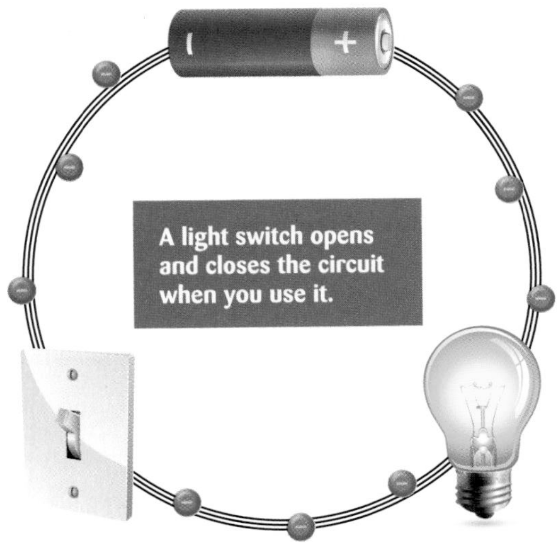

A light switch opens and closes the circuit when you use it.

Electromagnetism

Because electrons have a negative charge, electricity also has a negative charge. When negatively charged electricity flows, it creates what is called an **electromagnetic field.** This invisible field attracts anything with a positive charge. The more electricity there is, the greater the magnetic force.

STAYING SAFE AROUND ELECTRIC CURRENTS

Electricity can only travel through certain materials. We call materials that carry electricity easily conductors (For more on conductors, see page 163). Metals and water make very good conductors. Because humans are mostly water, we have to be careful when working with electricity. We can handle having small amounts of electricity travel through our bodies without harming us, but too much electricity can cause serious injury or even death. Using a small battery, like the one in the experiment on page 154 is safe.

A FEW TIPS TO KEEP YOU SAFE AROUND ELECTRICITY:

- Never use an appliance with a frayed cord.
- Unplug cords by pulling on the head of the plug, not by tugging on the cord.
- Keep water away from electricity and electrical appliances.
- Never put anything other than a cord into an electrical outlet.
- If you see that a power line has fallen down, do not touch it. Let an adult know about it.

ELECTROMAGNETIC FIELDS

This experiment allows you to explore the power of an electromagnetic field. How can you make an electromagnet stronger or weaker? How can you test it? Why do you think the wire gets hot?

Can a Battery Turn a Simple Wire Into a Magnet?

YOU WILL NEED:

- Metal bolt or screw
- Paper clips
- Insulated copper wire, 12 inches (30 cm)
- A battery
- Electrical tape
- Scissors

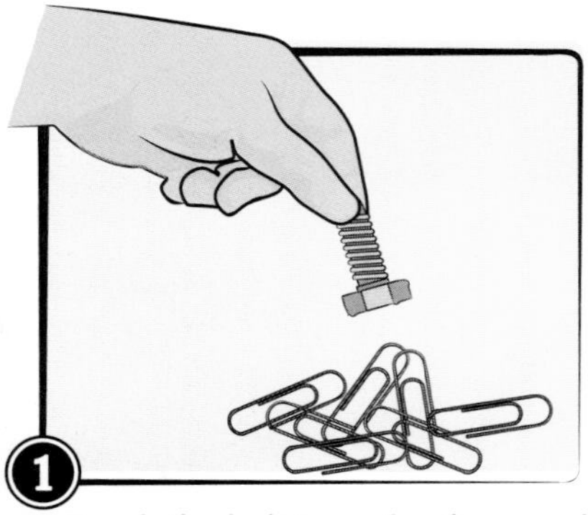

1 Touch the bolt to a pile of paper clips. Does it pick up any paper clips?

2 Wind the copper wire around the bolt several times to make a tight coil.

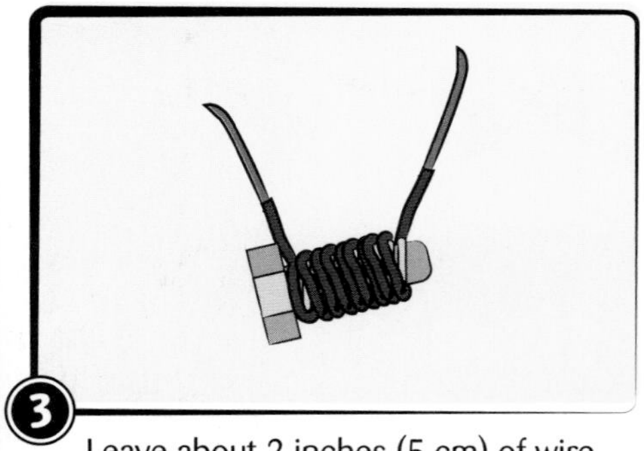

3 Leave about 2 inches (5 cm) of wire free at each end of the coil.

4 Tape each end of the wire to a battery end.

SAFETY NOTE

The bolt and wire may get hot when connected to the battery. Detach the battery when the experiment is done to avoid overheating.

BIG MAGNETS AND FLOATING TRAINS

Large electromagnets are used to pick up cars and propel monorails. Some countries, such as Japan, Germany, and China, have been investing in high-tech high-speed train systems called Maglev trains. The word *maglev* comes from the term *magnetic levitation*, and that's how they work. Instead of having an engine that pushes wheels along train tracks, these trains have large magnets along the bottom. There is a magnetized coil on the train tracks that propels the magnets forward. The train does not touch the tracks as it moves. It hovers anywhere from 0.39 inches (1 cm) to 3.93 inches (10 cm) above the tracks and can move faster than 310 miles (500 km) per hour. The trains of the future float—and fast!

Smaller electromagnets are used in motors, speakers, headphones, cell phones, and computer fans. They are also used to sort metal in recycling plants. Electromagnets are found in scientific and medical instruments, as well.

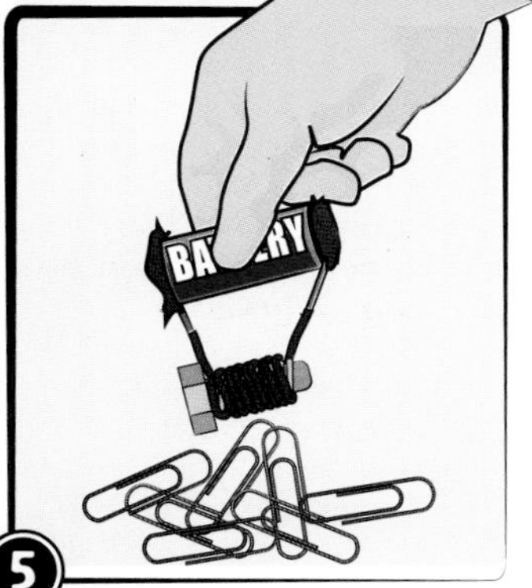

5 Hold the middle of the battery, and move the bolt so it touches the pile of paper clips. Does it pick any up now?

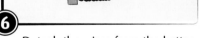

6 Detach the wires from the battery.

Change it UP!

What makes your electromagnet stronger or weaker? Here are some ways to alter your experiment:

- Change the number of wire coils.
- Use another type of battery.
- Try using several different sizes or types of bolt.

The SCIENCE Behind It

Electrons make a magnetic field as they run through the wire. A wire coiled around a core makes a bigger magnetic field. In this case, the core is the metal bolt. Scientists call this an electromagnet, because it is only magnetic when electricity flows through the wire coil. It is a magnet you can turn on and off.

USING THE POWER OF WATER AND WIND

We all use electricity. It powers our computers and televisions. It powers our lights, and helps us keep our homes warm. Electricity is produced at power plants, and travels to our homes and businesses through wires. The plants use many different fuels to produce power. But most power plants have one thing in common: They can't make electricity without turbines.

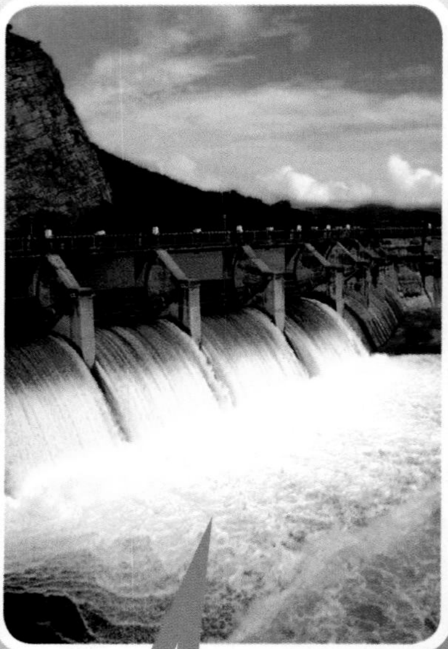

Turning Motion into Energy

A **turbine** is a machine that changes the energy of a moving substance (water or air) into mechanical energy. The turbine has a set of blades that rotate like the blades of a fan. When the turbine rotates, it turns a shaft. The shaft then moves a generator that makes electric current.

Making electricity in many power plants is all about boiling water. Most power plants burn a fuel, such as oil. The heat from the burning fuel boils water. When the water boils, it produces steam. A device directs powerful jets of steam against the blades of the turbine. The steam pushes against the turbine's blades. The blades spin, and the attached generator moves, too. The result is electric power.

Running water and wind can also turn the turbines of electric power plants. Instead of steam, the force of the wind turns a turbine's blades at a wind-powered plant. In a water-powered plant, the force of moving water turns the blades of the turbine. In both cases, the turbine spins a generator, just as in a plant powered by oil or natural gas.

Water power, also known as hydroelectric power, produces about 7% of the electricity in the United States.

In 2010, wind power accounted for a little more than 2% of the electricity in the United States. That number is on the rise.

Fossil Fuels

Burning coal produces about 45% of U.S. electricity—more than any other fuel source.

Most plants use a **fossil fuel,** such as coal, oil, or natural gas. These resources are burned to create the steam that turns the turbine. Fossil fuels such as coal, oil, and natural gas are nonrenewable. **Nonrenewable** energy sources have limited supplies. So one day they will run out. **Nuclear power** is a bit different. It is also a nonrenewable energy source, but the fuel in a nuclear plant doesn't burn. Instead, nuclear power plants use the element uranium. In a process called **fission,** atoms of uranium are split. This gives off great amounts of heat. The heat boils the water needed to make steam and turn the turbine.

Nuclear power provides about 20% of the electricity generated in the United States.

PREVENTING POLLUTION

Renewable energy sources have other advantages. Burning fossil fuels produces air pollution. Using uranium in nuclear power plants leaves behind harmful wastes. Renewable energy sources, such as solar energy, wind, and running water, do not give off pollution. Wind and water do not produce waste like other fuels.

Endless Energy

Many buildings use solar collectors on roofs to provide heat and hot water.

There are also **renewable** energy sources. Renewable energy sources have unlimited supplies. Wind and running water are renewable energy sources, because we will never use them up. We will also never run out of **solar energy.** Energy from the sun is free and constant. Solar furnaces use mirrors to direct the sun's energy to boil water or another fluid. The steam then spins a turbine at a power plant.

Geothermal energy is heat from within Earth. Some geothermal plants use natural steam from deep underground to drive turbines. At other plants, Earth's heat boils water to make steam.

THE BIG PUSH

Most power plants use turbines. But the turbines have different shapes. Do certain shapes work better with wind, while others work better with water? In this experiment, you will try to find the answer.

How Do Turbines Create Power?

YOU WILL NEED:

- 3 sheets of plastic paper (e.g., soft plastic report cover)
- Scissors
- Ruler
- Pen
- Pushpin
- Stapler
- 2 large metal paper clips
- Pencil
- Narrow drinking straw
- Tape
- Small paper plate
- 4 small waxed paper cups
- Hair dryer
- Watering can
- Big basin

SAFETY NOTE

Have an adult helper assist you in making the turbines.

Pinwheel Turbine

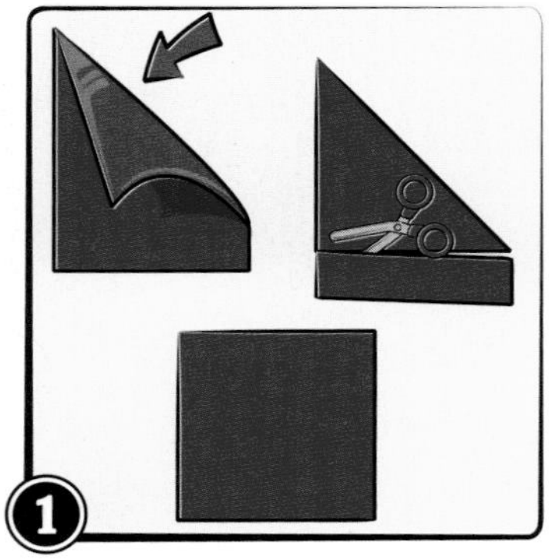

1. To prepare a pinwheel turbine with the plastic sheet: Lay the sheet on your work surface. Fold the top right corner to the left edge of the sheet to form a triangle with a rectangle beneath it. Cut along the edge of the triangle. Unfold the sheet and you will have a square.

2. Repeat step 1 using the long rectangular piece of sheet. Now you will have a much smaller square.

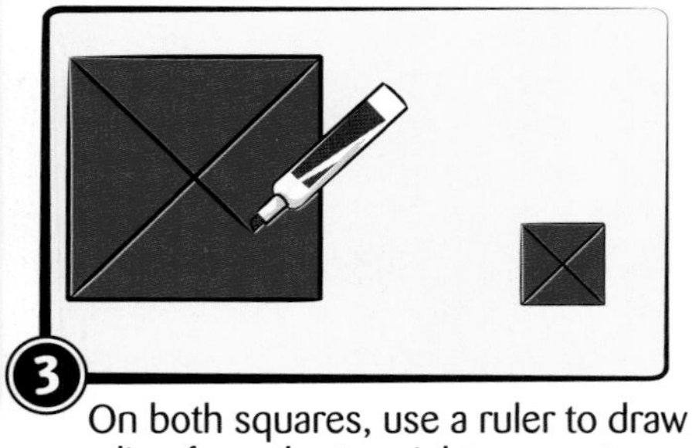

3. On both squares, use a ruler to draw a line from the top right corner to the bottom left corner. Then, draw a line from the top left corner to the bottom right corner.

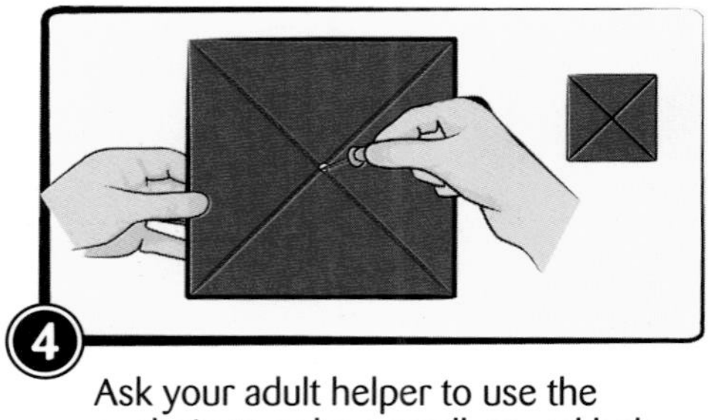

4. Ask your adult helper to use the pushpin to poke a small, round hole at the point where the two lines cross on each square.

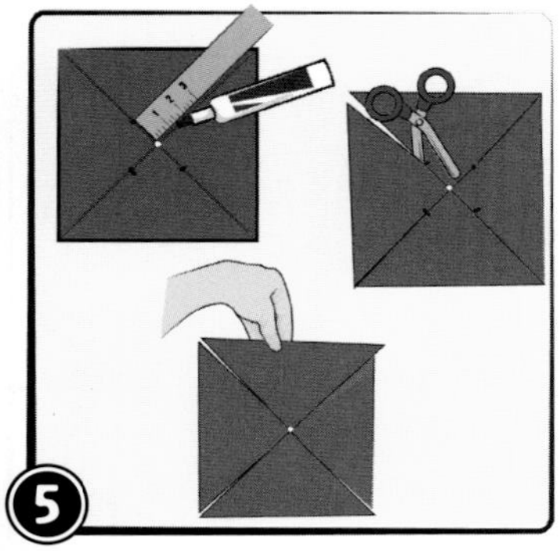

5

Mark each line about 1.5 inches (3.5 cm) away from where the two lines cross in the center of the larger square. Cut along the lines up to the marks.

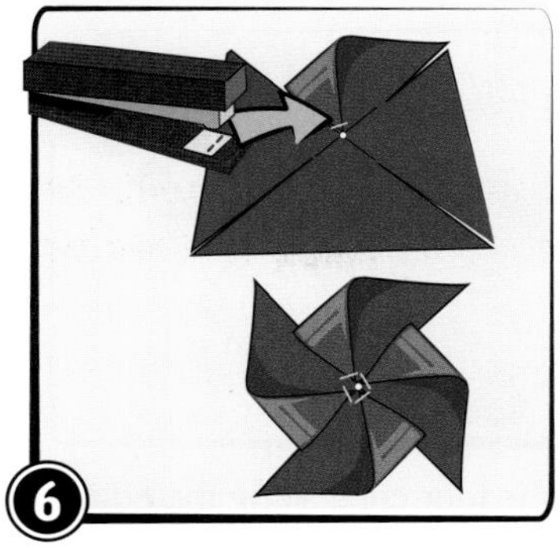

6

Bend the left tips of each corner toward the center of the sheet. Staple the tips to the center without covering the hole.

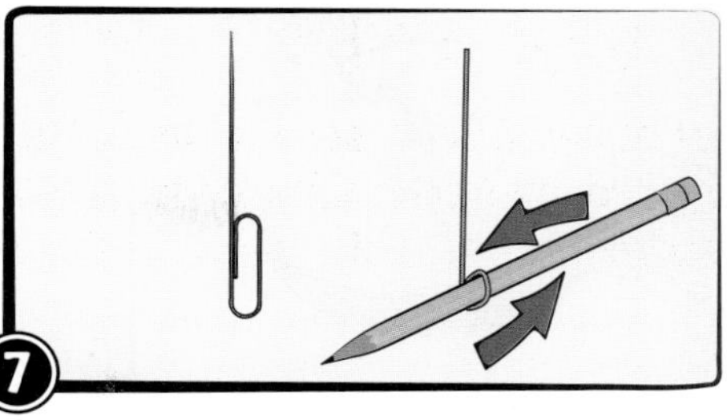

7

Unbend one arm of a large paper clip. Wind the other arm around a pencil to make a loop.

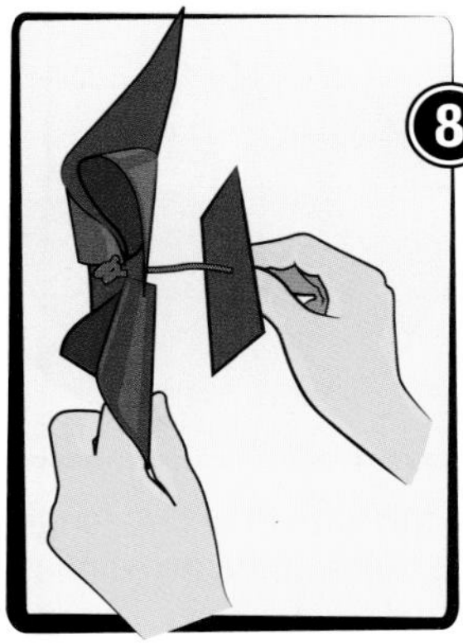

8

Fit the unbent arm through the pinwheel and then through the small square. The loop part should be on the same side as the pinwheel's flaps. Ask your adult helper to bend down the paper clip arm at the point where it exits the small square's hole.

9

Slide the straw onto the paper clip and tape it to the small square. Test your pinwheel. Hold it by the straw so that your fingers do not stop the blades. Spin the pinwheel to make sure it turns easily. Make adjustments if necessary.

Paddle-Wheel Turbine

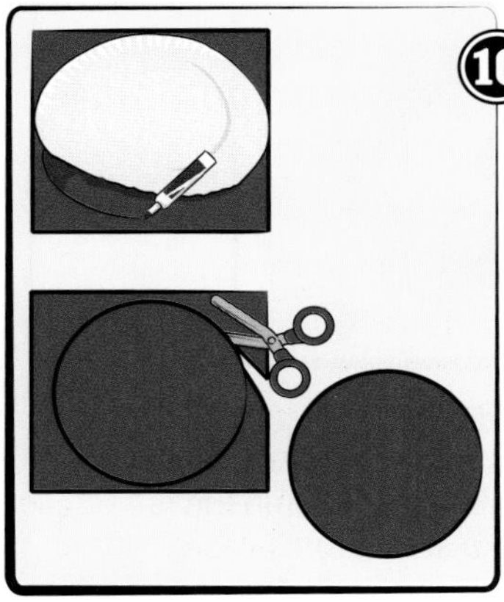

10

Prepare a paddle-wheel turbine with the cups, plate, and two plastic sheets: Draw an outline of the paper plate onto two sheets of plastic. Cut out the circles.

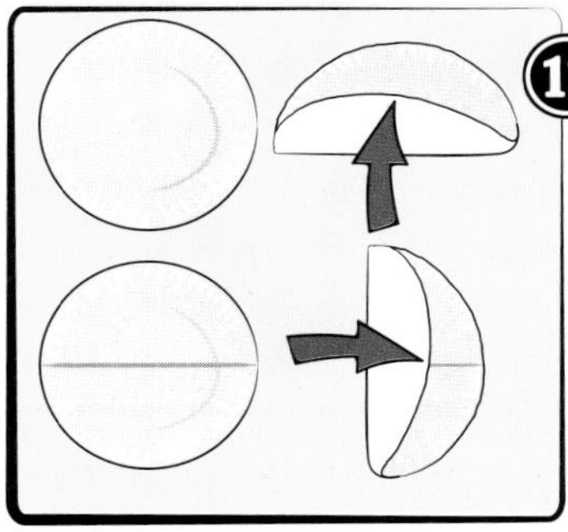

11

Fold the plate in half. Open the plate, turn it a quarter turn, and then fold it in half again.

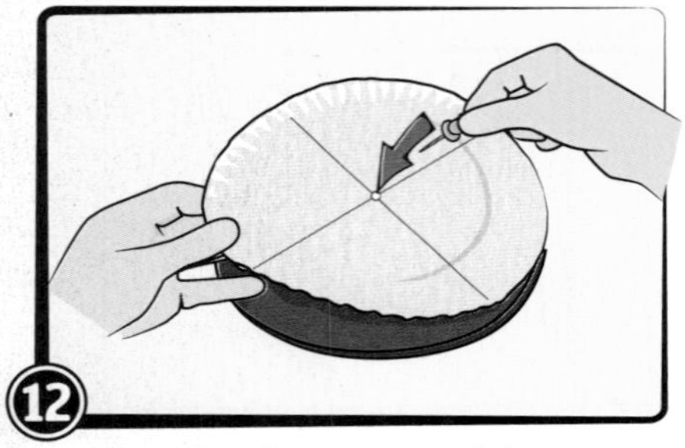

12 Place the plate on top of the two circles. Ask your adult helper to use the pushpin to poke a small, round hole at the point where the two fold lines cross.

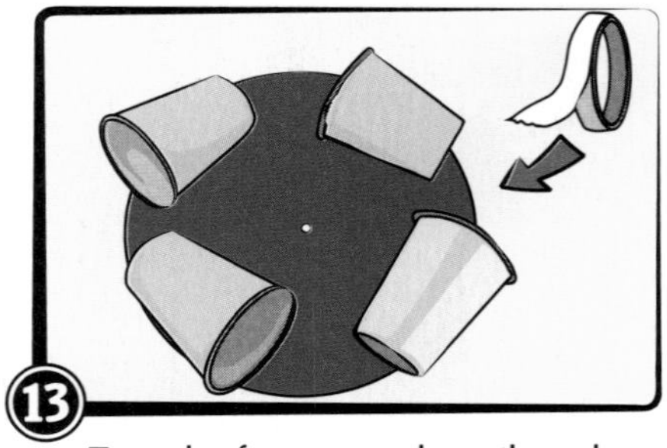

13 Tape the four cups along the edge of one circle. The cups should be in a circle so that the mouth of each cup faces the bottom of the cup in front of it.

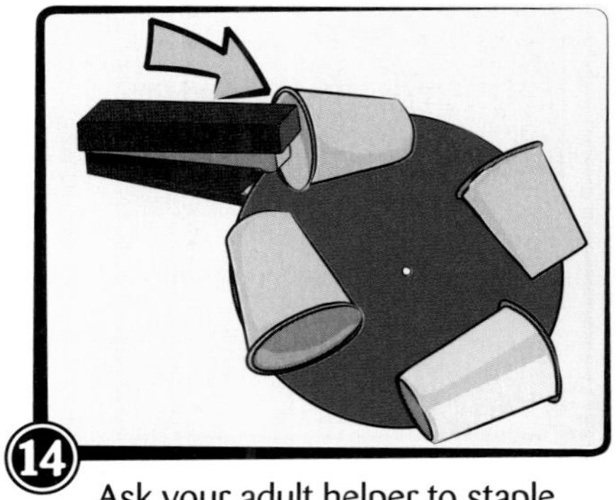

14 Ask your adult helper to staple the cups in place.

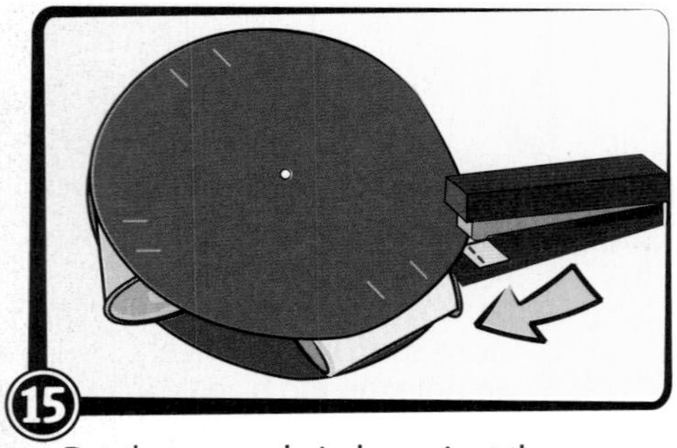

15 Put the second circle against the cups, and ask your adult helper to staple the circle onto the cups.

16 Unbend one arm of a paper clip. Pull up the bent arm.

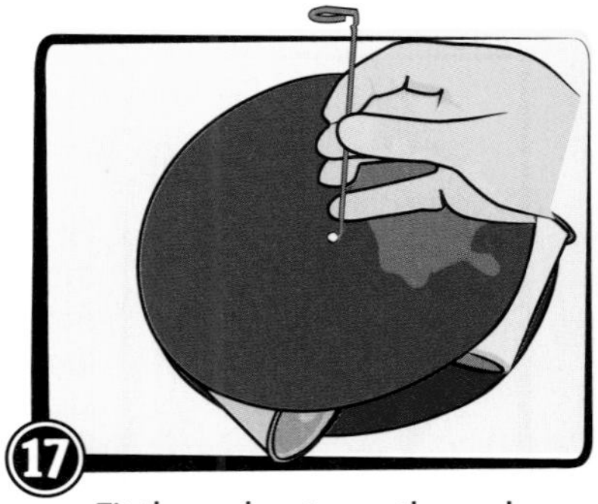

17 Fit the unbent arm through the holes in the two circles.

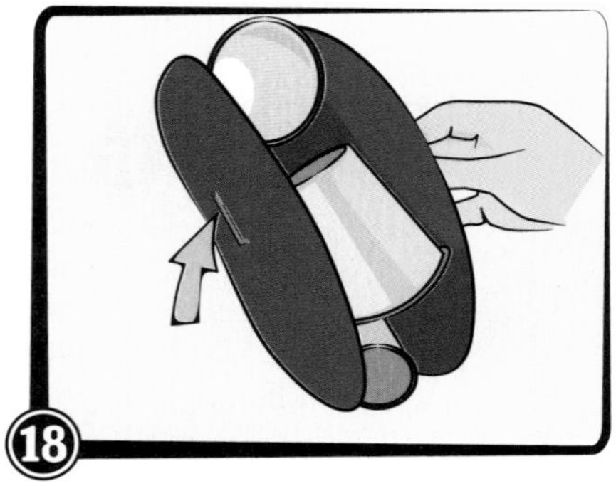

18 Ask your adult helper to bend down the paper clip arm at the point where it exits the second circle.

19 Test your paddle wheel. Hold it by the two ends of the paper clip, and ask your adult helper to spin the wheel to make sure it turns easily.

Turbines in Action

20

Test your two wheels with the wind. Hold the pinwheel facing forward, and walk quickly in a straight line. Does the pinwheel turn? Repeat with the paddle wheel.

21

Test your two wheels with water. Fill the watering can with water. Ask your adult helper to pour the water over the paddle wheel's cups as you hold it over the basin. Does the paddle wheel turn? Pour the water from the basin back into the watering can. Hold the pinwheel over the basin, and ask your adult helper to pour the water over the pinwheel.

FARMING WIND

The amount of wind energy Americans use to make electricity is growing. The number of wind turbines is growing, too. In places, thousands of wind turbines stand together in what are called wind farms. You can find wind farms in places where winds are strong and steady. Many wind farms are on wide plains or in windy mountain passes. Others are being built offshore in lakes and oceans. Winds can be steadier and stronger over water than land, so offshore wind farms may generate more power than ones on land. But experts want to make sure that the wind turbines do not harm migrating birds.

Another option for the future of wind power is to design and build wind turbines for extremely high altitudes. The higher up the wind turbines are placed, the stronger the winds. Flying wind generators could be placed high in the sky and attached to the ground only by wires. The electricity produced would travel back to power plants on the ground through these wires.

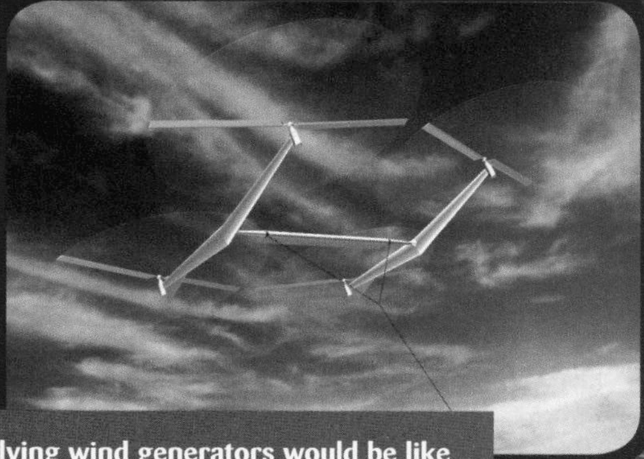

Flying wind generators would be like super-high-tech kites of the future!

Change it UP!

☞ Test turbine blades of different shapes and sizes. Try to find out which shapes and sizes work best with wind and which work best with flowing or falling water.

The SCIENCE Behind It

You're testing turbine blade efficiency. Turbines turn when a force pushes on their blades. An efficient blade turns well when pushed. Efficiency depends on the blade's shape and size—and what is pushing it. You tested the force of both wind and running water. The pinwheel has curled blades. A curled blade works better with wind. The paddle wheel has blades that are cup-shaped. Water turns a paddle wheel better.

HOLDING ON TO HOT AND COLD

It's a cold day outside. You want to dress in clothing that will hold in your body heat and keep you warm. Would you pick a cotton shirt or a wool sweater? You know the answer is wool. But why?

Thermal Energy

All matter is made of atoms and molecules—particles that are always moving. The energy of motion is **kinetic energy.** (For more on kinetic energy, see page 145.) The internal energy the particles produce as they move is **thermal energy.** The faster the particles in a substance move, the more kinetic energy it has. The greater the amount of kinetic energy, the greater the amount of thermal energy.

Does water have more thermal energy before it boils or after?

Heat and Temperature

Thermal energy often flows between objects. **Heat** is the transfer of thermal energy from one object to another. Yet heat does not move in a random way. Heat always moves from a hotter object to a colder one. Heat stops flowing when the objects are the same temperature.

Temperature is a measurement of the average kinetic energy of the atoms or molecules in a substance. In simpler terms, temperature measures how hot or cold an object is.

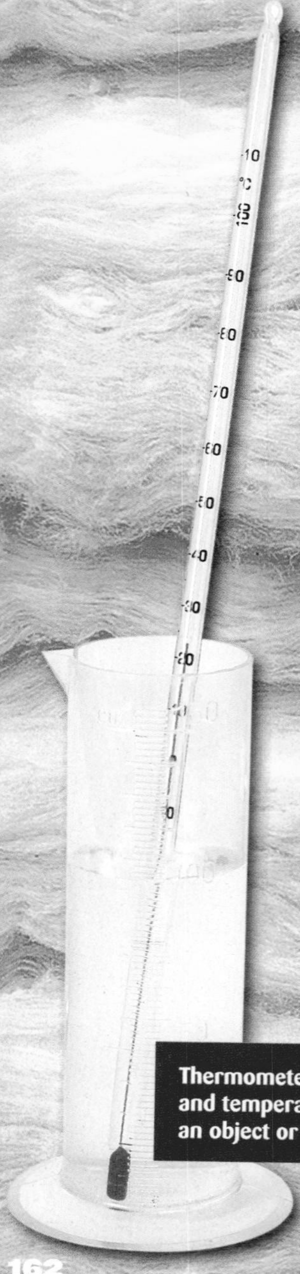

Thermometers measure temperature, and temperature indicates the heat of an object or liquid.

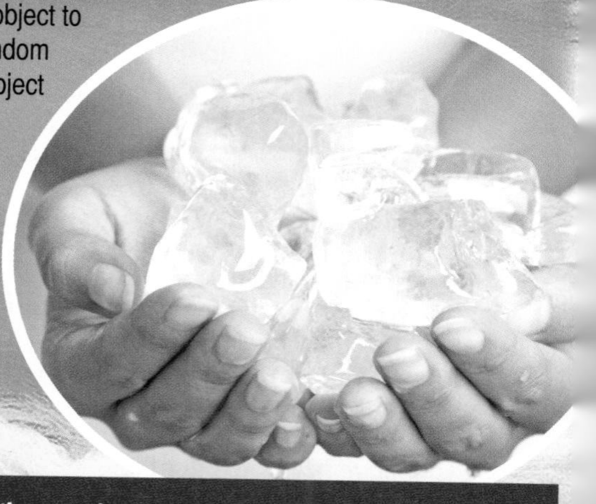

You may feel like your hands are freezing when you carry ice, but the ice cannot actually freeze your hands. The heat from your hands will always melt the ice cubes.

Insulators and Conductors

How well heat transfers from one object to another depends on whether the material is a conductor or an insulator. A thermal **conductor** is a material that heat can pass through easily. A thermal **insulator** is a material that is difficult for heat to pass through.

Picture a shiny stainless steel kettle with a black plastic handle. What happens when you fill the kettle with water and put it on the stove? Once you switch on the burner, the metal pot will heat up. In fact, it will get so hot that you won't be able to touch it. Because the kettle is made of metal, and metal is a good thermal conductor, the kettle will get hot and boil the water inside it.

When you take the kettle off the stove, you hold it by its plastic handle. Why doesn't the handle heat up, too? Because plastic is a good thermal insulator, heat does not pass from the metal part of the pot to the plastic easily. The handle stays cool to the touch. Materials such as cloth, glass, cork, wood, and rubber are good insulators. So is air. Some insulating materials, such as plastic foam or fiberglass, have pockets of air inside them. The air pockets make it difficult for heat to pass through the insulating material. Objects are designed with materials that are conductors or insulators, depending on how they'll be used.

Many pots and pans are made with special handles that won't get hot as you cook.

Oven mitts are often made of padded cloth. Fabric is an insulator. As an added layer of protection, there are small air pockets between the layers of many oven mitts, and air is also a great insulator.

KEEPING TEMPERATURE CONSTANT

Because a thermal insulator does not transmit heat well, the temperature of a well-insulated material will not change quickly. As a result, an insulator keeps a warm substance warm by holding its thermal energy in. An insulator keeps a cold substance cold by keeping out thermal energy from warmer substances around it. This is why thermos bottles can be used to keep soups or drinks warm or cool.

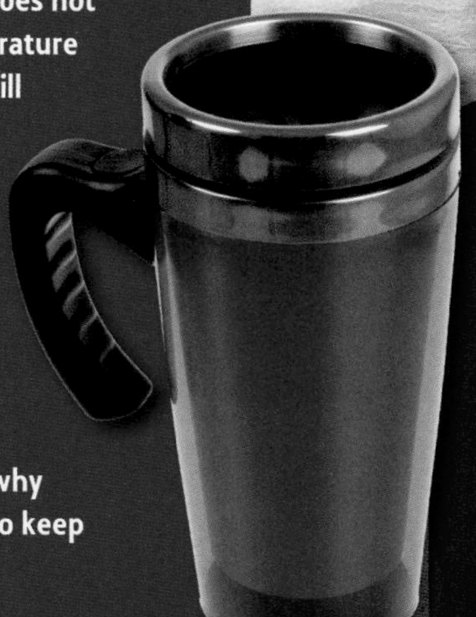

KEEPING IN HEAT AND COLD

A thermal insulator does not allow heat to flow through it easily. In this experiment, you will use the data you collect to determine which material is the better insulator.

Which Insulator Works Best?

YOU WILL NEED:

- 3 cans of soda at room temperature
- Tea towel
- Tape
- Resealable bag
- Petroleum jelly
- Thermometer
- Pencil
- Paper
- Refrigerator
- Clock

Leave three cans of soda out of the refrigerator and away from direct sunlight until they are all room temperature.

Wrap one can with a tea towel, leaving the top of the can exposed. Use tape to secure the towel.

Fill a small resealable bag about halfway with petroleum jelly. Place the second can inside the bag so the can is surrounded by the jelly. If necessary, add more jelly to fill the bag. Leaving the top of the can exposed, use tape to secure the bag.

Leave the third can unwrapped and uncovered. This is your control.

science fair tip

Use what you learned from your science project to find the materials that are best for creating a container that will keep a very cold jar of water cold. Design and "build" several different models that can be displayed along with your project.

Animals sometimes burrow into fresh snow, because it contains many air spaces that slow down the flow of heat. The animal stays warmer, because the snow insulation helps to keep its body heat in.

NATURAL PROTECTION

Insulating materials are important for keeping drinks cool and houses warm. But many animals that live in cold climates have natural insulation to protect them. Animals such as seals, chipminks, and walruses have layers of fat that insulate them from the cold. Some polar animals also have long hair or thick fur that traps pockets of air, which also help insulate them from the cold.

5 Open each can. Wait 10 seconds and insert the thermometer into each can to record its temperature. They should all be about the same.

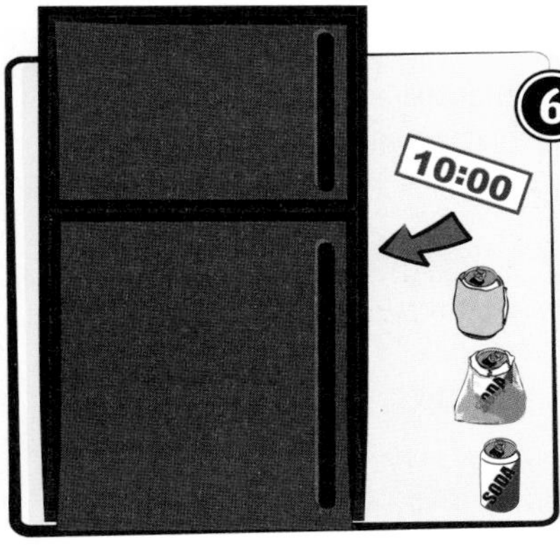

6 Place all three cans in the fridge, and record their temperatures every 10 minutes for an hour. Which can's contents cool down the quickest? The slowest?

Change it UP!

☞ You can try insulating warm cans of soda with other materials, such as:

Bubble Wrap	gel cold packs	refillable ice packs
mittens	plastic foam	

☞ Wrap several cold cans of soda with different materials to see which ones keep the soda cool longest when left out of the fridge.

The SCIENCE Behind It

Metals are great thermal conductors. The heat in the soda moves quickly through the uncovered metal can to reach the cold air in the refrigerator. Petroleum jelly and bunched-up cloth are both insulators. They stop the heat inside the can from moving to the colder air in the refrigerator. Based on your results, are all insulators equally effective? How do you know?

TYPES OF BRIDGES

Bridges have been around for thousands of years. Some of the earliest ones were just logs across streams. As time passed, engineers created better designs and found stronger building materials. Some of today's bridges are as tall as skyscrapers or stretch for miles. There are more than half a million bridges in the United States. In general, bridges fall into three categories.

Many highway bridges are beam bridges.

Three Main Bridge Types

BEAM BRIDGE

This is the simplest type of bridge. A **beam bridge** is just a beam or plank. It has two piers or columns for support at each end. Beam bridges get weaker as they get longer. The middle of the bridge bends under a heavy load. If the load is too heavy, the bridge can break. This is why most beam bridges are no more than 250 feet (76 m) long. Some very long bridges are just a series of beam bridges placed next to one another.

ARCH BRIDGE

An **arch bridge** has a roadway supported by an arch. The arch shape gives the bridge great strength. Because of the arches, arch bridges can be much longer than beam bridges. Supporting arches can be under the roadway or over it.

The Sydney Harbor Bridge in Australia is a famous arch bridge.

SUSPENSION BRIDGE

The world's longest bridges are **suspension bridges.** A suspension bridge has a roadway that is suspended or hung from cables. The cables are attached to two or more towers at the edges of the middle section of the bridge. The ends of the cables are connected to large concrete structures at each end of the bridge. Famous suspension bridges include the Golden Gate Bridge in San Francisco and the Brooklyn Bridge in New York City.

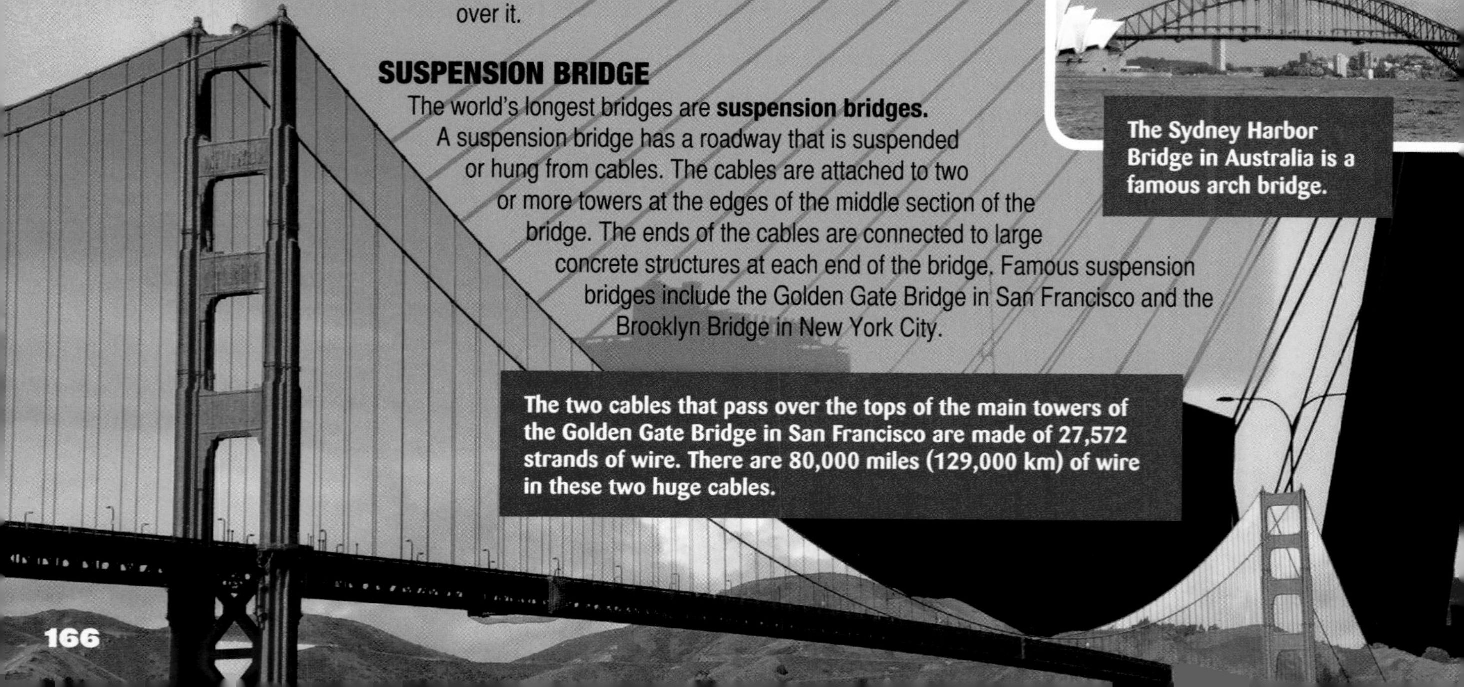

The two cables that pass over the tops of the main towers of the Golden Gate Bridge in San Francisco are made of 27,572 strands of wire. There are 80,000 miles (129,000 km) of wire in these two huge cables.

The Forces That Act on Bridges

Many forces act on bridges. Two of them are tension and compression. **Tension** is a force that pulls objects apart. When you pull two ends of a rope in opposite directions, the force on the rope is tension. **Compression** is the force that squeezes things together. When you squeeze a ball of clay between the palms of your hands, the force on the clay is compression. Because of the weight of the bridge itself and anything on it, these forces (and others) are always present. If the bridge is designed well, it resists these forces without cracking, buckling, or falling down.

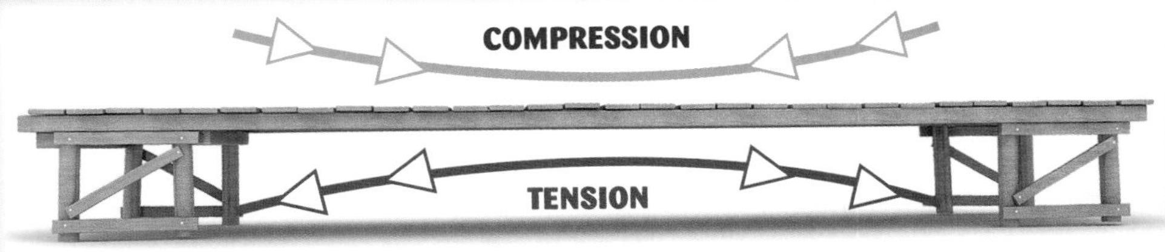

During a game of tug-of-war, the rope has a lot of tension.

Engineers began building truss bridges during the industrial revolution. But arch bridges have been used for more than 2,000 years.

Make It Stronger

Engineers choose the type of bridge to build based on where it will be and the load it will need to carry. See the way the forces of tension and compression act on a beam bridge in the diagram above. A beam bridge must be limited in length to overcome these forces.

Can an engineer strengthen a beam bridge? Yes. She can add trusses. A **truss** is a triangle-shaped structure placed above or below the roadway. Adding trusses turns a simple beam bridge into a truss bridge. Trusses strengthen the beam and help the bridge overcome forces, such as tension and compression. As a result, a truss bridge can be longer than a beam bridge. A truss bridge can also carry a heavier load.

When a truss is on top of a bridge, it is called a through truss. When it is below a bridge surface, it is called a deck truss.

BUILDING BRIDGES

Arches, suspension cables, and trusses are a few devices that architects and engineers use to make bridges stronger and able to carry heavier loads. Can you come up with creative ways to build a strong bridge out of construction paper?

Which Bridge Design Is Stronger?

YOU WILL NEED:

- 8 large books or blocks
- Construction paper
- Pennies

1 Create two stacks of four books each. Make a gap between the two piles.

2 Lay a piece of construction paper across the gap, with its edges over the two stacks so it lies flat. This is your first bridge.

3 Place pennies in the center of your bridge one at a time until it collapses.

4 Fold a piece of construction paper back and forth like the folds of a fan. This is your second bridge.

science fair tip

Bring construction paper and pennies to the science fair. Invite visitors to try to make bridges stronger than the strongest one you came up with. Take pictures of each try. Record the name of each person and the amount of pennies his or her bridge held.

STRONG SHAPES

Engineers and architects design bridges and buildings to resist forces from wind, tides, waves, earthquakes, and heavy loads. Look at bridges near your town. How are they built? You will observe the shapes that add strength—arches, triangles, cylinders—in their designs again and again. Notice where the shapes are. Think about how they strengthen the bridges you observe.

5 Place the second bridge across the gap. Line up the folds like roads going from one stack to the other.

6 Place pennies in the center of the second bridge one at a time until it collapses.

Change it UP!

☞ Try several different folding techniques to see how strong you can make a construction-paper bridge.

☞ Build two bridges with the same design, but with different materials. Compare a cardboard bridge to one made from glued-together craft sticks or toothpicks. See which bridge is stronger.

☞ Add supports, such as arches or columns, to make the bridge stronger. Find out which design is best.

☞ For a real challenge, make your own suspension bridge using straws and string. Keep track of the amount of weight each model will support before sagging, snapping, or collapsing.

The SCIENCE Behind It

The first bridge you modeled was a simple beam bridge. It wasn't very strong, and it probably bent easily under the weight of the pennies. Your second bridge was folded into semi-triangle shapes. Triangles and arches are shapes that make bridges stronger. The second bridge you made was a little bit like a truss bridge. The triangle shapes of the second bridge should have made it stronger.

There are three bridges over the Sanibel Causeway in southwest Florida. The spans are connected by man-made islands.

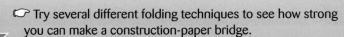

STAYING AFLOAT

Even in liquid, gravity is pulling things down. Gravity never quits, but some objects have the ability to resist gravity's downward pull and stay afloat. This is because of an opposite force that fluids exert on an object, pushing upward. This upward force exerted by liquid is called buoyancy.

Buoyancy

Buoyancy describes an object's ability, or tendency, to float. An object filled with air is less dense and more buoyant than an object filled with sand, meaning it's more likely to float. If the density of an object is more than the density of the liquid in which it is placed, it will not have enough buoyancy to float, and will sink.

It is easy to float on the water in a raft filled with air. A deflated raft would be no help at all!

Out of My Way!

When an object sinks, it pushes water out of its way. This is called **displacement.** Carefully drop a rock into a glass of water. You'll notice that the water level rises as the rock goes into the water. Because the rock takes up space, the water must move out of the way to make room for the rock. In a glass, there is nowhere for the water to go but up, so the water rises. The amount that the water rises, or the volume of the increase, is equal to the volume of the rock.

When an object is floating on water, part of it is submerged and therefore displacing water. If you place an ice cube in a glass of water, you'll notice that even though the cube floats, the water rises slightly. Push the cube down and the water rises even more. The more of the cube that is submerged, the more displacement there must be.

The small part of the toy duck that is under the surface displaces water.

THE COLOMBO EXPRESS

The *Colombo Express* is one of the largest container ships in the world. It carries tons of cargo, but it also has chambers in its hull (the main body of the ship) that are filled with air. The air-filled chambers make the ship less dense than the water underneath it, which allows it to float.

Float a Boat

The difference between a boat that sinks and one that floats has everything to do with density, the shape of the boat, and the volume of water being displaced. Boats are filled with air, and this changes their density. They are also shaped in a way that spreads their weight over a larger area. Regardless of its size, a boat weighing 1,000 pounds (454 kg) displaces 1,000 pounds (454 kg) of water. If the displacement is spread over a larger surface area, the boat can float.

It's also important that the boat be balanced. If one side of the boat is much larger or heavier than the other, it will tip over. Changing the shape of a boat can change its buoyancy.

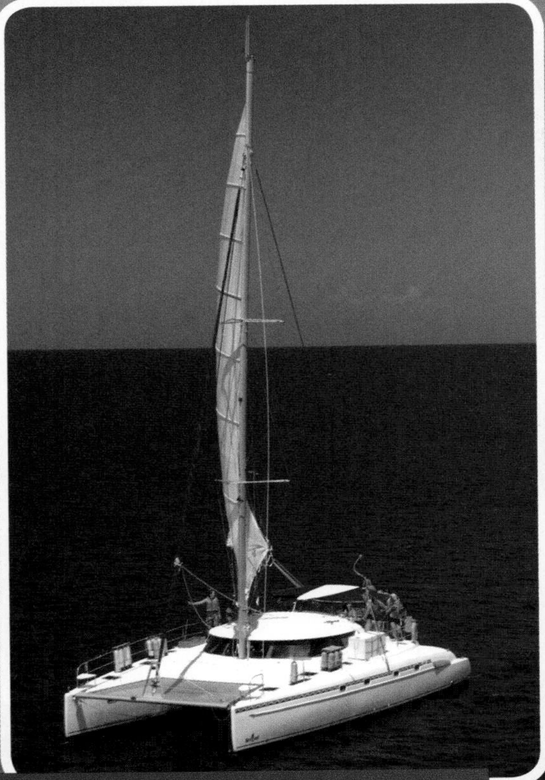

Can you see how this catamaran spreads its weight over the surface of the water? This wide boat design has been used for thousands of years because it's very stable, travels quickly, and carries a lot of weight for its size.

DENSE LIQUIDS

Fluids of different density provide different buoyancy. Mercury is a metal that remains a liquid when at room temperature. Mercury is so dense, that you can easily float a heavy coin in it. Salt water is denser than fresh water, so objects float more easily in salt water than fresh water.

WHATEVER FLOATS YOUR BOAT

Can you make a boat that floats out of aluminum foil? Can that same boat carry more than its own weight? In this experiment, you can explore the relationship between density, displacement, and buoyancy. What other materials could you use to make a boat? What shapes or designs work best?

Which Boat Shape Holds More Weight?

YOU WILL NEED:

- Scissors
- Aluminum foil
- Large bowl or sink filled with water
- Pennies

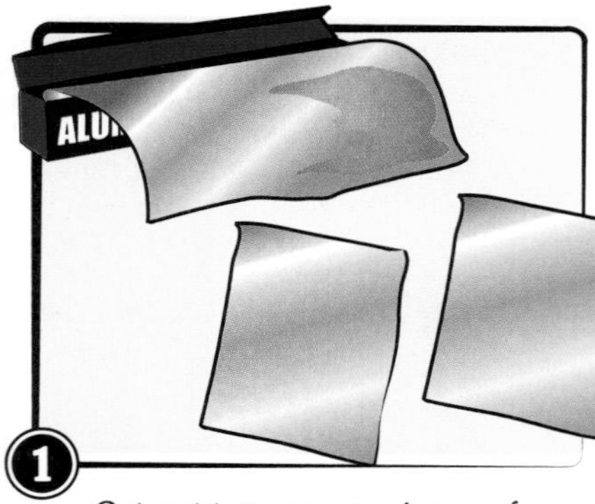

1 Cut out two square pieces of aluminum foil. Make sure they are about the same size.

2 Shape one piece of aluminum foil into a round boat shape.

3 Shape the other piece into a canoe shape, with pointed ends. These two shapes will be your model boat shapes.

A WATERY DISCOVERY

Archimedes was a scientist in ancient Greece. He knew that when an object was placed in water, some of the water was pushed out of the way, or displaced. It is said that he exclaimed, "Eureka!" when he discovered that the force of the water pushing up on the object is equal to the weight of the water displaced.

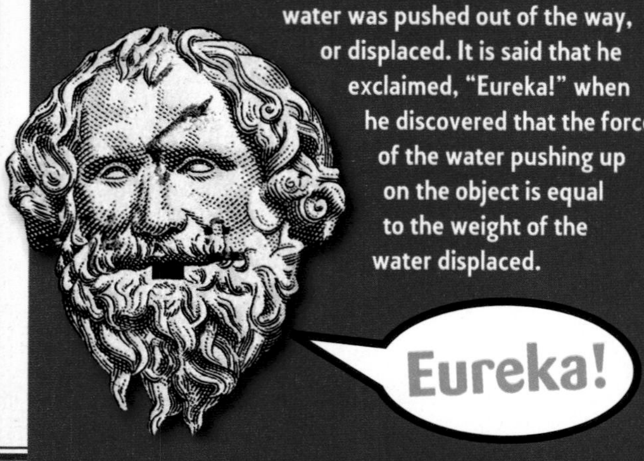

4

Float your boats in a large bowl or sink filled with water.

5

Add pennies to each boat, one at a time, until one boat sinks. Continue adding pennies until the other boat sinks. Which boat can hold the most pennies without sinking? Why do you think one boat shape worked better than the other?

Change it UP!

☞ Try your test again, but use teaspoons of water instead of pennies.

☞ Try making test boats with different materials, such as clay, wood, or empty recyclables.

☞ Research real boats, and create models to test their shapes.

SUBMARINES

Boats, ships, and submarines are engineered to have buoyancy. A submarine is specially designed so that the crew can change its buoyancy to dive or return to the surface. They do this by taking water in or pushing water out of compartments called ballast tanks.

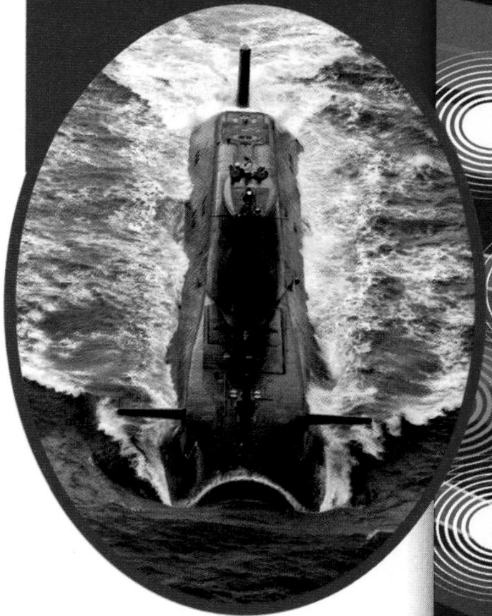

The SCIENCE Behind It

A material is buoyant and floats in water if it is less dense than the water around it. But aluminum is more dense than water! How does this work? A solid aluminum boat would definitely sink in water. But the boats in this experiment are both shaped to hold some air. That air is what gives the shape its buoyancy. An object can float in water if its overall density (including the air inside) is less than the density of the water. But a boat loses buoyancy when it becomes too heavy with coins, or when it tips and takes on water.

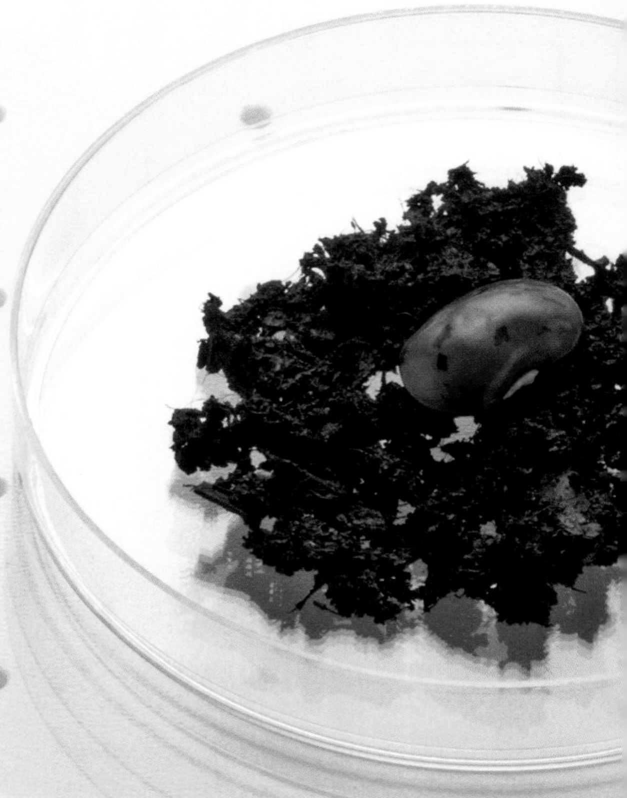

SCIENCE FAIR SUCCESS SECRETS

Schools, libraries, and clubs sometimes have science fairs. What exactly is a science fair? How do you make a project for a science fair? Read on for tips on writing interesting reports and creating eye-catching displays. You'll find lots of great ideas for impressing the judges in this chapter.

SHOW WHAT YOU KNOW

Schools, libraries, and clubs sometimes have science fairs. Participating in a science fair is a great way to challenge yourself, to learn new things about the world around you, to practice your reasoning and writing skills, and even to meet new, interesting people. But, what exactly is a science fair? And how do you make a project for a science fair?

Ask Questions

A science project is a way for you to use the same steps that scientists use to research a scientific topic. Begin with a question, like: How do different sediments layer to form rocks? How does the type of soil affect plant growth? How does the air pressure in a tire affect the way a bicycle rolls? Does a truss make a bridge stronger? Which cleaning product kills the most bacteria? Once you have a question, it's time to figure out the answer.

Research

Do some background research. Why should you conduct research before beginning to work? You might find some great information to help you better understand your question and how to answer it. Research will help you make a strong prediction. The research is also important because when you put your science fair project together, you'll be able to show the groundwork that you did first. If your project is in a contest, your research will impress the judges!

State a Hypothesis

Create a hypothesis. A hypothesis is a prediction about how something works. Your hypothesis needs to be something you can test. Your hypothesis might be something like, "If I keep one plant in a closet and one on a sunny windowsill, the plant on the windowsill will grow faster." It's important in your experiment to have only one variable. In the hypothesis about plants, the variable is the location of the plant—either on the windowsill or in the closet. It's important that the plants are the same in every other way. They should have the same soil, the same amount of food and water, and start at the same height.

Observe

Plan your experiment to test your hypothesis. You should do your experiment more than one time to be sure that the results are the same each time. Take careful measurements. Use your senses, observe, use tools to measure—and record your results.

Analyze

Analyze your data. Did you get the results you expected? What did you find out? Summarize your data and draw conclusions about it.

BE ORIGINAL!

Remember, you are doing science, not just reading about it! Researching what other scientists know about your topic is important, but you also need to come up with your own experiment.

GRAPHS AND TABLES

If you have measurable results, it's important to record and present them visually, with tables and graphs. A good title describes what kind of data, or information, you collected. A table shows what your results were. A blank table is also a helpful tool when you're collecting your data. Here is an example of what your table might look like for the experiment called "Where Do Plants Grow Best?" on page 34.

Plant Growth in Sun, Shade, and Darkness

	Carrot Top in the Sun 1	Carrot Top in the Sun 2	Carrot Top in the Shade 1	Carrot Top in the Shade 2	Carrot Top in the Dark 1	Carrot Top in the Dark 2
Day 1 height	.75 in	.75 in	.75 in	.75 in	.75 in	.75 in
Day 2 height	.75 in	.75 in	.75 in	.75 in	.75 in	.75 in
Day 3 height	1 in	.75 in	.75 in	.75 in	.75 in	.75 in
Day 4 height	1.25 in	1 in	.75 in	1 in	.75 in	.75 in
Day 5 height	1.5 in	1.25 in	.75 in	1 in	.75 in	.75 in
Day 6 height	1.75 in	1.25 in	1 in	1.25 in	.75 in	.75 in
Day 7 height	2.25 in	1.75 in	1 in	1.25 in	.75 in	.75 in
Day 8 height	2.5 in	2 in	1.25 in	1.25 in	.75 in	.75 in
Day 9 height	3 in	2.25 in	1.25 in	1.25 in	.75 in	.75 in
Day 10 height	3.25 in	3.25 in	1.25 in	1.5 in	.75 in	.75 in
Day 11 height	3.5 in	3.5 in	1.25 in	1.5 in	.75 in	.75 in
Day 12 height	4 in	4.25 in	1.5 in	1.5 in	.75 in	.75 in
Day 13 height	4.5 in	4.75 in	1.5 in	1.75 in	.75 in	.75 in
Day 14 height	5 in	5.5 in	1.75 in	2 in	.75 in	.75 in

Presenting Your Data

A graph shows the patterns or relationships you found with your data. Some common graphs include line graphs, bar graphs, and best-fit graphs. Graphs are drawn on a grid. Put the independent variable (e.g., time) along the horizontal x-axis. Put the dependent variable (e.g., height) along the vertical y-axis. Pie charts are also a useful way to show percentages. Choose a graph or chart that will best represent your results. You can draw graphs by hand, use a program like MS Excel, or search online for graph-making programs.

Bar Graphs

Bar graphs are helpful for showing how things have changed over time or for comparing different statistics. It is easy for someone to look at the data expressed on a bar graph and compare the rate of change of two or more things. In this instance, a simple bar graph helps us see how much each plant grew from the beginning of the experiment to the end. It also allows us to compare and contrast the growth of the plants in different locations.

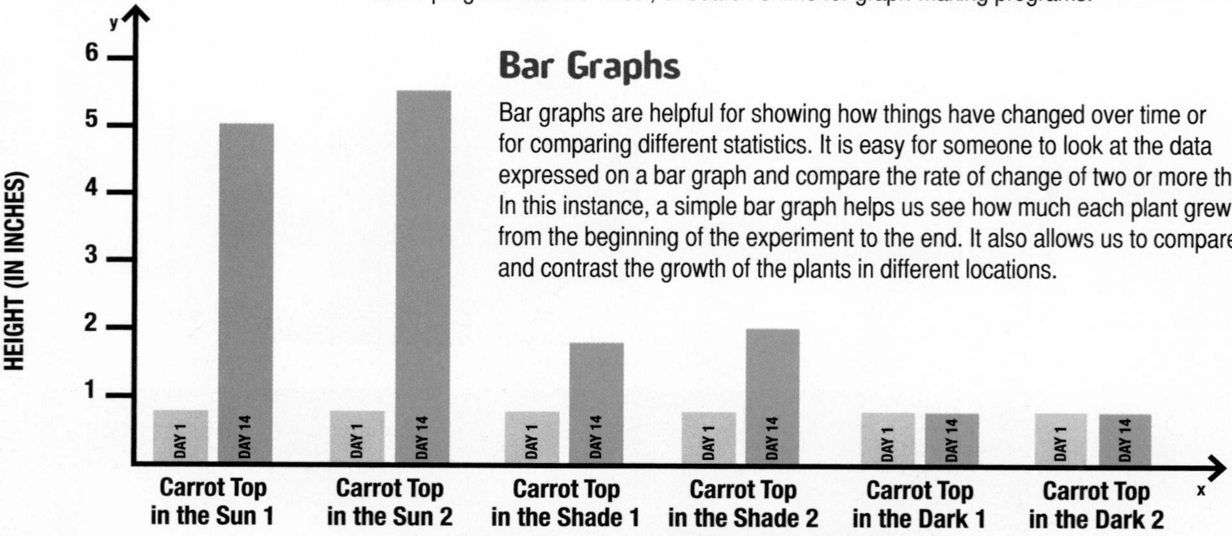

Growth Of Carrot Greens Over Time

Line Graphs

Creating a line graph is a simple way to display changes over time. In the line graph below, each of the carrot tops is represented by a different line. A quick glance shows us that the carrot tops in the sunny spots grew, while those in the dark did not.

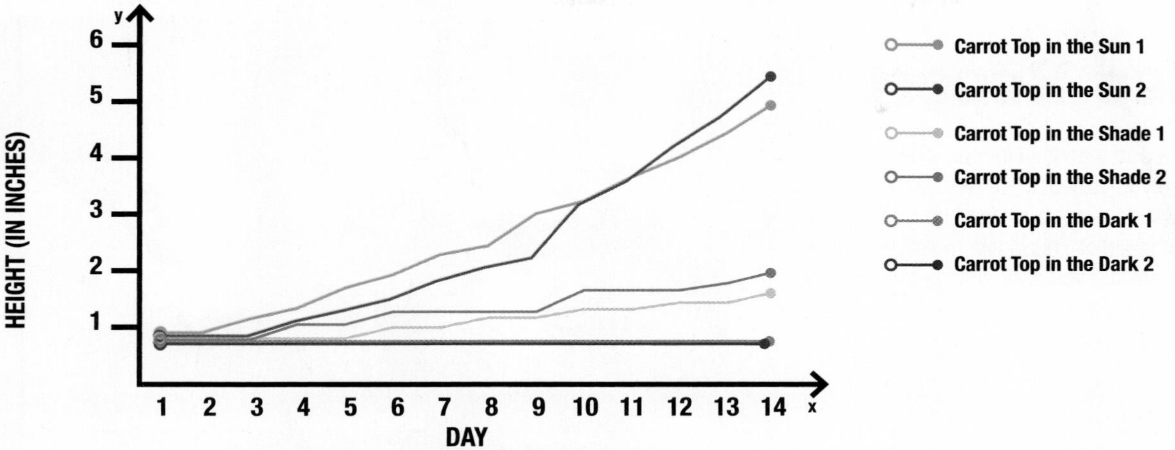

Growth Of Carrot Greens Over Time

X-Y Plots

You may choose to build an X-Y plot, which is also known as a scatter plot, to show how one factor affects another.

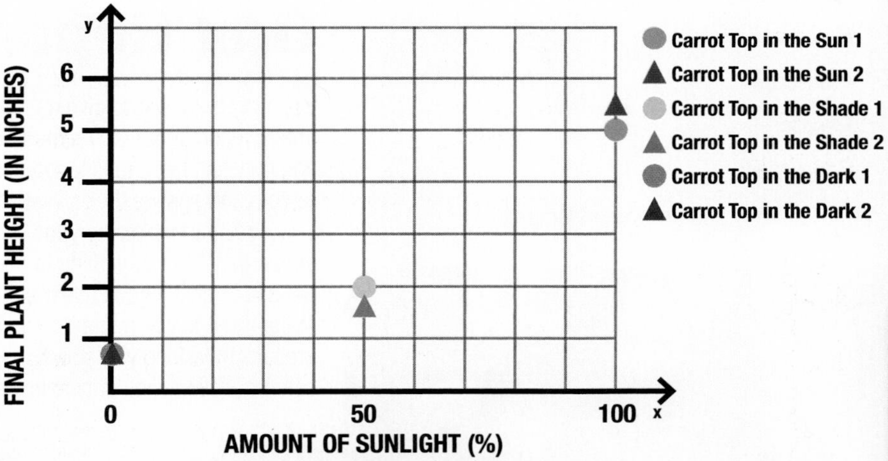

Plant Height After 14 Days

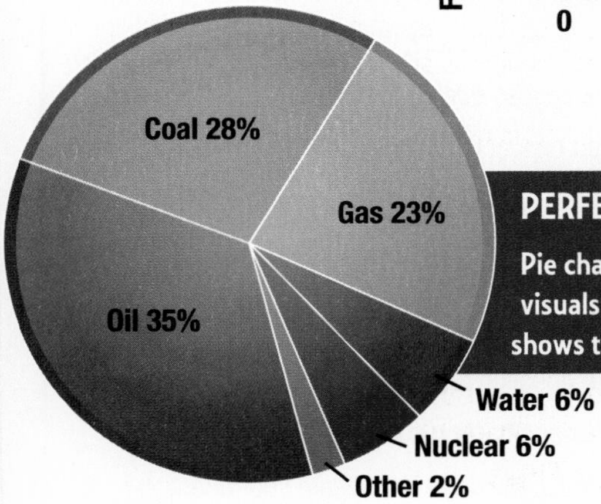

PERFECTING PIE CHARTS!

Pie charts are great for showing percentages. Unlike bar and line graphs, these visuals do not show how something changes over time. Here is an example that shows the amount of power a U.S. city gets from different sources.

SHARING YOUR PROJECT

A science fair project includes three important things: a typed report, a display, and a spoken presentation by you.

Typed Report

Your typed report stands in for you. It explains your project when you are not there. A science fair judge should be able to read your report and understand exactly what you did. This is where you put all the supporting details. Type and print your report and present it in a report cover or binder. Make sure you include headings like these in your report:

- Title
- Summary
- Question, variables, and hypothesis
- Background research
- Materials list
- Procedure
- Results
- Conclusions
- Bibliography and acknowledgements

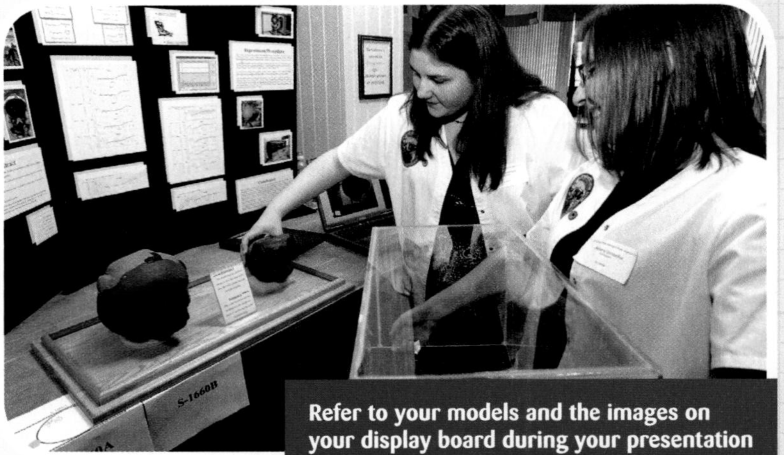

Refer to your models and the images on your display board during your presentation to support what you are saying.

Oral Report

Write down your key points on index cards to help you remember.

You may be asked to give a presentation about your experiment, or you may just need to talk about it with people and answer their questions.

Practice explaining your experiment from beginning to end. You should be able to give a good, clear summary of what you did in about three to five minutes. You can also ask a friend to help you prepare by asking you questions about your experiment. Here are some questions you should be ready to answer:

- What is your project about?
- Why did you choose this project?
- What did you expect to accomplish?
- Did you get the answers you were looking for?
- What was your plan, how did you collect your data, and can you explain your data?
- Do you think this was the best experiment to answer your question?
- What conclusions have you come to?
- What else could you do to investigate your question?

Display samples of the materials you used or models you created. Visitors will enjoy the hands-on experience of looking at, touching, or trying out parts of your experiment.

Display

Your display summarizes your project's key points in a visual, interesting way. How you present your experiment is just as important as the experiment itself. You need to include the key headings and points from your report, and use pictures, graphs, and tables to show your procedure and results.

Science fair display boards consist of three panels and are available at most office supply stores. Choose one that is made of a sturdy material that won't bend. Use bold, clear headings for each section on your board. These headings should follow the scientific method, like your typed report. The traditional way to set up the display board looks like this, but variations are acceptable.

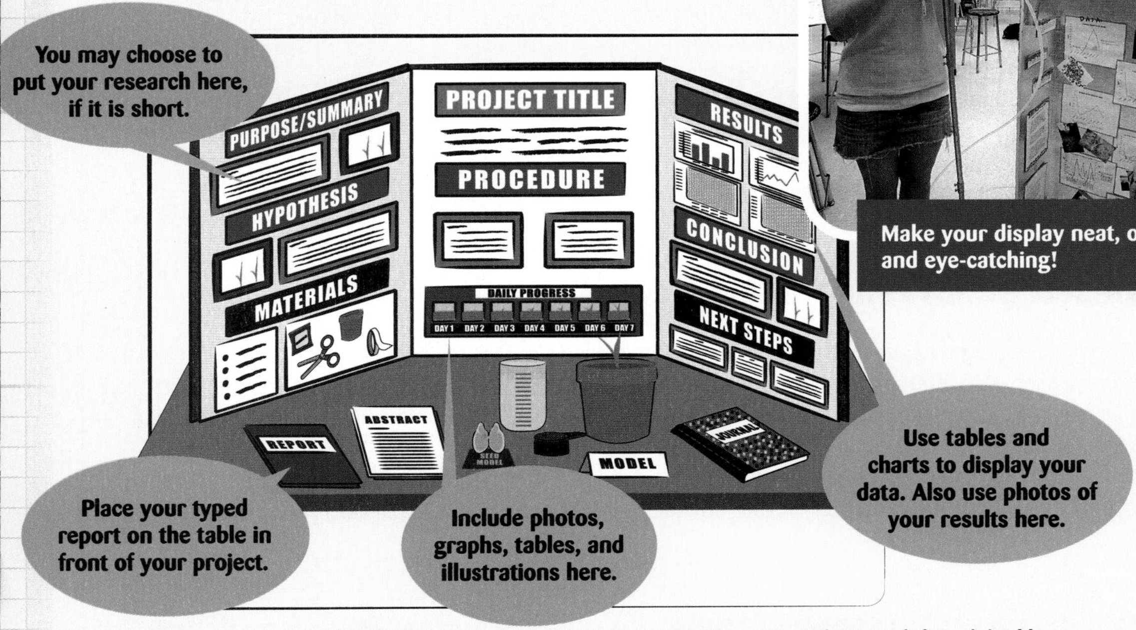

Make your display neat, organized, and eye-catching!

You can change this layout slightly, but make sure it is easy to read from top to bottom, left to right. Your typed report should be on the table, in front of the display. You may also have equipment from your experiment set up on the table, or a model of your equipment setup. See if you can find a way to make your presentation fun and interactive!

DISPLAY TIPS

- ✔ Check out the rules for your science fair. Are you allowed to use demonstration equipment as part of your display? Do the judges expect your display board to be a specific size? Make sure you follow the rules!
- ✔ Print out your text and headings and read them before gluing them to the board. You don't want typos up there!
- ✔ Use glue sticks or double-sided tape to attach your headings, text, and images to the display board.
- ✔ Printing on thicker paper or card stock will make your board look great, and it will prevent glue ripples or bubbles in the paper.
- ✔ You can use colored paper to highlight or frame your text and pictures.
- ✔ Use a font size big enough that it can be read from a few feet away—usually that means at least a 16-point font.
- ✔ For headings, use a font that can be read from across a large room. You want your display to pull people in.

A SAMPLE SCIENCE EXPERIMENT: FROM BEGINNING TO END

Let's see what a science fair project looks like from the first brainstorm to the final presentation.

Question: Be Curious, but Be Practical

At the beginning of any science experiment, the scientist needs to think about what he or she is interested in. What do you want to find out? Choose a topic you find interesting, because you are going to spend a lot of time on it. Next, brainstorm ways to find answers to your questions. What materials can you use? How much time do you have? You may wonder how close to the sun a rocket can get before it melts, but that might not be the easiest experiment to carry out. Choose an interesting question that you think you can answer with the time and materials you have.

Let's say you decide to do your science fair project on the experiment called "Where Do Plants Grow Best?" on page 34. Once you've chosen the question you want to answer, what steps do you need to take to complete your project?

Research: Investigate and Record

Start by doing some research to find out the science behind plant growth and sunlight. Check out scientific books, magazines, and websites. Write down the useful sources, and the key points you learned from each. Find some answers before you start your own investigation. What does a plant need to grow? What kinds of plant-growth experiments have other scientists done?

Begin keeping a record of your project in a notebook. This is your experiment journal. You may need to submit these notes as part of your project, so make sure you write everything clearly with dates and headings.

Hypothesis: Predict Your Outcome

Write down the question you want to answer. In this case, "Do plants grow better in sun, shade, or darkness?" Next, write your prediction or hypothesis. Do you think the carrot tops will grow best in the sun? That means your prediction is "The carrot leaves in the sun will grow taller than those in the shade or darkness."

Experiment: Create and Follow a Step-by-Step Plan

Design the experiment. Write down your list of materials and each step of your procedure in your experiment journal. Then make sure you have all the materials you need.

Carry out your experiment, and record as much information as you can. Write, draw, measure, and photograph what you see. Measure the leaf height for each plant every day, and record your measurements in a chart. You may also want to record other observations, like how much water each plant uses. Observing everything may help you think of other experiments you can do in the future.

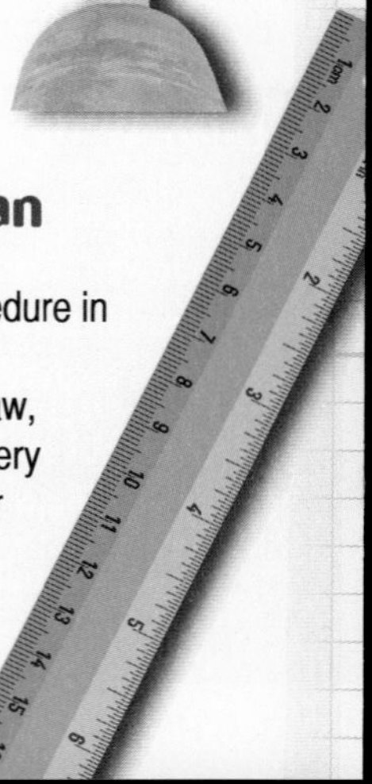

Analyze: What Happened and Why?

Look at your results. If the plants in the sun grow the most, then your results support your hypothesis. If the shaded plants actually grow better, your results do not support your hypothesis. That's okay! Scientists often learn more about their topic when they get unexpected results. Think about why you got these results, and write down your ideas and conclusions in your experiment journal. Maybe the sun was too hot for the plants, so the shaded plants grew better? Did your experiment raise new questions? If so, write them down and think about the experiments you could try next. To see if the hot sun had an effect, try another carrot top experiment where you test growth and temperature. You could also compare plant growth in cold, lukewarm, and very warm water.

Typed Report: Explain Your Method and Share Your Observations

Using the scientific method as your guide, type up an explanation of your experiment. Your written report needs to clearly describe the whole experiment so someone can understand it even if you are not there to explain. At the beginning of your report, include a title page and an abstract, which is a summary, or quick explanation, of the entire process in one paragraph. At the end, make sure to include a bibliography, or list of your research sources. Print the report and put it in a clean report cover or binder.

Display: Show What You Know!

Create a visual display of your plant-growth experiment on a tri-fold display board. Include the key points with eye-catching headings and colorful borders. Include a table of your measurements. Also include graphs of your results and pictures of your plants. Someone should be able to understand your experiment and your findings by looking at your display. If your science fair rules allow, you may also want to prepare a demonstration or model of your experiment. You could bring in carrot tops set up the way they were in your experiment, or a model explaining how sunlight affects plant growth.

Oral Report: Prepare a Lively, Informative Presentation

Practice and prepare so you can explain your experiment to people at the science fair. Write your key points on index cards. Practice so your presentation is interesting to listen to, and make sure you know your stuff! Be able to answer questions about what you did, why you did it, and what you learned.

Science Fair: The Big Day Has Arrived!

Bring your written report and display to the science fair and set it up at your table. Be ready to talk to everyone about what you did.

TIPS, TRICKS, AND BEST PRACTICES

How long will each step of your project take? Some experiments take a few minutes, and some take a few weeks. Write out each step of your project and how long you think it will take. Make sure you have enough time to finish and review it before the science fair!

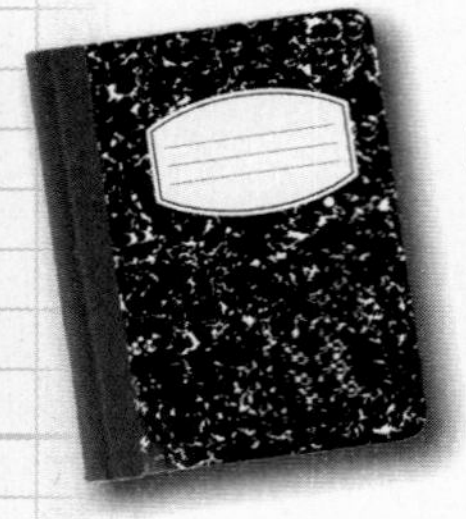

It's a good idea to keep an experiment journal or log book when you start working. Record everything with words and pictures. Then all you need to do later to write the report is organize your notes.

You can make a new experiment by choosing a different variable to change. Some common variables to test are: heat, cold, size, shape, wetness, dryness, light, saltiness, speed, friction, weight, color, stretchiness, amount, softness, hardness, and strength. Can you think of more?

Something that can change in an experiment is called a variable. Make sure that you test only one variable at a time. For example, if you want to see if more light makes plants grow taller, light is the only variable you should change. Expose the plants to different amounts of sunlight. Everything else about the experiment has to stay the same. The plants should all be the same species and size. They should all get the same amount of water. Make sure all the plants are healthy at the beginning of your experiment. Controlling all these variables lets you be sure that light is the only thing making them grow differently.

The variable you select to change is called the "independent variable." In your results, you need to show how changing the independent variable affected things. The effects are known as the "dependent variable." For example, to see the effect that water has on growing plants, your independent variable would be the amount of water you give the plants. Your dependent variable would be the amount of growth. Your results need to show whether there is a pattern connecting these two variables. Does more water lead to more growth?

Think Like a Judge

Wondering what the judges are looking for? Most science fair judges score projects based on five big questions:

1. **DID YOU USE A SCIENTIFIC APPROACH TO THE PROBLEM?**

   Follow the scientific method, and design a good test with one variable you can measure.

2. **IS THE PROJECT ORIGINAL AND CREATIVE?**

   Come up with a new, interesting experiment idea, and make your display visual and exciting!

3. **IS IT THOROUGH AND ACCURATE?**

   Write down all your steps and observations, and check your results twice!

4. **IS IT CLEAR?**

   Write everything out and use pictures so anyone could understand your experiment, method, and observations.

5. **DID YOU LEARN FROM IT?**

   Show that doing this project helped you learn something new about science.

Every science fair has its own list of rules and regulations. Make sure you read them and follow them!

SUPER SCIENCE PROJECT CHECKLIST

- ✔ You should change only one variable.
- ✔ You must control all other variables to be sure they stay the same.
- ✔ You should repeat the experiment at least three times to be sure your results are correct.
- ✔ Describe the setup of your experiment well. Draw pictures to include in your report.
- ✔ Think carefully as you write. Be sure to include the details of every step in your experiment.
- ✔ Have fun! It's exciting to conduct your own science investigations.

Image Credits

All step-by-step illustrations by Darin Anderson/Shay Design.

Front Cover: Darin Anderson/Shay Design (illustrations); pzAxe/Shutterstock.com (magnifier); Alias Studiot Oy/Shutterstock.com (plant and beaker).

Contents: 2–3: VIPDesignUSA/Shutterstock.com (large flask). 5: R. Gino Santa Maria/Shutterstock.com (beakers and flasks). All other photos repeated in the interior. *See individual pages.*

Introduction: 6–7: iladm/Shutterstock.com (background); Nicemonkey/Shutterstock.com (border). 6: AP Photo/Joerg Sarbach (paleontologist); Scott Bauer/USDA Photo Library (agricultural engineer). 7: Monkey Business Images/Shutterstock.com (boy with laptop); Laurence Gough/Shutterstock.com (girl); Monkey Business Images/Shutterstock.com (boy writing).

Earth Science: 8–9: Ikunl/Shutterstock.com. 10–25: Neo Edmund/Shutterstock.com (border). 10–13: Sergey Mironov/Shutterstock.com (background). 10: Steve Cukrov/Shutterstock.com (soda); Shutterstock.com (branch); Sari ONeal/Shutterstock.com (icicle). 11: Bruce Raynor/Shutterstock.com (cloud forest); Jan Kaliciak/Shutterstock.com (distillation). 13: Anthony Jay D. Villalon/Shutterstock.com (desalination plant); M Rutherford/Shutterstock.com (albatross). 14–17: SSSCCC/Shutterstock.com (background). 14: AISPIX/Shutterstock.com (wrinkles). 15: ©Can Stock Photo Inc./chris74 (sunburn); Sonya Etchison/Shutterstock.com (applying sunscreen); Martin Allinger/Shutterstock.com (boys). 16: winnond/Shutterstock (hat and glasses). 17: Vynogradova/Shutterstock.com (paint and wood). 18–19: Scott Prokop/Shutterstock.com (background). 18: Bryan Busovicki/Shutterstock.com (Colorado river); Library of Congress Prints and Photographs Division (Dust Bowl); Jerry Sharp/Shutterstock.com (flood). 20–21: Pichugin Dmitry/Shutterstock.com (background). 20: Sergey Tarasenko/Shutterstock.com (seal); AND Inc./Shutterstock.com (rain forest); Jan Martin Will/Shutterstock.com (penguin); Nataliya Hora/Shutterstock.com (mountain). 22–23: Barbara Delgado/Shutterstock.com (background). 22: iofoto/Shutterstock.com (clouds); Steshkin Yevgeniy/Shutterstock.com (lightning); Rudy Balasko/Shutterstock.com (Chicago). 23: Alexey Stiop/Shutterstock.com (barometer). 24–25: Alex Zabusik/Shutterstock.com (background). 24: Awe Sashkin/Shutterstock.com (magnet); Dr_Flash/Shutterstock.com (Earth); ©StockTrek/SuperStock (North Pole). 25: Marty Ellis/Shutterstock.com (geese); Inspiring Images/Shutterstock.com (magnet).

Life Science: 26–27: Oleg Znamenskiy/Shutterstock.com. 28–93: Johan Larson/Shutterstock.com (border). 28–31: patpitchaya/Shutterstock.com (sunflowers). 28: Darin Anderson/Shay Design (seed illustration); Bogdan Wankowicz/Shutterstock.com (sprouting sequence). 29: Fotoline/Shutterstock.com (strawberry); haveseen/Shutterstock.com (seedling). 31: AP Photo/John McConnico (vault); Galayko Sergey/Shutterstock.com (chickpea); Abel Tumik/Shutterstock.com (almonds). 32–35: laurent dambies/Shutterstock.com (background). 32: Dreamy Girl/Shutterstock.com (transpiration); Jordan Tan/Shutterstock.com (giraffe); Volodymyr Krasyuk/Shutterstock.com (sun); Yellowj/Shutterstock.com (grass); Ulrich Mueller/Shutterstock.com (cow); Dmitry Melnikov/Shutterstock.com (boy). 33: Steve Cheeseman/Shutterstock.com (algae); Christina Richards/Shutterstock.com (trees with green leaves); Kochergin/Shutterstock.com (fall trees). 35: NASA (astronaut); Madlen/Shutterstock.com (carrots). 36–39: R_R/Shutterstock.com (background). 36: Peter Gudella/Shutterstock.com (leaf); D. Kucharski & K. Kucharska/Shutterstock.com (leaf close-up); ©iStockphoto.com/Oliver Sun Kim (vascular bundle). 37: Matthew Cole/Shutterstock.com (plant illustration); marilyn barbone/Shutterstock.com (oak tree). 39: xJJx/Shutterstock.com (house); ©SOMOS/SuperStock (plants). 40–43: Roman Pyshchyk/Shutterstock.com (background). 40: Alexonline/Shutterstock.com (cell illustration); Arto Hakola/Shutterstock.com (mangrove tree). 41: Leigh Prather/Shutterstock.com (paint); AP Photo/Patrick Semansky (oil spill). 42: Angel Simon/Shutterstock.com (oil and spoons); Ivaschenko Roman/Shutterstock.com (oil bottle); Artur Synenko/Shutterstock.com (lettuce). 43: Lepas/Shutterstock.com (lettuce); AP Photo/Jim Urquhart (worker in oil); AP Photo/The Houma Courier, Matt Stamey (dispersant in oil). 44–47: zhu difeng/Shutterstock.com (background). 44: Keith Weller/USDA Photo Library (scientist with grapes); sakhorn/Shutterstock.com (farmer spraying). 45: Michael A. Grusak/USDA Photo Library (golden rice); Scott Bauer/USDA Photo Library (rice varieties); tomato (schwarzhana/Shutterstock.com); lineartestpilot/Shutterstock.com (fish); Perutski Petro (seed). 46: Art Vector/Shutterstock.com (groceries). 47: AP Photo (exploding watermelon); Nikola Bilic/Shutterstock.com (cookie). 48–51: Scorpp/Shutterstock.com (background). 48: Steve Gschmeissner/Science Photo/Getty Images (yeast); andersphoto/shutterstock.com (bread). 49: Danny Smythe/Shutterstock.com (measuring cup); Christopher Elwell/Shutterstock.com (grain sack); xpixel/Shutterstock.com (yeast); burly/Shutterstock.com (dough); fdimeo/Shutterstock.com (kneading dough); Dewitt/Shutterstock.com (bread in oven); Zurjeta/Shutterstock.com (boy); Bridgeman Art Library/Getty Images (Egyptian art); North Wind Picture Archives via AP Images (Pasteur). 50: Petr Malyshev/Shutterstock.com (bread slices). 51: Kachalkina Veronika/Shutterstock.com (baker facing out); ©Otnaydur/Dreamstime.com (baker facing oven). 52–55: loisik/Shutterstock.com (background). 52: ©Cooper5022/Dreamstime.com (dung beetles); Dani Vincek/Shutterstock.com (mold); Steven Russel Smith Photos/Shutterstock.com (mushrooms). 53: ©iStockphoto.com/Laurie Knight (dog vomit slime mold); Alekcey/Shutterstock.com (mushrooms). 54: gsplanet/Shutterstock.com. 55: Denis Dryashkin/Shutterstock.com (pills); Joerg Beuge/Shutterstock.com (pepper). 56–59: Maksym Protsenko/Shutterstock.com (background). 56: fusebulb/Shutterstock.com (red blood cells); Ronald van der Beek/Shutterstock.com (Earth); Photodynamic/Shutterstock.com (glacier). 57: SPB photo maker/Shutterstock.com (pipe); s-ts/Shutterstock.com (shower); Steven Coburn/Shutterstock.com (woman); alterfalter/Shutterstock.com (plastic bottles). 59: Piotr Marcinsky/Shutterstock.com (girl). 60–63: Vibrant Image Studio/Shutterstock.com (background). 60: Selyutina Olga/Shutterstock.com (disco ball); Yuriy Kulyk/Shutterstock.com (window); Brigida Soriano/Shutterstock.com (road). 61: mcherevan/Shutterstock.com (sun); leodor/Shutterstock.com (car); Asaf Eliason/Shutterstock.com (sand). 62: Elena Elisseeva/Shutterstock.com (drinks).

63: AP Photo/Matt Rourke (roof); AP Photo/Pablo Martinez Monsivais (Chu); Hannah Eckman/Shutterstock.com (shirts); ©iStockphoto.com/Diana Hirsch (girls). 64–67: Evgeny Karandaev/Shutterstock.com (background). 64: Juriah Mosin/Shutterstock.com (girl); Andrjuss/Shutterstock.com (potatoes); Roxana Bashyrova/Shutterstock.com (bread); Luti/Shutterstock.com (boy). 65: nikkytok/Shutterstock.com (milk); Sandra Caldwell/Shutterstock.com (meat); Chris leachman/Shutterstock.com (lentils); Mike Flippo/Shutterstock.com (bacon); helza/Shutterstock.com (cheese); XAOC/Shutterstock.com (nutrition label); zimmytws/Dreamstime.com (boy). 66: D McKenzie/Shutterstock.com (boy). 67: Basheera Designs/Shutterstock.com (food groups). 68–71: ARENA Creative/Shutterstock.com (background). 68: Zurijeta/Shutterstock.com (girls); leonello calvetti/Shutterstock.com (digestive system). 69: Elena Elisseeva/Shutterstock.com (girls); Matthew Cole/Shutterstock.com (intestines); ©iStockphoto.com/Alyn Stafford (boy). 71: Olinchuk/Shutterstock.com (baby); Tyler Olson/Shutterstock.com (bacon). 72–75: marekuliasz/Shutterstock.com (background). 72: Monkey Business Images/Shutterstock.com (sleeping); Lerche&Johnson/Shutterstock.com (boy stretching); Aleksandr Markin/Shutterstock.com (girl stretching). 73: David Young-Wolff/Riser/Getty Images (sweaty girl); Edyta Pawlowska/Shutterstock.com (boy); Galina Barskaya/Shutterstock.com (tennis); Kzenon/Shutterstock.com (family). 75: Jason Stitt/Shutterstock.com (girl); oliveromg/Shutterstock.com (group). 76–77: itsmejust/Shutterstock.com (background). 76: Jerry Sharp/Shutterstock.com (hurdlers); Arcady/Shutterstock.com (skeleton); kuehdi/Shutterstock.com (x-ray); Stacy Barnett/Shutterstock.com (arm in cast). 77: Edyta Pawlowska/Shutterstock.com. 78–81: Fedorov Oleksiy/Shutterstock.com (background). 78: Vladimir Wrangel/Shutterstock.com (girl); Andrey Nyunin/Shutterstock.com (finger); Anita Potter/Shutterstock.com (skin layers). 79: Anneka/Shutterstock.com (foot); ©iStockphoto.com/Jason Lugo (boy); Sashkin/Shutterstock.com (bacteria); caimacanul/Shutterstock.com (hands). 81: Alsu/Shutterstock.com (braille). 82–85: Elena Leonova/Shutterstock.com. 82: ©Flash45Me/Dreamstime.com (girl); Hulton Archive/Getty Images (Mendel). 83: R-photos/Shutterstock.com (green pod); Madlen/Shutterstock.com (yellow beans); Peter Arnold/Getty Images (albino crocodile). 84: Sergio Ponomarev/Shutterstock.com (scientist); ©Macmoss/Dreamstime.com (cleft chin); Sparkling Moments Photography/Shutterstock.com (widow's peak); Andrea Slatter/Shutterstock.com (boy). 86–89: Nattavut/Shutterstock.com (background). 86: Felix Mizioznikov/Shutterstock.com (Adam's apple); Benis Arapovic/Shutterstock.com (two boys). 87: Reflekta/Shutterstock.com (family); Francisco Caravana/Shutterstock.com (boy); ©iStockphoto.com/Flashon Studio (girl). 88: Sonja Foos/Shutterstock.com (teens comparing height). 89: ©iStockphoto.com/Sean Locke (doctor measuring height); Tracy Whiteside/Shutterstock.com (girls); Lisa F. Young/Shutterstock.com (boy). 90–93: italianestro/Shutterstock.com. 90: Booka/Shutterstock.com (DNA); Sergej Khakimullin/Shutterstock.com (boys); ©iStockphoto.com/Peter Kim (dusting for prints). 91: Tatiana Makotra/Shutterstock.com (eye); ©iStockphoto.com/Hans Laubel (arch); Aliisik/Shutterstock.com (loop); ©iStockphoto.com/Hanquan Chen (whorl); PRNewsFoto/IBM via AP Images (hand scan). 92: Tatiana Popova/Shutterstock.com (magnifier). 93: Lobke Peers/Shutterstock.com (dog).

Physical Science: 94–137: Wang Jie/Shutterstock.com (border). 94–95: Jose Antonio Perez/Shutterstock.com. 96–97: Dmitro2009/Shutterstock.com (background). 96: Margo Harrison/Shutterstock.com (bike); Roman Kholodov/Shutterstock.com (apple); magmarcz/Shutterstock.com (Statue of Liberty); Glenda M. Powers/Shutterstock.com (camera); Anton Albert/Shutterstock.com (boy); Richard Griffin/Shutterstock.com (onion); Andrey Burmakin (dynamite). 97: Kinetic Imagery/Shutterstock.com (pennies). 98–99: Ng Yin Chern/Shutterstock.com (background). 98: holbox/Shutterstock.com (boy); Stasys Eidiejus/Shutterstock.com (color spectrum); C&OPhoto/Shutterstock.com (lemon); Crisp/Shutterstock.com (soda); Horiyan/Shutterstock.com (soap); Tobik/Shutterstock.com (baking soda). 100–103: David David/Shutterstock.com (background). 100: Jag_cz/Shutterstock.com (snow crystals); Dmitri Vervitsiotis/Photographer's Choice/Getty Images (diamonds); Robert D Pinna/Shutterstock.com (quartz). 101: Douglas Knight/Shutterstock.com (stalagmites and stalactites); Vladi/Shutterstock.com (geode); drfelice/Shutterstock.com (spoon); Danil Balashov/Shutterstock.com (empty glass); Aaron Amat/Shutterstock.com (spoon in glass). 103: Chris May/Shutterstock.com (candy); Luis Carlos Jimenez del rio/Shutterstock.com (sugar beets); Swapan/Shutterstock.com (sugar cane). 104–107: Graham Prentice/Shutterstock.com (rainbow). 104: Eric Isselee/Shutterstock.com (zebra); Hannamariah/Shutterstock.com (painting); ©iStockphoto.com/setixela (light dispersion). 105: Melinda Fawver/Shutterstock.com (trail mix); Andy Crawford and Tim Ridley/Dorling Kindersley/Getty Images (chromatography). 107: ©iStockphoto.com/Rubén Hidalgo (shopping list); Inhabitant/Shutterstock.com (perfume); AP Photo/HO/Photo: Bayer AG (scientist); artproem/Shutterstock.com (markers). 108–109: B747/Shutterstock.com (background). 108: Andreas Gradin/Shutterstock.com (fish); Phil MacDonald Photography/Shutterstock.com (cherry); Subbotina Anna/Shutterstock.com (soda). 110–111: Pitcha T./Shutterstock.com (background). 110: Tom Begasse/Shutterstock.com (pot); Steve Schwettman/Shutterstock.com (beach); Layland Masuda/Shutterstock.com (girl). 112–115: topseller/Shutterstock.com (background). 112: Batareykin/Shutterstock.com (balloon on left); botazsolti/Shutterstock.com (center balloon); ©George Burba/Dreamstime.com (balloon on right). 113: ©Kalsers/Dreamstime.com (girl); David P. Smith/Shutterstock.com (star balloon); Todd Shoemake/Shutterstock.com (tornado). 114: trailexplorers/Shutterstock.com (microwave). 115: Fred Goldstein/Shutterstock.com (woman); Elena Elisseeva/Shutterstock.com (popcorn); Igor_Gubarev/Shutterstock.com (boy). 116–119: Matt Gibson/Shutterstock.com (background). 116: Ase/Shutterstock.com (ice cubes); Bob Falconer/Shutterstock.com (beach); Volodymyr Goinyk/Shutterstock.com (iceberg). 117: Aleksandra Duda/Shutterstock.com (fork); Andi Berger/Shutterstock.com (girl); travis manley/Shutterstock.com (acetone); fotogiunta/Shutterstock.com (oil). 119: AP Photo/Darron Cummings (man); Vereschagin Dmitry/Shutterstock.com (antifreeze). 120–123: mashe/Shutterstock.com (background). 120: Atovot/Shutterstock.com (pan); Sue Robinson/Shutterstock.com (insect); Lana Langlois/Shutterstock.com (soap); kostrez/Shutterstock.com (detergent). 121: Michael C. Gray/Shutterstock.com (meat); Monkey Business Images/Shutterstock.com (laundry); wim claes/shutterstock.com (bird); AP Photo/Bill Haber (cleaning bird). 123: Toranico/Shutterstock.com (man). 124–127: Ken Sato/Shutterstock.com (background). 124: Viniius Tupinamba/

Shutterstock.com (metal box); Jo Lomark/Shutterstock.com (wooden box); NASA (astronaut). 125: Cynthia Farmer/Shutterstock.com (girl); Filipe B. Varela (oil in water); J. Helgason/Shutterstock.com (bucket); Kletr/Shutterstock.com (pumice); Elena Koulik/Shutterstock.com (floating). 127: Joyce Marrero/Shutterstock.com (river); Craig Wactor/Shutterstock.com (penny). 128–129: Kataleewan interachote/Shutterstock.com (background). 128: Dimitriy Shironosov/Shutterstock.com (walking); frantisekhojdysz/Shutterstock.com (diver); Sergey Popov V/Shutterstock.com (underwater). 129: AP Photo (diving bell). 130–133: Jason and Bonnie Grower/Shutterstock.com (background). 130: NASA (shuttle); Matthew Benoit/Shutterstock.com (balloon); Corbis/SuperStock (foursquare). 131: Manchan/Digital Vision/Getty Images (swings); Talvi/Shutterstock.com (elephant); Felix Mizioznikov/Shutterstock.com (boy). 133: MO:SES/Shutterstock.com (plane); Karen Givens/Shutterstock.com (horse). 134–137: Bernd Juergens/Shutterstock.com (background). 134: afitz/Shutterstock.com (stones); Stasys Eidiejus/Shutterstock.com (color spectrum). 135: Steve Gschmeissner/Science Photo Library/Getty Images (fly close-up); ©Gbh007/Dreamstime.com (girl); Dorling Kindersley/The Agency Collection/Getty Images (eyeball diagram). 136: Masson/Shutterstock.com (girl). 137: Valentyn Volkov/Shutterstock.com (honey); Glenda M. Powers/Shutterstock.com (man).

Technology and Engineering: 138–139: Delmas Lehman/Shutterstock.com. 140–173: Keo/Shutterstock.com (border). 140–143: Denis Babenko/Shutterstock.com (background). 140: ©Vaeenma/Dreamstime.com (coconut); terekhov igor/Shutterstock.com (bowling ball); Alex Staroseltsev/Shutterstock.com (apple). 141: NASA (astronaut); Dmitriy Shironosov/Shutterstock.com (boy); Orla/Shutterstock.com (toy). 142: Shutterstock.com (egg). 143: Glenda M. Powers/Shutterstock.com (egg); Steve Broer/Shutterstock.com (girl). 144–147: jaymast/Shutterstock.com (background). 144: Viktor1/Shutterstock.com (pizza); ©Wjphoto/Dreamstime.com (roller coaster); xfox01/Shutterstock.com (sun). 145: Jhaz Photography/Shutterstock.com (lightning); B. Franklin/Shutterstock.com (boy); Andresr/Shutterstock.com (rolling ball); Shutterstock.com (ball with pins). 147: Ariusz Nawrocki/Shutterstock.com (foil ball); Sonya Etchison/Shutterstock.com (boy); Morphart/Shutterstock.com (catapult). 148–151: LianeM/Shutterstock.com (background). 148: Bonita R. Cheshier/Shutterstock.com (baseball player); Eric Limon/Shutterstock.com (snowboarder). 149: Diego Barbieri/Shutterstock.com (skater); Lane V. Erickson/Shutterstock.com (treadmark); Mirenska Olga/Shutterstock.com (basketball); AYAKOVLEV.COM/Shutterstock.com (ballet); romarti/Shutterstock.com (engine). 150: Lizard/Shutterstock.com (boots). 151: Lipsky/Shutterstock.com (tread); R.S.Jegg/Shutterstock.com (hiker). 152–155: Anettphoto/Shutterstock.com (background). 152: Goodluz/Shutterstock.com (yelling boy); fzd.it/Shutterstock.com (atom); Vasca/Shutterstock.com (copper cable); ©Showface/Dreamstime.com (cold boy). 153: Roman Sotola/Shutterstock.com (sign); tuulijumala/Shutterstock.com (light switch); baldyrgan/Shutterstock.com (battery); MilaLiu/Shutterstock.com (lightbulb); hkannn/Shutterstock.com (electrocuted man). 155: AP Photo/Eugene Hoshiko (train); ansar80/Shutterstock.com (boy). 156–161: Paul Maguire/Shutterstock.com (background). 156: Belinda Pretorius/Shutterstock.com (water power); Stephen Meese/Shutterstock.com (wind farm). 157: James M Phelps, Jr/Shutterstock.com (coal power plant); Thorsten Schier/Shutterstock.com (nuclear power plant); ssuaphotos/Shutterstock.com (renewable energy); GorillaAttack/Shutterstock.com (solar house). 161: Ben Shepard (flying wind generator). 162–165: Madlen/Shutterstock.com (background). 162: Andrei Nekrassov/Shutterstock.com (thermometer in cylinder); Steven Coling/Shutterstock.com (boiling water); Maridav/Bigstock.com (ice). 163: Ivancovlad/Shutterstock.com (kettle); photomak/Shutterstock.com (girl); Jaroslaw Grudzinsk/Shutterstock.com (thermos). 164: Nils Z/Shutterstock.com (top of can). 165: Margaret M Stewart/Shutterstock.com (chipmunk); Vladimir Melnik/Shutterstock.com (walrus). 166–169: Christian Delbert/Shutterstock.com (background). 166: iofoto/Shutterstock.com (highway bridge); Regien Paassen/Shutterstock.com (Sydney Harbor Bridge); M Reel/Shutterstock.com (Golden Gate Bridge). 167: Gorilla/Shutterstock.com (girl); z0w/Shutterstock.com (wooden bridge); LSqrd42/Shutterstock.com (truss bridge). 168: Aaron Crawford/Shutterstock.com (pennies). 169: Jeff Kinsey/Shutterstock.com (top left bridge); Caitlin Mirra/Shutterstock.com (top right bridge); Sheri Armstrong/Shutterstock.com (Sanibel Causeway bridge). 170–173: Diana Taliun/Shutterstock.com (background). 171: erlire74/Shutterstock.com (duck toy); MaszaS/Shutterstock.com (boy). 172: AP Photo/Christof Stache (*Columbo Express*); tubuceo/Shutterstock.com (catamaran); MarcelClemens/Shutterstock.com (mercury). 173: Mark Yuill/Shutterstock.com (boat); blinow61/Shutterstock.com (Archimedes). 174: AP Photo/BAE Systems, HO (submarine); Charles Ostrand/Shutterstock.com (boats).

Science Fair Success Secrets: 174–175: Image Source/Getty Images. 176–185: iladm/Shutterstock.com (border). 176–185: Nicemonkey/Shutterstock.com (background). 176: Horiyan/Shutterstock.com (bike), R-photos/Shutterstock.com (plant), Stephen Coburn/Shutterstock.com (girl). 177: tazubraX/Shutterstock.com (plants); Orange Line Media/Shutterstock.com (boy); AP Photo/Northwest Herald, Lauren M. Anderson (girl); imagebroker.net/SuperStock (two boys). 178: Iconica/Getty Images (girl). 180: Tracy A. Woodward/The Washington Post/Getty Images (girl); Mark Gail/Washington Post/Getty Images (two girls). 181: AP Photo/Oscar Sosa. 182: Phase4Photography/Shutterstock.com (boy); notkoo/Shutterstock.com (rocket); Vertes Edmond Mihai/Shutterstock.com (sun); mikeledray/Shutterstock.com (clipboard); Zloneg/Shutterstock.com (carrot); Alhovik/Shutterstock.com (ruler). 183: Konstantin Yolshin/Shutterstock.com (girl); rlat/Shutterstock.com (binder); AP Photo/Don Ryan (boy on right); AP Photo/Alamogordo Daily News, Ellis Neel (boy on left). 184: Hank Frentz/Shutterstock.com (journal); Katrina Leigh/Shutterstock.com (plant); Leian/Shutterstock.com (measuring cup); Sean Reilly/Shutterstock.com (water drop), Alhovik/Shutterstock.com (ruler). 185: Tracy A. Woodward/The Washington Post/Getty Images (girl with judge); Rubberball/Nicole Hill/The Agency Collection/Getty Images (girl with display).

Back Cover: Dr_Flash/Shutterstock.com (Earth); MilanB/Shutterstock.com (magnet); ©iStockphoto.com/Oleg Prikhodko (thermometer in glass); Jiang Hongyan/Shutterstock.com (pinwheel); Chris May/Shutterstock.com (candy).

Index

Family Tree

The chart below will help you create a personalized family tree. Begin with your grandparents and add entries for your uncles, aunts, cousins, brothers, and sisters. Write the names of men and boys in rectangles and the names of women and girls in circles. Use your own family tree to complete the experiment "Which Traits Do You Share With Your Family?" on page 84.

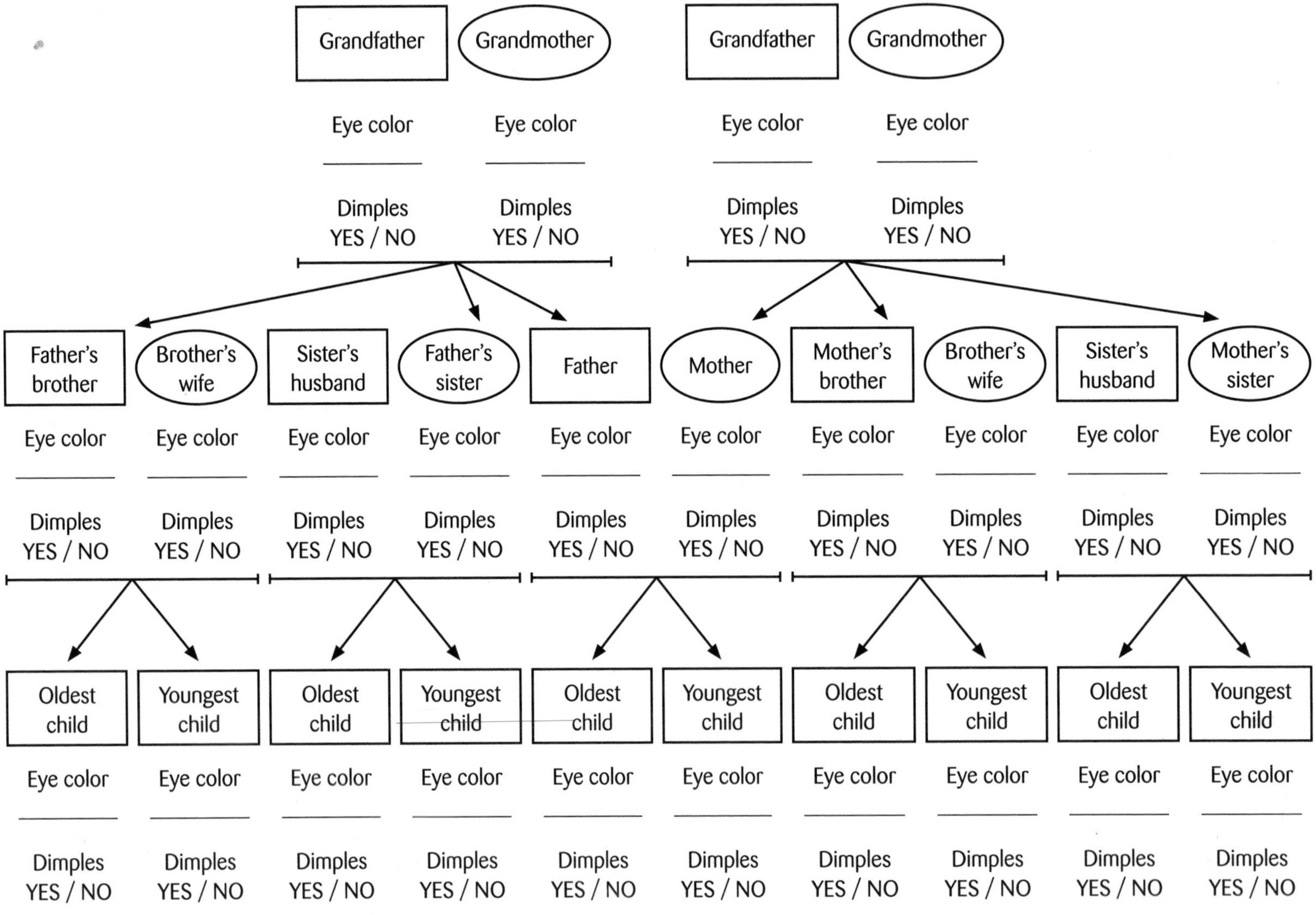